SPEAKING OF NOËL COWARD

SPEAKING OF NOËL COWARD

Interviews by Alan Farley

Edited by Ron Lazar

AuthorHouse™ LLC
1663 Liberty Drive
Bloomington, IN 47403
www.authorhouse.com
Phone: 1-800-839-8640

© 2013 by Alan Farley. All rights reserved.

No part of this book may be reproduced, stored in a retrieval system, or transmitted by any means without the written permission of the author.

Published by AuthorHouse   09/09/2013

ISBN: 978-1-4817-7325-6 (sc)
ISBN: 978-1-4817-7324-9 (hc)
ISBN: 978-1-4817-7326-3 (e)

Library of Congress Control Number: 2013914312

Any people depicted in stock imagery provided by Thinkstock are models, and such images are being used for illustrative purposes only.
Certain stock imagery © Thinkstock.

This book is printed on acid-free paper.

Because of the dynamic nature of the Internet, any web addresses or links contained in this book may have changed since publication and may no longer be valid. The views expressed in this work are solely those of the author and do not necessarily reflect the views of the publisher, and the publisher hereby disclaims any responsibility for them.

CONTENTS

Alan Farley's Obituary.................................xi
Introduction by Ron Lazar..............................1
Sir David Attenborough.................................7
Leonard Bernstein......................................9
Judy Campbell...10
Joyce Carey...29
Charles Castle and Stanley Hall.......................43
Stanley Hall..57
Roderick Cook...70
Mary Ellis..75
Peter Greenwell.......................................80
Norman Hackforth......................................94
Derek Jacobi...124
Geoffrey Johnson.....................................126
Evelyn Laye..132
Joe Layton...138
Moira Lister...162
Peter Matz...179
Joe Mitchenson.......................................204
Sheridan Morley......................................212
Sheridan Morley......................................226
Ned Sherrin..235
Graham Payn..246
Graham Payn..272
Helene Pons..278
Donald R. Seawell....................................283
Neil Simon...290
Alan Strachan..293
Elaine Stritch.......................................312
Harry Alan Towers....................................328
Wendy Toye...334
Barbara Waring.......................................352

"Speaking of Noël Coward"
Interviews by ALAN FARLEY
Edited by Ronald I. Lazar

ALPHABETICAL LIST OF INTERVIEWEES

SIR DAVID ATTENBOROUGH
Broadcaster and brother of Sir Richard Attenborough, who starred in Coward's wartime film *"In Which We Serve"*.

LEONARD BERNSTEIN
Conductor and composer.

JUDY CAMPBELL
Actress who toured with Coward.

JOYCE CAREY
Actress and longtime friend, who acted in many Coward productions.

CHARLES CASTLE
Author and broadcaster, who filmed Coward's last interview.

RODERICK COOK
Actor and creator of *"Oh Coward!"*

MARY ELLIS
Actress and singer, who appeared in Coward's *"After the Ball"*.

PETER GREENWELL
Pianist and composer, who was Coward's last accompanist.

NORMAN HACKFORTH
Pianist and songwriter, who accompanied Coward during and after World War II.

STANLEY HALL
Wigmaker and longtime Coward friend.

DEREK JACOBI
Actor directed by Coward in *"Hay Fever"* at England's National Theatre.

GEOFFREY JOHNSON
Casting director and Stage Manager for *"Sail Away"* and longtime consultant to the Coward Estate.

EVELYN LAYE
Actress who starred in *"Bitter Sweet"*.

JOE LAYTON
Director and Choreographer, who worked on *"Sail Away"* and *"The Girl Who Came to Supper"*.

MOIRA LISTER
Actress who played with Coward in *"Present Laughter"*.

PETER MATZ
Pianist, arranger and composer, who accompanied Coward in Las Vegas and worked on *"Sail Away"*.

JOE MITCHENSON
Co-Editor of *"The Theatrical Companion to Coward"*.

SHERIDAN MORLEY
Author of the first biography of Coward and longtime adviser to the Estate.

NED SHERRIN
Author, broadcaster, director and theatre historian.

GRAHAM PAYN
Actor and Coward's longtime companion, and former head of the Coward Estate.

HELENE PONS
Costume designer for *"Sail Away"*.

DONALD SEAWELL
Producer of *"Sail Away"* and founder of The Denver Center of the Performing Arts.

NEIL SIMON
Playwright.

ALAN STRACHAN
Director, involved in creating *"Cowardy Custard"* and *"Noël and Gertie"*.

ELAINE STRITCH
Tony winning actress, star of *"Sail Away"*.

HARRY ALLAN TOWERS
Film and radio producer, who produced *"The Noël Coward Radio Programme"*.

WENDY TOYE
Director and choreographer, who worked on *"Sigh No More"* and *"Cowardy Custard"*.

BARBARA WARING
Actress who appeared in *"Cavalcade"*.

Alan Farley dies—popular KALW host
by Joshua Kosman—San Francisco Chronicle

Oct. 23, 2012

(10-23) 23:01 PDT—Radio host Alan Farley, whose lively, erudite and versatile broadcasts on literature and the performing arts were a staple of the Bay Area airwaves for more than four decades, primarily on public radio station KALW, died Sunday of pancreatic cancer at the San Francisco home of a friend, Louis Dorsey. He was 76.

Mr. Farley joined the staff of KALW in 1975 after a stint as a volunteer and staff member at KPFA in Berkeley, and immediately began to put his personal stamp on the station's offerings.

Among the programs he created and hosted were "Book Talk," a weekly interview with writers; "Explorations in Music" and "Open Air," which often featured interviews with visiting luminaries in the worlds of music, dance and theater; and "My Favorite Things," on which Bay Area notables were invited to play and discuss their favorite musical recordings.

He was the host for the station's broadcasts of concerts by the Berkeley Symphony Orchestra and other performing arts specials. Each week he indulged his passion for the works of Noël Coward (Mr. Farley's car was instantly recognizable for its California vanity plate, which read SIRNOËL) by providing a "Noël Coward Entr'acte" between two Friday night programs.

He spoke eloquently and often about his love of baseball and his zeal for the Giants. And as one of the station's on-air hosts, he could be heard regularly bringing clarity and verve even to such mundane assignments as cueing the traffic report or regaling listeners with the daily lunch menu of the San Francisco Unified School District.

"Alan's passing is a huge loss for us here at KALW," wrote station manager Matt Martin on the station's website. "So many people were touched by Alan's voice, by his skill and generosity as an interviewer, and by his infectious enthusiasm for music and theater and books."

Off-air, Mr. Farley was a tireless devotee of the performing arts. He was a regular at opening nights for the San Francisco Symphony, the Ballet, Opera and American Conservatory Theatre, as well as many smaller cultural institutions.

"He considered that part of doing his homework," said his friend Fred Lipschultz, who often accompanied him. "He'd go because he knew there was someone he had just interviewed, or was planning to interview, on the radio."

Mr. Farley was born Jan. 24, 1936, in Lewiston, Idaho, and grew up in Seattle and Los Angeles. He studied mathematics as an undergraduate at the California Institute of Technology and as a graduate student at the University of Michigan and UC Berkeley. From 1964 to 1969 he was chairman of the math department at Morehouse College in Atlanta.

His resume included a stint as Richard Pryor's road manager. After moving to the Bay Area, he taught at Merritt College in Oakland before moving into the world of radio full time.

Mr. Farley's illness came on abruptly, friends said. He took a week's vacation at the beginning of August to attend performances at Shakespeare Santa Cruz and the Cabrillo Festival of Contemporary Music, where he began suffering from stomach pains. He was diagnosed with cancer shortly after that and did not return to work.

Mr. Farley is survived by two nieces and a nephew of Saipan in the Marianas Islands. Plans for a memorial service are pending.

Joshua Kosman is The San Francisco Chronicle's music critic. E-mail: jkosman@sfchronicle.com

INTRODUCTION

We are in San Francisco. It is 7 PM, March 26th, 1983, exactly ten years since Noël Coward died and became the eternally blithe spirit we celebrate in this book of interviews.

Tonight is an unusually warm evening. The waiters fan themselves with the table card announcements that The Plush Room Cabaret at the Hotel York is happy to have its hit Coward and Cole Porter revue extended into its third year. Alan Farley was the show's greatest champion, returning to see it with a willing initiate so many times, that I would bet on a stack of NPR producers, that for two years he attended more performances of the show than anyone else in town.

[Editor: This is where I first met Alan. It was later in 1987 that he was given a copy of my play, "Blue Harbour Honeymoon" (in which Noël appears as a character), and asked me to direct it for a Noël Coward birthday special he was producing for NPR.]

I expect the first audience member to arrive tonight will—as usual—be Alan Farley, and speaking of Alan Farley, he is now breezing towards us in casual white pants, smartly creased, wearing his trademark mock turtleneck shirt, and a sport coat draped from his squared shoulders. He is tall with a good head of straight, baby-fine white hair, pink skin and professorial demeanor, until he smiles a boyish grin, and lights up the faces of the staff. "He's here again!" chortles one of the graceful lads, martini en route,

From then to the day Alan Farley passed away, just before Thanksgiving, 2012, Noël Coward was a central artistic passion, a fascination that has manifested in this stunning collection of interviews.

This is a book of stories, told to one of Noël's most dedicated enthusiasts, about a man who modestly owned his genius by famously understating it—"the most I've had is just a talent to amuse." I would like to add that for Alan, it also would be an understatement that all Alan had was a talent to *ask questions*. His larger talent in evidence in this collection of interviews was his talent to *listen*.

INTRODUCTION

How did Alan come to his passion for Noël? Let me answer with this story:

Dick Cavett once asked Noël, "When did you first know that you were going to be a performer?"

Noël replied, "When I was four years old, my aunt and mother took me to church. The minute the organ started playing, I was in the aisle dancing. They took me home and put me straight to bed. Hardly an auspicious beginning, but it showed which way the wind was blowing."

That is not completely unlike Alan's first encounter with Coward's songs. Alan, too, was soon in the aisle at intermission, enthralled, humming the music, recalling those sparkling lines, and imitating the tone and gestures. Alan knew he had encountered a master artist, and fell hopelessly in love. Afterwards, Alan went to bed—not straight away, because it was three o'clock in the morning by the time the opening night party ended, but his lifelong revelry with Noël never ended.

It is easy and natural, and one would think—permissible and encouraged somehow by Noël's spirit—for Alan to interject into conversation inside references about Noël's friendships and associations. Alan loved to share stories he picked up through these interviews, so he broadcast them, and rebroadcast them, told them from memory at parties, over breakfast, lunch and dinner, between innings at the baseball game, and finally, naturally he thought it would be a very good idea to publish an edited version of the hundred plus hours of tape.

Alan believed these interviews give us the privilege of having a close encounter with an extraordinarily gifted man, seeming somewhat unapproachable, yet actually surprisingly accessible. The subjects are keen to tell us about Noël's empathy for the troubles of his intimates and associates. What often comes through in these interviews in rich detail are exquisitely expressive examples of how Noël impressed them with his insights of how very much alike we human beings really are. Noël's affectionate lampooning of British colonial eccentricities, and his poking fun at social conventions aside, Noël mostly endeared himself to people with his plainspoken and memorably precocious handling of delicate personal interactions, revealing his thoughtful character and lightning wit that electrifies his frequently amusing upbraids.

Should I take a moment to mention a charming character trait of Alan's—his frequent puns? Well, some were very good. Some were absolutely painful, so much so that he made himself groan, however, I enjoyed them. I recall how the eight o'clock show was late getting started, and since I was the entire technical crew for the club, he called me over and with a smile in his well-loved velvet tenor voice said into my ear, "Will the show be tonight at eight? Or, *'Tonight at 8:30'*?" We chuckled and tell the waiter, who laughs, who then tells the bartender, and so Alan is brought a martini on the house.

Noël and Alan did share the commendable trait of having intense focus, determination, and real emotional muscle, absolutely loved to be in control, but with a chocolate bunny for a heart. Alan was not a confrontational person, but needed a way to handle obstinate or judgmental people. Since he truly admired Noël's passionate put-downs, he often had one of those famous one-liners at the ready for any deserving bore who had the misfortune to cross him. Though, I never once heard Alan actually say any of them to their faces, he would tell me afterwards how he wanted to flatten the irritating person with one of Noël's lines, like a pointed putdown from "The Vortex"—"Poor ____, she's under the terrible delusion that she actually matters."

So, it is easy for me to feel that this collection of memories is really a treasure map. Where will this map take you? That sort of depends on where you want to go. For Alan, it led him to the heart of the answer to his questions, "Why did Noël make such a deep impression, and what did Noël mean to so many people?" Also, great stories. Noël was a man who himself is a treasure, obviously, but, for his dedication, Alan is the treasure-bearer. It was entirely of his own vision to embark on this odyssey so long ago. One soul seeking connection through a deep appreciation of another soul worth admiring. Noël was for Alan, what he is for me, and I believe many people, a wise and understanding friend, a guide, a confidant. Alan made it his joyful mission through his life to discover Noël Coward through the loving eyes of those who knew

INTRODUCTION

something special about Noël, and in these pages, his efforts are fulfilled.

Alan went to these interviews with no less curiosity than Darwin had in his obsession with the Galapagos. Likewise, this fascination runs through these interviews like the equator runs through islands of actors, continents of critics, countries of culture, and oceans of audiences. What is materially known to have been collected on these journeys by Alan, he left in his vast archives.

The unedited interviews were over 500,000 words of transcription. So, in case you were wondering what an editor of a book of interviews *does* with half a million words, he tasks himself with cutting out all that seems extraneous, or boring. This book is the essential result of carefully culled moments, to the more reasonable length of 112,850 words. They need not be read sequentially, or chronologically, and one might enjoy opening the book up to any page that catches your interest.

Theatrical people have a wide variety of verbal patterns, often giving much variety of dramatic emphasis. Some subjects easily sparkle with details and digressions, speak in asides and parentheticals, meander off track and back again. In one interview, Alan continued a conversation for over three hours with a progressively inebriated interviewee. I found it quite amusing. It reminded me of the scene in "Fallen Angels" when Julia and Jane get plastered. It seems sometimes life imitates Noël Coward.

I have taken care to do my best to invoke the particular inflections, attitudes, emotions, and vocal characteristics of each person, by the theatrical device of how dialogue is often written in a play—specific punctuation helps, even if it is grammatically incorrect, as best serves the speech of the subject, and the free employment of font enhancements.

Alan sat on a park bench in Central Park, New York to have a candid conversation with the compelling, energetic, and grounded realist Elaine Stritch. Alan flew to Switzerland to Les Avants for an intimate and sublime, and sometimes spiritual discussion with Graham Payn. Alan went wherever there was an interview worth having. There are many tales set in the atmosphere of pure fun in the backstage hurly burly world of actors, designers, friends and admirers.

Alan's style of interviewing has a consistently cordial and relaxed tone. He never pries or digs for dirt. His subjects are at ease and eagerly open up to him. If one is particularly interested in such techniques, Alan cultivated a fantastically subtle and truly sincere approach, sharing a love for Noël, and creating a safe, confidential space in which people embraced the opportunity to talk about Noël's humanity. As the editor, I often felt that there was more being said obliquely, so, I hope you will read between the lines, too. By that count the book is still easily over half a million (implied but unspoken) words.

This book will probably be appreciated most by those folks who are already familiar with Noël. For them, this book will be a banquet of gourmet delicacies. If you have no idea who Noël Coward is, well, *first,* I am surprised that you would think this book the place to begin; *second,* that you somehow came upon this book at all; and *third,* please consider accepting this as your invitation to the ball and feast. You are likely to enjoy his aficionados as much as you enjoy Noël's wit and music.

Personally, (and worth noting here, for it certainly affected how I responded to these interviews, and therefore, how I chose to edit them), I love how he stood up to and mocked pomposity, dismissed narrow minds, banished prudes, dispatched ersatz talent, ("next!"), admired a kimono as revenge [See the interview with Leonard Bernstein] and celebrated, often to music, all human struggles of the heart worthy of theatrical attention.

Alan brings us Noël's inner circle who understood him, his eccentricities, his creative tempo and artistic gestation process. Even after a lifetime of knowing Noël, they never stopped to wonder at how Noël's ideas came to life—sometimes giving birth in astonishingly few days (*"Hay Fever"*), (*"Private Lives"*) and sometimes a notion would take years to see the light of the stage. The great interpreter of Noël's music, Steve Ross, has recently released a recording of over two dozen songs by Noël that have never been recorded previously! Are we not all a bit breathless at Noël's output that is both wondrous and seemingly endless? Alan also uncovered some rare material during the course of his quest.

Alan's curiosity was also a hunger for knowing *how* an idea became a song, or *what* happened in the course of creating

INTRODUCTION

a hit show. Like a soap bubble that could travel the globe and never burst, Alan's interest in Noël never died, no matter how Alan's tribulations preoccupied him. In fact, he would find himself seeking comfort in Noël's music, as it seemed to bring him closer to the answer of how to handle darker times. There is a potency that heals one's hurt in some of Noël Coward's songs, and Alan turned to them, finding they gave him strength to persevere.

I remember when Alan came to visit me at my Oregon home for Thanksgiving 2004, and we took a long drive up the beautiful coast. I knew something was bothering him, and when I asked him if he wanted to talk about it, he said "no." Then he began singing "Sail Away." We both knew all the words, and by the end, he was better and hopeful again. Noël was there for Alan, with a heart and a sense of humor, even when there were bad times just around the corner.

I hope the interviews gathered in this book, that Alan ventured thousands of miles to do, and broadcast on NPR KALW over a span of twenty years, will serve his legacy well, as one of the most devoted chroniclers of those who love speaking of Noël Coward.

Ron Lazar, Editor
May 2013

SIR DAVID ATTENBOROUGH

b. May 8, 1926

Interviewed on October 3, 1995

SIR DAVID ATTENBOROUGH is a well-known and popular television broadcaster on both sides of the Atlantic. He is the brother of Sir Richard Attenborough, who played in Noël Coward's wartime film, *"In Which We Serve"*. I spoke to him when he was in San Francisco to talk about his new book and television series *"The Private Life of Plants"*. The interview was recorded at the KALW studios.

ALAN FARLEY: Did you know Noël Coward?

DAVID ATTENBOROUGH: Well, I *met* him.

AF: Because I think he was instrumental in Sir Richard's acting career.

DA: Oh, very much. My brother *revered* him, and thought that he was *The Master.*
    Well, I don't know whether I should be telling this story on air, but the very first film my brother made was directed by Noël Coward, in which Noël Coward starred, *"In Which We Serve"*. It was about a British destroyer during the war that was sunk.
    I was, I suppose, fourteen at the time. Big brother left. We grew up in a city called Leicester.
    My big brother had gone out to the big city, you know, and working with Noël Coward! Noël Coward!! My goodness! So, we were FRIGHTFULLY thrilled with all this!
    In due course, Dick said, "Why don't you come down? Would you like to see the studios, so you can see where I've been?"
    Well! Thrill upon thrill! So, I put on my school cap and my short trousers, and off we went, down to the studios in London.
    They were shooting a scene in a big tank, which had a floating raft in it, and hanging on this raft was my brother, and

Noël Coward, and various other people like John Mills, and Bernard Miles, and various people who were big actors of that time.

    We waited for what seemed hours, when eventually, they got what they wanted, they said, and they climbed out of this tank sopping wet and covered in oil and stuff, to my slight apprehension. I was slightly aghast that this demigod, Noël Coward, was clearly going to come over and SEE us! How did you deal with, you know, such an ENORMOUS figure? I mean, as I say, a HERO of utmost glamour!

    My brother said, *"Mister Coward,"* of course, "may I introduce my young brother, *David?"* Noël Coward said (and I can't really imitate his clipped voice) but he said, *"Delighted to meet you. I think if I'd stayed in that tank another tiny minute, my little nuts would have dropped right off!*

    I was astounded—amazed—that a grownup spoke to ME about such THINGS!

    I wished that the floor had opened and swallowed me up!
    [laughter]

AF: Wonderful story!

LEONARD BERNSTEIN

b. August 25, 1918   d. October 14, 1990

Interviewed in February, 1984

Leonard Bernstein, renowned American conductor and composer, told an anecdote about Noël Coward during a visit to San Francisco with the Vienna Philharmonic Orchestra; recorded after a press conference in Davies Symphony Hall, San Francisco, California.

ALAN FARLEY: Did you get to know Noël Coward well?

LEONARD BERNSTEIN: Yes, well, not *that* well. I tell you what, though, the time that I spent—the longest unbroken time—was a few hours one night at dinner.
    He came to our house in Martha's Vineyard [Massachusetts]. I don't know what he was doing in Martha's Vineyard, but we invited him to dinner, and *he played the score of "Sail Away"* that night. He was just about to open on Broadway.
    I remember—I don't usually remember what I say, and I never quote myself—but, I remember being *very hung up for something to say,* after he'd played the score, and I heard myself say, "Noël, it sounds like it's *always been there."*
    Which can be variously interpreted—like a *classic,* or like an *unoriginal* piece of music, which it *really was.* It was his last feeble days.
    But, the *main* thing about that evening was that I had just come back from Japan, and I had this *marvelous kimono* that had been made for me there, with *my initials* in Japanese, with beautiful decorations, and he admired it enormously, 'cause I wore it to the dinner table, and I said, "Oh, would you like to wear it through dinner?"
    "Oh?" He asked, "Could I try it on? Such wonderful silk." Well, he wore it through dinner, and *left with it, and I never saw it again! Never been mentioned!*

JUDY CAMPBELL

b. May 31, 1916   d. June 6, 2004

Interviewed on September 28, 1990

Judy Campbell, actress, worked extensively on stage with Noël Coward during World War II, and has appeared in Coward works in the theatre and cabaret in the years since. The interview was conducted in her London home.

JUDY CAMPBELL: I *dreamed* of meeting him.
　Oddly enough, in those days I could sing. I roughed up my voice very badly during the long, long tour of a play called *"Idiots Delight"* with Vic Oliver, that the Lunts had done in America. There was a lot of screaming and shouting in it, and I had tonsillitis, and Vic wouldn't let me be off. So, I played for weeks on end with screaming tonsillitis in very, very big theatres, and by the end of the tour I'd lost my top register altogether.
　And because I'd not been to drama school, and I'd never had lessons in voice production, I didn't know how to husband it. How to *breathe* from the stomach and do all those things you're supposed to do, so I used to just—Awk!—on the vocal chords and really messed them up. By the time I was made a present of *"Nightingale"* [Ed. Note: *"When The Nightingale Sang In Berkeley Square"*] my first reaction was, "I can't sing!" because I was UNtrained, *of course,* but I had had a reasonably large range. And it had gone. I just had a range of about an octave. Do you want to know about *"Nightingale"?*

ALAN FARLEY: Yes, because it's the fiftieth anniversary, isn't it!

JC: Yes it is! And it was just so extraordinary, because I'd been in rep for years and I was the leading lady at Liverpool.
　The idea was that apart from the opening number and some quartets and some trios, I would do a monologue by Dorothy Parker for my star turn and nobody could find Dorothy Parker. She

had disappeared into the Arizona desert or something, and we had a war on.

So, one day sitting 'round in the Cafe Royale with Jack Davis and Eric Maschwitz, they said, "I think you'd better sing *"When the Nightingale Sang in Berkeley Square"*. Eric had written it with another composer, Manning Sherwin.

So, we went up to the music publishers with me saying, "I'm terribly sorry, I can't sing," and went through it.

In the end, it was agreed that I *would* take it away and rehearse it with Elsie April, who is the most amazing lady. She'd done *all* of Coward's orchestrations. I did go to a music teacher and he said, 'If you came every day, I might give you a voice, but if you are opening in a couple of weeks, then remember—*talk* what you can't sing, and gargle with port and the best of British luck.

I went back to Elsie and she put a bit into waltz style, and she switched keys and thought of all sorts of clever things. I made up a dance, and all this time I wouldn't do it in front of anybody. I wouldn't show it to *anybody,* and at last—we were within days of opening and the director said, "I've got to make you a dress."

Joan Davis, who was doing the dances, said, "I've really got to look at it."

So, I did it.

I was wearing a jacket and when I came to the end, I threw my jacket into the air and ran off laughing instead of singing the last line.

And they said, "Keep it. Keep it just like that."

Joan helped me clean up the turns a bit, so that I wouldn't get too dizzy in my little dance, which was all sort of, for me, it was very happy.

I think that Harold Hobson wrote these lovely articles about it, about how it was the song that kept up everybody's morale during the air raids. How it was the most romantic thing. He wrote a sweet thing, if I can quote it, about myself, saying that "the pressure of recollected *happiness* that she put into her husky voice."

That *is* what I tried to do. For me, the whole thing was immensely happy.

Later on, when it was made into records, by Bing Crosby in America and Vera Lynn here, it was a quite different thing. They did it extremely well, of course, but it was *crooned* and it was a bit *sad*, I thought. Whereas, for me it was immense *happiness,* and I hope I brought humor to it, and even a little dance.

I imagined that I was being waltzed around in his arms, and that we were laughing and enjoying ourselves. My mother found a feather boa that I could throw into the air. We tried a bit of chiffon and it didn't work. She found the last feather boa in London, and I used to throw it up into the air, and after that it got imitated in another revue, and it sort of caught on. It was a success. It was lovely.

Then the air raids started.

Soon after we opened in late Spring, early Summer and around May or June, I remember standing outside the stage door and watching a dogfight in the sky. Then they got worse and worse.

To begin with, when the sirens went on, the stage manager used to come onto the stage and say to the audience that the air raid sirens had gone, and if they wanted to take shelter, the nearest shelters were in Leicester Square, but if they liked to stay in the theatre, we would do our best to entertain them.

Of course, the "all clear" [siren] used to not go till one o'clock in the morning sometimes. So, there we were. When we finished the revue, we did a great deal of it all over again. Then the stage manager did his conjuring tricks and then we led the audience in community singing. This went on, I can't remember, three or four weeks, maybe longer, and then the raids got really heavy and were all night jobs. So, that was a bit different.

Then the government *closed* the theatres and sent us off on tour. We only went on tour for about a month, but I do remember we did Coventry, Liverpool—wherever we arrived, they either had just had the worst air raid ever, or they were just about to have it.

In Liverpool the smell of fish was overpowering because they'd bombed the fish market, and we, none of us, had anywhere to sleep because they'd bombed the Adelphi Hotel. That sort of thing.

Then the government decided it was all a *mistake*, and we must have the theatres *open*. So, we came *back*.

Alas, with two pianos, instead of that *lovely* orchestra. I had *flutes* in my introduction, it was so magical. Like the opening of *"L'Apres-Midi"*. It was *magic* for me and I hope for the audience. I kind of created a persona, and acted it, to tell the audience what a wonderful night it was when the *"Nightingale Sang in Berkeley Square."*

AF: But how come *you* didn't get recorded?

JC: By that time I'd gone into a straight play. I think I'd gone into *"Watch On The Rhine"*.

You know, one has to remember that there was a war on, and an awful lot of the time was spent—I narrowly escaped being in the Cafe de Paris the night that it was bombed. When the whole thing was coming to an end, because it ran for over a year right into 1941—It was Charlie's idea [Producer, Charles Cochran].

He said, "Let's take a recording studio" which you could do for ten shillings or something, and "I'll play the piano for you."

So, we made this little record. My mother had a copy and I had a copy. Somehow, one of them survived, covered in scratches, and now it's been lifted, so it's slightly less scratched. It had *brought me so much, "Nightingale"*. After all, if it hadn't been for the war, I wouldn't have been in the revue. I would have come to London, one assumes, in a straight play. Probably something perhaps that we had done at Liverpool, or something like that, because there was a war. It was light entertainment, that was all. There were about four or five revues running in London. We had to keep on changing it, too. When Paris fell, we had to take out—I had another number called *"Paris Is Not The Same"*—we had to take it out and put in *"Room Five Hundred and Four"* We had a lot of rather French flavored numbers, and when the Germans got France, you know, there was just a hasty rehearsal, and of course, we did troop concerts on Sundays and all of that.

But, do you see? It brought me Noël.

He came to see it, *and* came 'round to see *me*! I thought at first it was—I knew he was in front—I didn't dare hope that he'd come 'round to see me, because he was my—I've told you I think—my most admired, to me, the most glamorous, marvelous figure as a writer, as a playwright, everything.

So, when there was a knock on the door, I thought maybe somebody was pulling my leg, but they weren't.

He said, "It takes considerable talent to put over a song without a singing voice. You must come and act with me in my plays."

He was as good as his word. A year later I *did*.

I did *"Watch On The Rhine"* and I did another play, but I was only in it for three months, because the call came to go and play Joanna in *"Present Laughter"* and Ethel in *"This Happy Breed"* and, also, he had the idea of doing *"Blithe Spirit"*.

But I wasn't free of *"Nightingale* because we did an immense seven-month tour. Unheard of! [Producer] Binky [Beaumont] wasn't at all keen. He wanted to do it all at The Haymarket.

But Noël said, "No, no, no! There is a war on. The provinces can't come to the West End anymore, therefore, the West End must go to the provinces!"

We opened in Blackpool, and then we went further and further north. We were in Scotland for Christmas and the New Year. We were in Inverness for the New Year, and Noël had to go to the Mayor to try and get a radiator for Joycie [Joyce Carey] and me because we were so cold. War time regulations, you could only have *four inches* of bath water!

So, ALL of us had roaring colds!

One night we were playing *"Present Laughter"* in Inverness, and a very small fire broke out in a wardrobe that was *under* the stage. Spires of smoke came *up* into the orchestra pit, and without pausing in the scene, Noël got up and began *pushing* the sofa downstage. We *both* pushed the sofa.
He said, "May as well get *nearer* the fire."

[laughter]

And we went on with the scene!

He used to wear this silk dressing gown. I wore my Molyneaux dress that you've seen photographs of, under which I could wear nothing. I couldn't even wear a bra, and so it was very, very cold indeed.

Everywhere we went Noël had taken on to entertain the troops. We were going to Scapa Flow, and at the last minute we couldn't. We went to an island nearby. It was the first time I'd ever flown in an airplane. It's tremendously exciting for me. Sometimes we sang in the Sergeant's mess, and sometimes we sang in a destroyer. Sometimes we entertained the commandos on a mountainside, and the snow was so deep up in Scotland that we couldn't get back to the hotel, and Noël and I had to go and stay the night in a sort of shooting lodge, that belonged to a rather crazy man, who was in the commandos, and we stayed there and it was extraordinary.

The whole thing was lit by paraffin stoves, and when we came down to breakfast in the morning, we wore *papal vestments*, because this slightly crackpot, sweet man collected papal vestments, and as we had *no luggage* with us, and no dressing gowns, he gave us these long cardinal robes and things to wear. **I always remember Noël coming down the stairs in a purple cassock!—clasping his box of a 'Hundred Players' [cigarettes] to his chest saying, "My tiny hand is frozen."**

[laughter]

It was funny. He used to take me along. You see, really the thing was, he was going to do it, but he was going to do an hour, which is a hell of a long time, and so we toured with a pianist, and he always had a piano in his room, or his sitting room, of course, the big hotels were still open the Midland Manchester, so, in a way, you could have a sitting room, so that he always had a piano, and he did a great deal of *composing.*

On tour we had a pianist, not Norman Hackforth, but Robb Stewart, who was amazing.

Noël conceived the idea that he would take me along so that I could give him a break and a rest, and I would sing for six or seven minutes, maybe. Well, you know a number doesn't last very long, so, after *"Nightingale"* it meant I had to learn some other things.

Then, he would do a terrifying tease that was really a challenge for me.

Sometimes we'd gather after the play in his hotel sitting room, and he usually had visitors, maybe Coley [Cole Lesley] would come if he had a bit of leave, friends from the London theatre, Joycie maybe would be coming along for the troop concerts, maybe visiting firemen of various sorts.

Then the cars would come and collect us to take us off there, and Noël—this didn't happen *every* time, but you know, quite a few times, especially when we first started up in the north, and he'd say, "Well, we've got five minutes to wait for the cars. What are you going to sing for us this evening?"

And he would *make* me get up and *sing* in the sitting room, in a hotel!

I've never been so *scared* in my life! I used to *hate* it so. And he *knew* how scared I was, but it was a challenge and you did it.

It's like, *"IF* for Girls", you know Rudyard Kipling's *"IF"*? There's a version for girls . . . *"can sing, when asked, without excuse or stammer,"* is one of the things in it. It was a challenge.

Then, once the cars arrived, he was very, very good.

He would always just be alone with me. 'Cause he knew I was scared, and, sometimes, we'd have a little *nip* out of a hip flask. Drinking in the theatre was always, quite rightly, absolutely *forbidden*. Noël had seen *too* many actors go to pieces with drink, and so, never, never, *never* did he have the drink before the show, but, *on the way* to the *troop* concerts we *would* have a *little* nip.

He used to give me wonderful advice. *Wonderful* advice.

He used to say, "You know, I know that you're frightened, but walk out onto that stage, and look around at the audience, and give a *smile*, as *if* you are *pleased* to see them, and let Robb *start*, and wait, wait, *wait* until you've got their *total* and *entire* attention, and *then*, and not before, START! And *if* you want to make a gesture, you *must* make it *above the waist*, never below."

He was quite right. He was quite right.

He said, "*Act* the confidence that we know you haven't really got, but you must walk out there *confidently*, taking your time, as *if* we are all going to have a lovely time."

Well, then of course, the whole thing collapsed when we got to the midlands, because we had to sing to the factories, to the munitions workers, and they weren't even in the room with us. They were scattered about hearing the thing over *loudspeakers,* and they were used to music while you work.

Noël said, "There, they all are, *deeply* regretting that we're *not* Vera Lynn." [laughter]

It was awful.

When we got down to the south, to Portsmouth and Plymouth, and those places, there were big naval hospitals there, and there was one that was really—it had been a mental hospital in peace time, and it was being used, for the Navy, for people who were mentally ill, more than physically impaired. People who'd cracked up under the strain or whatever.

So, Noël had done *"In Which We Serve"* and he'd use people from the Navy in that scene where he says goodbye to the men, after the HMS Kelly is sunk.

When we did this hospital in particular, all of them, actually, we would go around to the beds to visit the men who were bedridden, and couldn't get to the concert. He would go up one side of the ward, I would go up the other, we'd cross over at the top, and come down the other side. I found that when I went down the side that Noël had already visited, at least half the men would say, "Captain Coward remembered me."

Because they'd been *in "In Which We Serve"* and he *did*, he *remembered* them! Nine times out often he remembered their names. It was quite extraordinary and wonderful. I loved doing that with him. I loved it.

We went to a ward for bad cases and they'd got one man who'd been shipwrecked three times doing convoys to Russia, and had been left in icy cold water with others, of course, somehow survived, and had then come back and then got another, and it happened again, so that he was in pretty bad shape.

They were going to give him something fairly new then, it was the 'deep sleep treatment'. He asked if the treatment need start till after Noël had been there.

Perhaps he had been one of the *"In Which We Serve"* people, I don't know. But, they'd got him alone in a darkened

17

room, and Noël was ordinarily a very punctual *leaver*, he would do his stuff marvelously at a party or anywhere else.

Then he would say, "Time to go," and *go*.

But, on this occasion, they told him about this man—and we stayed on.

I stayed and talked to the others while he went in and talked to this man for about half an hour. When we got the usual 'letter-of-thanks,' which, of course, came to Noël, and he would show me, it said that "Your visit did such immense good for morale and for the morale of this man, in particular, it might no longer be necessary to give him 'the deep sleep' treatment."

Noël's visit had had such a tremendous *therapeutic* effect! Isn't it marvelous? It's something that people don't know about him, *I* think.

His love for the Navy, and his immense patriotism, of course, and his love for the theatre—I know he was very social, and he had lots of The Royal Family, and dukes and duchesses, and all of that very glamorous stuff, but he also *always* remembered *old* friends from earlier days.

Once, he took me with him because he was going to see a musical comedy actress, who'd married *somebody*, who ran a farm, and they were *up there*—somewhere outside Carlisle—and she'd *written* to him when she heard he was coming there.

He took *me* because my parents were in the theatre. He knew *I* liked talking 'greasepaint talk,' and so we went out and had lunch in the farmhouse kitchen, and just talked about the old days—about musicals of the twenties, which I'd only seen as a little girl, but *I* knew about that sort of world immensely through my father and mother. He was just as outgoing for her as he was for any duke and duchess.

I'd like to have that said, too, because so many people *think* that he was rather a *snob*. There is *another* side to it. *I* think he loved the theatre really more than anything.

AF: Let's talk a little bit about creating those roles—in *"Present Laughter* for instance.

JC: It really was quite something because time was very short, and we were going to do *three* plays, and we still only had a rehearsing time of four weeks. We did a play a week, and then a week of dress rehearsals. We had a reading in Noël's studio.

He said, "Would you all please do your best to *learn* it *beforehand.*"

We were all pretty young. Joyce [Carey] had been in on the writing of a great many of the plays, you know, so it wasn't too hard. I'd been in weekly rep and was awfully used to learning very fast, so it wasn't too hard.

Something made it much, much easier, because Binky [Beaumont] *took* the theatre, which was dark at the time, and had all the sets built! Although we didn't have the clothes for *"Present Laughter"* we did have a few bits and bobs for *"This Happy Breed"*, but we had the sets and props and everything. So, I always remembered that the *first* play we rehearsed the first week was *"Blithe Spirit"* because that was already running and they'd worked out all the technicalities of it. I always remembered being swept on at the first rehearsal through *real* French windows by a wind machine—and then, of course, we *hadn't* learned the words perfectly, but, all the same, we *were* able to do *"Blithe Spirit"* in a week.

Then, the next one was—I think it was probably *"Present Laughter"*.

When we came to do that, Noël said, "I've worked out some positions for the scenes that involve more than two people, because that's obviously going to be a shortcut." He said that when we come to the 'two-handers' we'll work it out.

So, that long love scene we worked out as we went along, and then Noël would say, "Next time, you know, tomorrow, try moving down to the fireplace earlier," or something like that.

The next day, yes we did that. We rehearsed it for a week. On Saturday we went back and picked up *"Blithe Spirit"* so we wouldn't forget it.

Then the third week, *"This Happy Breed"* was absolutely astonishing! It was so amazing having the props, because, every time, the *first* scene I had with him was emptying packing cases, (because we'd moved into our new house), and so, one was unpacking things out of bits of newspaper, and he'd come over and give me a kiss!

We'd go on unpacking these things and darting around the room. We had the packing case. We had things all wrapped up in bits of newspaper. In the other scenes, we had tea trays, enormous, great trays of tea or something rather like that. It was amazing to *have* the trays.

So, as I say, one wasn't really anything like 'word perfect' on the first rehearsal, but all the same, we had a great working notion of it. You've done your homework as best you could, and to have the props, and above all to have *Noël* there—so that when you ordinarily rehearse a play with a director who isn't in the play, and you come to a knotty spot and he says, "Well, I'll ask the author, and I'll ring him up tonight" and you know, but—well, Noël was *there*. He was *playing in* the play. He'd *written* it, *and* he was *directing* it. So, it was an *amazing* short cut. So, that it wasn't—you know, when one says to people, "We rehearsed each one in a week"—yes, it was, it was *extraordinary.*

Then the last week of all, in the daytime we had dress rehearsals, and then in the evening we'd have *public* dress rehearsals. Everybody used to come. The nurses, the firemen, *everybody,* also the Oliviers, anybody who wanted to see the plays, which was a great, great many people. So, that last week was a sort of foretaste of what was to come.

AF: How did he direct himself? How could he get an idea of how *his* performance was going?

JC: I think he had a pretty good idea. He *wrote* it. [laughs] I think the only one that for him was extraordinary was that he was doing *"Blithe Spirit"* partly, he said, because he wanted to play Charles Condomine, and then when he came to do it, he said, "I had no *idea* what a bloody *awful* part it is! ft is extremely long, and Cecil Parker is quite brilliant to have sustained it on that level," he said, "because *I* do all the work, and you get all the laughs!"

You know, Madame Arcati and the wives get all the laughs, and he said, Tm there, *never* off the stage, doing *all* the work! Great mistake!" [laughs]

He was terribly kind. He took me out to lunch before the play started, or sometime in the first week or other, and *I was* very afraid of his *acid wit,* because I'd heard a lot about it, and *I* was very nervous of being the butt of his *acid wit* if *I* did something wrong.

So I virtually *asked* him to be kind, and he promised he *would* be, and indeed, he *was.*

Anything he said to *any* of us, it was much *more.* It came about, actually, you were *working,* you were *doing* the stuff, and he would alter moves, or just stop and suggest something, but really, he *didn't* criticize one's performance, except if he wanted to, say, sharpen something up, he was very good about doing it *not* in front of everybody, which was wonderful, and lovely to work with, absolutely lovely.

Then during the performance, of course—as I say, we did seven months—the thing began growing. Especially *"Present Laughter"* because Gary Essendine is meant to be himself [Noël] and with Joyce [Carey]—in the play, she's his ex-wife, and in real life, as you know, his dearest friend. So, it was all written about himself really. He built that up like anything.

At the end he just collapsed on the sofa saying, "Leave me, leave me, all of you."

Suddenly, when we'd been doing it for a few weeks—*months* on tour, this began to get longer and *longer.* And he made a sort of tirade speech.

One night he launched into a great long speech from *"Cyrano de Bergerac"!* [laughs] We were all absolutely *stunned! Instead* of collapsing on the sofa, he collapsed onto the floor!

Everybody who was leaving had to step over him! Which made it terribly funny!

You know—"good night!"—"Garry, I really think you've behaved in a most extraordinary fashion," they said, as one stepped over his recumbent body. It was terribly funny.

That all came about in *performance.* It was *not* rehearsed. We didn't have—as far as I can recall—I don't think we had any rehearsals while we were out on tour. Everything that happened, happened during *performance,* and sometimes he would go faster, and then he used also to do a thing to keep us on our toes, which *only* he could do.

He would *cut you off short!*

He would *interrupt* your line, so that you had to *push* it out, and make it very strong. *I* remember Beryl Measor, who was quite brilliant playing Madame Arcati, she also played Monica in *"Present Laughter"* and where she's going home, he actually *stood* in front of the door and refused to let her go home—until, in the end, she was saying, "Well, *really,* Garry!" and forcing her way off. That kind of thing. So, it meant you were mentally alert the whole time.

Also, he used to do the opposite. He would *not* come in on a broken sentence, forcing you to finish it, which is very, very good for any actor, really. I don't mean on things that needed frightfully careful timing, or wonderful laughs.

There was a bit, I remember, in a wedding scene of *"This Happy Breed"* when I had to say something about—"Oh, really, I don't know where Frank's got to! He was meant to be"—and then *Noël* was meant to break in and say, "Don't fuss, Ethel."

He didn't. He just *sat* there.

I said, "He was meant to be—going—to see what's *happened* to the *taxi,* and *I don't* know what's happened to the *taxi,* and *I don't* know what's happened to *him"*

And Noël said, "Go on, Ethel, you're speculations fascinate me strangely."

[laughs]

And I had to go on.

He didn't do it *every* night. We didn't keep that in, but it's just an example of something he might do.

On Saturday nights, actually, we did *"This Happy Breed"* and it was the longest one of the plays, and we used to hurry it up a bit so that we could catch the late night train back to London on a Saturday night, when possible. So, he would start cutting and leaping ahead, and all of us were on our toes and did the same.

He gave you a wonderful liberty to put things in yourself.

He would sometimes build on things that did stay in. Like—I began *rubbing my shoulder* out of tiredness, the way you do, doing my mending in *"This Happy Breed"*. He nodded to the actress who was playing my daughter and he said, "Give your mother's shoulder a rub, Vi." And she came over and began rubbing my shoulder and it was good. We kept it in. That sort of thing, you know, just built up while we were doing it, so that by the time we opened in London it was fantastic.

Oh, but I was telling a story against myself. In *"Blithe Spirit"*—I adored playing Elvira—and I became more, and *more,* and *more FLUTTERING* about like a ghost.

One night in the wings he said, "I've never, never criticized your performance, but there is just a tiny thing I want to say. You really are getting too bloody *graceful*. I know you're a tall girl, so you've studied to move gracefully."

I took it very badly. I said, "I don't know what you mean. It just comes to me naturally. I never studied to be *graceful.*" Very *miffy*, like that.

And so, he said, "Well, okay . . . but just, you know, one *less* turn on the way to the piano would make the scene a *great* deal funnier, because the whole *point* about Elvira is that she's a ghost, but you're *made up* like a ghost, and the audience *accepts* you as a ghost, but you don't have to *fly about* like a ghost, because it *stops* it being funny. You must *walk* onto the stage when you are in a sulk. You must *stamp* about as if you are wearing *gum-boots*. That's what makes it funny."

"Ooh-hoo! All right!" I said.

Then we went on to play the scene, and I had to follow him on for that scene where Elvira's in a temper about something, and I was so put out I *tripped* over the hearthrug, and I nearly fell flat on my face! Noël was delighted! 'Hee, hee, hee!'

After that, I was in a *real* rage, and I *stamped* about, and of course, he was dead *right*. It was a great, *great* deal funnier! Much funnier. [laughs]

He would sometimes say as one sat in the wings, "Let's try and make it faster tonight" or "We seem to have lost that laugh on . . ." something or other; never, never called a rehearsal.

To work for him was never quite the same. I did his play, *"Relative Values"* with Gladys Cooper, after the war, around the early 1950's, I think. Noël badly wanted a success.

He was furious at Gladys Cooper, who either wouldn't, or *couldn't* learn her lines, though he adored her, really, and she gave a *brilliant* performance. and it was all wonderful. During rehearsals, she just didn't seem to learn her lines.

In fact, she said, "I never had the book out of my hand till the dress rehearsals for [actor-manager] Gerald [du Maurier], I'm damned if I'm going to start for you!" [chuckles]

When she'd gone one day, Noël said, "I'm sorry, I'm going to have to start having *word* rehearsals, because otherwise, I know *what* is going to happen. We shall open and there will be a dull crack from the back of the dress circle, and it will be *me*—shooting myself. [laughs]

And Gladys said, *not gone,* "Careful what you say, I'm still here!"

She was amazing, but we *did* have to have evening *word* rehearsals, because he *did,* by then, have that *thing,* that he wanted everybody to *know their lines* before rehearsal.

A lot of people don't agree with it. They'd rather write in the moves, and build the thing up. If you've got three or four weeks to do it, why not? But of course then he came down to visit us when we were on tour, and began worrying all of us, and then, in the end, Binky came and smoothed it all over, and of course, we opened in London, and Gladys was absolutely magnificent and perfectly wonderful! The thing was a great success and ran for a year!

I'm only saying it because I don't know how other people have found being directed by Noël, but it was *not* the same as working *with* him. Working *with* him was a dream! One *learnt* more from working *with* him. He was wonderful.

AF: When you sang to relieve Noël in those troop concerts, did you ever sing any of *his* songs in that interval?

JC: No. No. *I* sang, at his suggestion, *I* sang, *"Let's Do It"*—

AF: He *almost* made that his!

JC: He *made* that his! As far as actual singing, I was quite good if the thing had got rhythm. *I* used to sing a version of *"On the*

Bonnie, Bonnie Banks of Loch Lomond" I used to sing Gertie's song from *"Nymph Errant" ["The Physician"*—she sings some of the song very quickly.] Oh! It was absolutely divine! Heavenly number!

AF: [quoting from the song] "But he never said, he loved *me!*"

JC: That's right! [laughs]

AF: Oh, I think that is one of Cole Porter's greatest songs.

JC: Greatest songs. Absolutely marvelous! Marvelous! Yes, those are the sort of things I did.

AF: Just as a member of the audience, or as a fan, what were some of his songs that were your favorites?

JC: *Where are the songs we sung?*
When love in our hearts was young
When in the limbo of the passing years
Lie all our hopes, and dreams, and fears.
I think it's the most amazing lyric and the most beautiful, beautiful tune.

And then I loved [Yvonne] Printemps singing—the one she sings after she says, *"It doesn't feel like my birthday anymore."* [in *"Conversation Piece"*] *"Nevermore"* was the song she sang; it ends something like—
Others may regain their freedom,
But for you and me,
Never,
Nevermore.
And she went *up!* And, oh, how *I* wish *I* could *really* sing. Printemps did amazing things with it.

I've heard Patricia Routledge, oh, she's so funny, she's so good! She's an amazing actress, and she's also got a wonderful, wonderful voice. She sang it for Noël's birthday celebration, and *I* hadn't heard it for years, and, oh, it was beautiful, beautiful.

Then, when I'd first met him, and *I* was still in *"New Faces"* and then afterwards, *I* was in a play—it didn't run for very long, it was directed by John Gielgud. And Clemence Dane, beloved Winifred, who was Noël's great friend, used to give parties at her flat in Covent Garden.

I went to stay the night with her once, because wherever I was, I couldn't get back to, there was such an air raid, and she painted the city in flames from her window, while the air raid was going on! She was an extraordinary woman. She gave picnics and things, and Noël came. There was a wonderful picnic she gave in Hyde Park and Noël came and Joyce [Carey], I think. There was Winifred, who had made sausage rolls, and I helped her pack it all up.

She said, "The gypsies, you know, would have baked a hedgehog, but we can't do that. They baked them in clay," according to her, "and then all the prickles fall off when you take the clay off, and you're left with a little *hedge-pig,* which tastes like *chicken"*—according to Winifred.

Anyway, we had this picnic in Hyde Park, and a wounded sailor came by, and he'd served with Mountbatten, and it was at the time that Noël was doing *"In Which We Serve"* (I get terribly muddled up with dates.) So, he was invited to come and join us. It was lovely. We all sat on the grass and he joined in the picnic.

Winifred of course, *wrote.* She was part scriptwriter on that film with Noël. I didn't realize it until I saw it again. I saw that she had a credit as having written the script.

AF: I didn't know that.

JC: Anyway, she used to give parties in her flat in Covent Garden, and I was invited to two or three of them. There were all these lovely luminaries. Noël would play the piano. He played a song called *"I Travel Alone"* I believe he subsequently has recorded it, because I've heard it since, but I'd never heard it before, and it was lovely—

Free of the places and faces I've known,
When the journey's over and passion has flown,

I travel alone.

It was lovely. He sang quite a lot of those songs that weren't the big hits—*'one-off'* songs. Do you remember that film he made called *"The Scoundrel"?*

AF: Yes.

JC: I'd seen it when I was in rep. It played at Coventry, I think, and I used to go every afternoon and see it. It seems terribly dated and peculiar now, but then it was pretty good.

I remember, there was a scene where a composer came, and he [Noël] said, "What have you written lately?"
The composer said, "Oh, only a few small pieces."
Noël said, "Play me some of the smallest."

AF: [laughing] I don't remember that!

JC: [laughing] That's what Noël did with Winifred. Played a few small pieces, some of the smallest.

AF: That's interesting because that film is the one in which Mary Martin first saw Noël Coward, where she was *first* impressed by him, and wanted to meet him after seeing him in it. She was just a teenage girl in Texas at the time.

JC: That's right. That's right.

AF: Well, you've been very generous with your time.

JC: I've loved it. I've loved it. I hope I haven't left out things that I wish I'd told you, because you know, you talk off the top of your head, but it's a time I remember so well.

AF: As you say, people just do not write lyrics like that.

JC: They don't. Very few ever did. And when you think that he wrote lyrics that were as good as Cole Porter's, and music, and wonderful, wonderful, musicals! *"Bitter Sweet"* and then he wrote *"Private Lives"*.

I've never known an all-around man of genius like him. It is extraordinary. Extraordinary. To have that output. I think it's a super, super amount of energy. They say that genius is ten percent inspiration, and ninety percent perspiration, but *my god* the *inspiration!* As he's written himself, you know, the waltz from *"Bitter Sweet" dropped* into his mind, while in a *taxi, whole* and *complete,* and he couldn't wait to write it down.

[her voice soft, reverent]

Amazing! Wonderful, amazing man.

JOYCE CAREY

b. March 30, 1898   d. February 28, 1993

Interviewed on May 4, 1989

Joyce Carey knew Noël Coward for nearly fifty years; from their first meeting in 1924, when her mother, Lilian Braithwaite, [Dame Lilian Braithwaite DBE 9 March 1873-17 September 1948] played a leading role in Coward's breakthrough play, *"The Vortex,"* until his death in 1973—She was a constant confidant, colleague, and companion. She appeared in some of his greatest film works, including *"Brief Encounter"* and *"In Which We Serve."* She was interviewed in her Eaton Square flat.

ALAN FARLEY: It seemed to me, from reading *"The Diaries"* that you must have been just about one of Noël's closest friends for the longest time.

JOYCE CAREY: Well, I did have the amazing good fortune to be, I think, well, he was certainly my dearest friend, you know, he's marvelous. Did you know him?

AF: No. I never did.

JC: Never met? Oh, what a shame! What a shame.

AF: It is. I wish I had been as interested then as I am now, because I could have.

JC: It's so extraordinary, because you're supposed to get over losing people. But I don't ever feel that he's gone. I constantly think how he will enjoy something. It sounds silly, but you know, it isn't. It's a very, very live personality.

AF: After all the reading I've done, and people I've talked to, I get to feeling that way myself, too. I think, "well now, what would he have thought about this?"

JC: You feel you know him.

AF: When did you first meet him?

JC: I first met him, when I lived with my mother, Lilian Braithwaite. Did you know about her?

AF: Yes. She was in *"The Vortex"* the first time.

JC: That's right. That's when I first met him. I was working in something, can't remember what, not anything very important, I imagine, but important to me, naturally, and I came home and found my mother very excited with a script. She had lots of scripts, and she didn't generally get very excited over them.

She said, "This *strange* young man had been 'round" to see her, and wanted her to play. And, of course, it was *"The Vortex"*. I am not surprised she was excited because it was a marvelous part, and she was used to being offered "nice ladies" you know, in *drawing rooms*. And so this was quite a surprise.

AF: Well, that was a very controversial play in 1924.

JC: It was, indeed! And she *wouldn't* accept it! We lived at one end of Pelham Crescent. And Kate Cutler, who was rehearsing it, lived at the *other* end.

Lilian said, "He must make quite sure that she was refusing it."

Anyway, he went back and made quite sure that Kate Cutler would renounce, and then, they did it.

But of course, I met Noël then. I was allowed to go to a dress rehearsal in Hampstead, because I couldn't go to the first night because I was working, and they were all terribly depressed after the dress rehearsal, as companies are. They were at the Everyman Theater, Hampstead, and the whole company was sitting around a stove. It was rather a Russian effect. Not that I've ever been to Russia, but I was not accustomed to giving my opinions, or anything, but all that went by the board.

I flew in and said, "It is wonderful!" and "You're all marvelous!" And Noël was sitting there, you see, and Lilian and everybody.

And I said, "It will be a huge success!" and, "You'll just be here for the allotted week, or whatever it is, and you'll go straight to the West End! And it's wonderful!"

And of course, I think, it started us off on a fairly amiable basis. And he was so good to Lilian. He loved her and was very sweet to her. I went to see them off when they were going to America, and to my horror, I burst into tears on the platform and said, "I want to go, too!"

And the dear, dear man, but I don't suppose it was anything to do with that, but not very long after I was given the part in *"Easy Virtue"*. You've seen *"Easy Virtue"* I think.

AF: Yes, I saw it at the King's Head, last year.

JC: That's right. I took the boat and went to New York and played Sarah in *"Easy Virtue"*. It was marvelous! And of course, one got to know him a little more and a little more. He was a wonderful person, and he had millions of friends, perhaps. Very kind, and it was wonderful having him there with Basil Dean, you see, who was directing. My memory of Basil as a director was of him saying, "No, no, no!" And, of course, that's terribly discouraging.

AF: I guess, a lot of people thought he should have been knighted long ago, long before that [1970].

JC: Oh, he was meant to be knighted years before. Somebody stopped it. You know, when you have enormous success very young there are a lot of people out to make sure you don't get too much celebrity. 'Enough for Noël, I think, that's it.' And he was knighted the same year Lillian got her "dame" and he was so nice about it.

AF: I think he felt, didn't he, that a lot of the critics were envious of him.

JC: Oh, the critics! How ghastly they can be—later they see some sense when they see the public flocking—oh! And then, they also, of course, can be very good.

AF: You and he went out a lot, didn't you? Went to theatre, went to films.

JC: Oh, yes, we went to everything.

AF: What kind of an audience member was he? During a performance, watching somebody else's work, was he critical?

JC: Never disturbing in any way, you know. Well, I might have heard, once or twice a few . . . [She makes a sound, imitating Noël's "tsk tsk tsk"] . . . or something like that, but he might have given me a little *kick,* or a *pinch,* or something.

Of course, I went with him on an enormous tour during the war. We went as far north as Inverness, and of course, people were so glad to laugh, and it was so wonderful to hear them, it really was. Amazing, splendid job for the war.

AF: What were you playing?

JC: We played three plays. *"Present Laughter" "This Happy Breed"* and *"Blithe Spirit".*

AF: How is he to work with as an actor?

JC: Oh, wonderful, lovely! Absolutely lovely!

AF: Did he always know his lines? Did he ever forget his lines?

JC: No, not really much. We did laugh occasionally, as much as actors will, especially if you're playing with him.

AF: So you played?

JC: I played Ruth, in *"Blithe Spirit"*. That's a tease! Liz, in *"Present Laughter"* that's a nice part. Actually, he never wrote a bad part. It was wonderful!

AF: Were you ever with him when he was painting?

JC: Oh, yes, indeed I was. There was a splendid morning in Jamaica when he said, "So, we'll go up the mountain and I'll paint you."

So, up the mountain we went, you know, above Firefly, and he set up and painted. And, in a comparatively short time, he really had caught an extraordinary look, not only of me, but, of my mother, just slight. And it was fascinating going along wonderfully. And suddenly, the sun went in, and he was *furious*.

[She laughs]

It changed all the light, you see. We fussed around for a little while. But he knew the climate too well, and he said, "It's not coming out again. It's not coming out."

And I was furious, because I thought I saw a very strong likeness. He was very clever you know.

AF: I didn't know he did any portraits.

JC: Oh, he was very, very clever. I mean they weren't studio portraits, you know, but a strong look, and so it turned into being quite a jolly visit there. I remember the way one always greeted the sun in Jamaica. But it was funny when the sun disappeared, because it was always there. So, I don't think he tried much more, just a very little, and then he said, "No, it's ruined. No good."

AF: So you haven't got a portrait.

JC: So, I never got that. No, for a long time it joined the army of canvases that pursue anybody who paints. At last, I remember, it was back at Goldenhurst, long ago, and it was known there as "I'm worried about my hair," because it hadn't been finished ever.

AF: He was very happy in Jamaica, wasn't he? He was happy the time he spent in Jamaica?

JC: Oh, yes, very happy painting. Oh yes, very happy.

AF: He loved to travel, didn't he?

JC: Oh, yes, loved it. Marvelous traveler. *Very* good. Of course, he did *heaps* of traveling, oh goodness me, yes, and wonderful, I got lovely postcards from him.

AF: In fact, I think he wrote at one time he was considering doing a travel book. But he never really did it—a different kind of travel book, not the standard kind.

AF: He didn't do much. He just read, sort of read and—

JC: He was very good about all that sort of thing, and he had absolutely no, oh, I don't know what to call it—false modesty? I don't know. He *didn't* have to *be funny* all the time.

AF: Tell me a little bit about Cole Lesley. I have heard so much about him.

JC: Oh! That, I think, is one of the things arranged from *above*! Did you know him?

AF: No.

JC: He was the person in the world who was right for Noël. Quite wonderful. And also, he had a gift for writing. He wasn't a writer by nature. His book *["The Life of Noël Coward"]* is the only book you should ever read about Noël.

AF: It's the best.

JC: He was perfect for Noël. He had humor. Extremely good taste. He was a village boy, from North Folkstone. He was the most charming character—utterly unselfish, brilliant humor, wonderful, affectionate, charming—not stupid for one second.

You know, people may have thought that he was just a valet. And he wasn't *at all*. And there is no reason why somebody shouldn't be just a valet, he was a very exceptional valet—able to understand that complex character—but clearly was *born* for Noël. He really was. Well, you know all that is necessary for you to know. You really do. Marvelous.

AF: He comes through very well, and everyone I've met and talked to says the same thing. That's *his* is the best book and he was just such a wonderful person, Coley was.

JC: Any other things written about Noël are always certain to get me into a temper, because it was not like that, and it's all wrong. Isn't it strange? It is odd. And now when everybody is having things written about them, I even get quite cross about other people who haven't loved Noël like I've loved Noël.

AF: I just read some of the bits in a book [Richard Huggett's] about [producer] Binky Beaumont.

JC: Oh, I had a postcard from John Perry [Beaumont's companion] saying, "Don't read about Binky."

AF: I hadn't known, before, that that *you* were a playwright, till I read about your play, *"Sweet Aloes"* in the book about Binky.

JC: Oh. Is it nasty about it?

AF: No, no, not at all. It's just that he first objected to your playing in your own play, and then someone said, "Well you wouldn't object if it was Noël Coward playing in his own play"—so he, ultimately, allowed you to perform in your play. But you'd written it under another name.

JC: Yes, they told me to do that. Binky. I don't know why, really, he said that it was not good to have a play by a rather young actor.

And I thought I'd thought of rather a good pseudonym—Jay Mallory. I thought it could really have saved a certain amount of trouble if I'd just used Joyce Carey, but still, that was all right. Noël was very critical of it when he read it, at first.

AF: But it was a success.

JC: It ran over a year in London, but then it had Diana Wynyard at her sort of peak of beauty, and Tony Guthrie directed it!

AF: Oh, yes.

JC: Oh, yes! And of course, he was so marvelous!

AF: Why didn't you write more plays?

JC: I wrote another one, and it wasn't too bad, but it wasn't very good, and it didn't have Tony Guthrie to direct it.

AF: Did you see the new production of *"The Vortex"* in the West End?

JC: Yes, indeed. And I am most fascinated to think that *that boy* [Noël] thought all that about life when he was twenty four!

AF: Twenty four.

JC: He got it right, too! Didn't he? [laughs]

AF: Yes, and here it is—what?—sixty five years later? And it's *still* contemporary.

JC: Still entertaining people. Now, I have a great friend at Cambridge, George Rylands, you've probably never heard of him, he's almost in the theatre, it doesn't matter about him, but he, to my great fascination, said "Oh, there's no question about Noël Coward!"

He said "There isn't a question about Noël. He *is* the *follower on* of Congreve."

I always thought that he was a little bit jealous of Noël. I don't know why, but that is a bit of an *enormous compliment,* isn't it?

AF: Yes, it is.

JC: And I'm beginning to think he was right, because, you see, people don't have their plays redone. You see, even Terry, who was a smashing writer—

AF: Terry Rattigan?

JC: Yes, even *his* plays don't take *instantly* like that. I mean, I really do think Noël's plays have an enduring quality. Isn't it interesting about humor? It seems to last. Doesn't it?

AF: Yes. The interesting thing about his humor, I think, and his plays especially, *"Private Lives"*—it's not a play of jokes, it's the situations and relationships, and it depends, perhaps, more on good acting. It's the situations. He didn't write one-liners like Oscar Wilde.

JC: It's curious, isn't it? Yes. It's wonderful! It is remarkable.

AF: Let's talk a little bit about *"In Which We Serve".* What did you think about the film at the time when it was being made?

JC: Marvelous.

AF: Because there was some objection to it in the government, because it involved the sinking of a ship, and some people felt that was not patriotic; some short-sighted people.

JC: I don't think I heard about that. They took such trouble over it. Everything was nearly as it was, and of course, Mountbatten was wonderful over it. I saw it not long ago. I was amazed at how good it was.

AF: I did too. I just saw last year, again, and it's such a strong film. It's really one of the best films about war.

JC: It's a wonderful movie. I wish they'd show it again. It wasn't very long ago that I saw it. And we'd all been in it. Marvelous.

AF: Quite a cast in that film. John Mills, Celia Johnson.

JC: Oh, yes, he was very good.

AF: Richard Attenborough, the young Richard Attenborough.

JC: Oh, how good they were, the boys, awfully good. And there was that terribly moving scene when they, you know when they came back. Floods of tears always, when the troops came back.

AF: The Queen Mother was a good friend of Noël's, wasn't she?

JC: She adored him. They got on marvelously. Real friends. Charming.

AF: She even visited him in Jamaica, didn't she?

JC: Yes, she did. I wasn't there then. I was doing a job, or something. She is a lovely, lovely lady, isn't she?

AF: You must have gone to see Noël Coward's final stage performances in London in *"Suite in Three Keys"*.

JC: Oh, yes! Yes! Of course! He was staying in the flat just around the corner.

AF: He wasn't very well at the time, was he?

JC: He was all right for playing, you know. It was an effort.

AF: Let's talk, then, about your playing with Noël in *"Present Laughter"*. Some people think it was very autobiographical, the character he played, Garry Essendine.

JC: No, no, I don't think so. I don't think anything was. I think that everything was a *little* bit of his own life, and *none* of it was *all*. Can't think if he had a pet character. He loved to make people laugh. He also liked to make them cry, which he succeeded in doing very well. Yes, and you know that was a wonderful experience, that tour. I mean, everyone who was in it, it was really ghastly when it came to an end. I mean we didn't know how to behave. [laughs]

AF: It's like a death, in a way, like a death in the family when a run of a play ends.

JC: It was marvelous. And then he got ill, and there was a pause, and then we had to play a lot of rather Navy places that we had to skip because he was ill. And that was all lovely, because it was all tremendously successful, and everything, but, of course, it culminated in good-bye. And that was very, very hard. He wasn't bound to linger over those sort of things, you know, just "Good-bye." [laughs]

AF: Do you remember the songs of his that he liked to play on the piano? Which of his own songs did he like to play?

JC: When they were new, you see, he always liked to play the new ones, and I remember—*"Imagine The Duchess's Feelings"*. Do you know that one?

AF: Yes.

JC: Well, now that one is not a sort of particularly *general,* [well known] is it?

AF: No. It's not as well-known as his more famous songs.

JC: He played that a great deal at the time. He played what was in his mind, at the time, mostly, and then out popped something else.

AF: Were you ever with him when he thought of some lyrics or when he was working on the music for a song?

JC: You mean when he was stuck for something? Listening to him compose was *not a soothing, beautiful dream.* He would *BANG* on the note, and he would, "AHHHHH!!" It was not beautiful. And then, of course, ultimately, it WAS! It would disturb him, too. He would make faces and then *out* would come something very nice.

AF: But it was hard work.

JC: He was a great believer in *hard work.* He was very surprising in many ways. *That* was a nice platitude! BUT HE *WAS!*

AF: Did you start acting because your mother was an actress? Is that what got you interested in theatre?

JC: I don't know. I always *intended* to be an actress from the age of *three,* I think. No, she didn't want me to be an actress. They never do, I don't think. My father was gone by then, so he didn't have as much say. I mean, not gone, but *left.* They didn't last as a couple. Well, very difficult thing in the theatre. She was very successful, and he *wasn't too* bad, he was very musical.

AF: When you visited Noël in Switzerland, what did you do? What would the typical evening out be, if you went out? Or did you just stay in the chalet?

JC: Oh we were much, much more likely to stay in. I wasn't a great one for going out in Switzerland. What did we do? Talk.

AF: Gossip?

JC: Gossip? Well, he *wasn't* a terrific gossip, you know. I mean, yes he was, but he wasn't a scandal monger, particularly.

AF: Just the latest news about what was happening to all his friends.

JC: Yes. I don't think there were awkward silences ever. [laughs] No, it was very nice, very lovely. I was extremely fortunate.

AF: Tell me about Gertie Lawrence.

JC: Gertie! Oh dear! How splendid! All I can tell you is Gertie was an absolute dear in the theatre.

AF: Well, you know that Mary Ellis, and Evelyn Laye, and Dinah Sheridan have recorded *"Waiting In The Wings"* for the BBC radio. It hasn't been broadcast yet, but they've recorded it. It is going to be coming out either this Summer or in the Fall.

JC: A pity Graham couldn't have done it. He has sung that song so well.

AF: Oh, that's a wonderful song! *"Come The Wild, Wild Weather"*.

JC: And one of my favorite songs, I think, it's the most charming song.

AF: The funny thing was when I interviewed Evelyn Laye, who has a little hearing problem—

JC: She's quite a friend of mine. I'm quite fond of her.

AF: A couple of times I asked her a question and she answered a completely different question. [they laugh] Which was still a good answer, but it wasn't the answer that I expected. What did you play in San Francisco?

JC: I think I went there with Noël. Yes I did, once. I think it was *"Present Laughter"*.

AF: Did you like San Francisco?

JC: Adored it. Absolutely loved it. I thought it was a wonderful place.

AF: Did you ever write an autobiography?

JC: Yes, I did. But I wrote it at a very bad moment. Nobody would publish it, and I never did anything about it, which is very silly of me.

AF: So, where is it?

JC: I should think it's in the back of a wardrobe somewhere. It's an awful business.

AF: Maybe you should get it out.

JC: No. It's too old.

AF: You've lived through such interesting times. When did you write the biography?

JC: Three or four years ago.

AF: Well, I think it would be interesting

CHARLES CASTLE
and
STANLEY HALL

Interviewed on February 27, 1988

Charles Castle is an author and documentary filmmaker. Stanley Hall was a makeup artist and wig maker who worked on film and stage productions in London for many years. The interview was recorded in their home in Kent, England, in front of a roaring fire.

ALAN FARLEY: Charles, when did you first meet Noël Coward?

CHARLES CASTLE: It would have been in 1962, or longer before than that, I would say, through Stanley Hall.
　I'd done a film on Richard Tauber, the opera singer, (a *Veritas* singer), and a book. It was his life story, a biography. There were lots of *stars* in it. It was the first of that sort of biography where lots of celebrities talk about the actual subject. Evelyn Laye and many other stars were in it talking about Tauber.
　When Noël Coward came to dinner, he saw it, and said, "One day, I'd like you—"
　I asked if I could do his life story.
　He said, *"Well,* we'll *see* about that."
　He wasn't well at the time, so he couldn't, and he didn't want to give any immediate answer. In the fullness of time, Cole Lesley telephoned and said, "Well, The Master said, 'okay."
　So, that really was through knowing him *socially,* moving on to knowing him *professionally,* in—first of all, making the film, *["This Is Noël Coward"]* which became the definitive biography that has, of course, been seen in America, and all over the world, and ultimately was nominated for the international award then, in Monte Carlo, and later on, won the Hollywood Television film festival award for best documentary. It is introduced by John Gielgud and has many people, including Richard Tauber, Yul Brynner—interviews with them.

I was the last one to film many of the people who are no longer with us, including Maurice Chevalier and strings and strings and strings of people. Sadly, I'd planned it as *two* 90-minute films, but we couldn't get the network time. So, it was condensed to 90 minutes for Britain, and then finally condensed to 60 minutes for America.

In the making of it I went to *Switzerland* to film Noël at his home. Richard Burton in the *south of France,* Maurice Chevalier in *Paris!* It took one *all over Europe* to tell the story, and then the film became a book called *"Noël",* which became a bestseller over here for about 16 weeks.

AF: I always wondered about the relationship between the two, because the book is certainly not just a transcript of the television program.

CC: No, there was a *great deal* of material, obviously, that *couldn't* be used in the film. See, it was to be *two* ninety-minute, so, I couldn't use all of the material in the film, so all that I couldn't use as well as what I did use went into the book—*plus* a lot of other things.

Once people found that I was making the film and doing the book, they *all* wanted to be in it. They were, like, *queuing* up. Douglas Fairbanks Jr., for instance, years later when he asked me to write *his* biography, he said, "I was very disappointed that you didn't include me in the film. Didn't you realize that I was one of Noël's *greatest friends?"*

And, in a way, that was the yardstick for the book and the film, because if you had to include *all* of Noël's friends from *all over the world*—you may have interviewed *Gandhi.* It just *wasn't* possible to include *everybody* that Noël Coward knew.

AF: How did you decide *whom* to interview?

CC: I did a chart, saying—Noël as *producer,* as *playwright,* as *lyricist,* as *composer,* as *actor,* as *director,* as *wit.* Then I made a *list*—that was the top column—to be careful that I wasn't *duplicating* interviews—I would only talk to them *specifically* about him as a *producer*, some of them about him as a *composer*, some of them about him as an *actor*.

If I'd put a column in of *friends*, it would have been a column the size of the Manhattan telephone directory! That really was the yardstick, people who had actually *worked* with him professionally, who had *known* him. Like Hermione Gingold, and Dame Edith Evans, since childhood, and *that* was the yardstick! That they shouldn't just *waffle* on and say, 'He was such a marvelous friend. He was such a good host.' He *was* a marvelous friend to **everybody!** And he was a good host, too. To the ones whom he'd entertained.

AF: Aside from Gertrude Lawrence, who would you have liked to interview, but didn't have a chance?

CC: Well, oddly enough, he didn't perform in any of his works, but he was a friend in a different way. I did try to contact Frank Sinatra, and had a very, very polite letter from him, not from a bevy of secretaries and aides, and so forth, but to say that at the time when I planned to be in America, he wouldn't be there. But, he was *very fond* of him.

There was another one, which I absolutely loved, and that was Fred Astaire, because Fred Astaire choreographed a work of Noël's way back, *way* back long ago.

AF: *"On With The Dance"* or something like that wasn't it? [*"London Calling"* in 1923]

CC: I can't remember exactly—in the *twenties*—but *way* back. So, therefore, you see, you have the connection of somebody who *worked* with him, and then became a great *friend*.

I remember being in Beverly Hills, where we had a preview of the film, and I'd been given the telephone number of Fred Astaire. I telephoned and said I was "a friend of Noël Coward's. We were previewing the film. Would he like to come?"

And, again, that element that I found very *good*—generally, celebrities of that *caliber*, because of security, because of privacy, and so forth, *don't* come to the telephone. And he *did* come to the telephone!

I said, "Well, would you like to come to see the preview of the film, and then be interviewed?" because we could still include him in the book, without having filmed him.

He said, "Oh, I'd like to come very much, indeed, but unfortunately, I'm in-between funerals right now."

[Castle laughs]

That was one meeting about Noël that I really would have liked to make.

Another one is Elizabeth Taylor. While I was filming Richard Burton in Monte Carlo—their yacht was based in Monte Carlo—and she had done the movie *"BOOM"* with him—Tennessee Williams' *"The Milk Train Doesn't Stop Here Anymore"*—which *wasn't* a big success, but they were great *admirers* of one another, and it would have been interesting to talk to her about Noël as an actor, because he didn't write *"BOOM"*.

Apparently, he *did, in fact, write his own dialogue* for it, which is one of the *conditions* that he did the film called *"BOOM"*. Right up until the eleventh hour, she was, she *wasn't,* she was, she *wasn't,* and from the Hermitage Hotel in Monte Carlo, we could, in fact, *see* their yacht from the terrace. He said it would come at an appointed time, which it did, being very punctual, and so did *David Niven.* They came within about a half an hour of one another. In fact, when filming began, they saw one another, because, of course, they knew one another very well indeed.

I said, "Would Miss Taylor be here?"

David said, "Well, she's not very keen on being interviewed at all, much as she loves Noël, but she'd rather *not* be interviewed."

And, in fact, she gives very, very few interviews. Nowadays, she does, because she's commercializing various products, as well as her own books and so forth, but then, fifteen years ago, it was like getting to interview, I have to say again, Gandhi.

AF: Did Noël see the film?

CC: He did, yes! He was very, very pleased with it, indeed. The interesting thing about it is that we had to take it *to* him in

Switzerland, of course, where he lived, and it was in its rough-cut stage. It was agreed that before it was transmitted he would have *approval* on it, which was fair and fine.

We took it on the plane and it was quite extraordinary! The *projector,* on which it had to be shown, was an ENORMOUS projector! Half the size of a *coffin!*—and we *carried* this thing on the plane! Can you believe it? Right through *Customs,* right through *Immigration,* right up the *aisle* of the plane! We had to leave it at the end of the aisle, because there was nowhere else to leave it. You couldn't put it in the *hold,* because the sound was on *one* section, and the film would be on *another* reel on the *other* section, so you couldn't run the film on a regular projector.

So, this ENORMOUS thing was carried on, and *not one person* stopped us and said, "What are you doing with that? Where is that going?"—and so forth.

But, when we got to Geneva airport, they *impounded* the film! They *didn't* look at the projector—there *could* have been a *bomb* in it, there *could* have been *diamonds,* there *could* have been *contraband, gold,* there *could* have been *drugs,* there *could* have been nearly a*nything.* This thing is half the size of a coffin standing upright, but the *film,* they ***impounded.***

We only had about forty-eight hours in Switzerland to show him the rough-cut before we did the finalization of the actual film, and there we were, *without the film.*

Lord Mountbatten, I had filmed, and was *in* the film. Fortunately, he was staying with Noël up until the night before. So, we went to the British embassy in Geneva and said, "Look, this film has been impounded, and there's *nothing* in it. It's not a *blue* movie, so to speak. I think I've got a feeling maybe *that's* why it was impounded. They *didn't know* what was in it."

The Embassy said that *they,* Customs, "gave *you* a receipt for it."

I said, "No, they simply took it."

So, the Embassy said, "Right. We've got a jolly good case against them." Then they telephoned the embassy in Geneva airport. And time is running really short, because to *get* from the airport to Geneva itself, and then *back* to the airport, *collect* the film and *go to* Noël at Les Avants, it was quite a feat having to get *back* to get flight connections, and then do the editing, and so forth . . . so we really were punching a clock.

Finally, the Embassy telephoned Customs, and said, "Look, you've impounded this film without a receipt. You've got to *release* it until they leave the country. Give them a receipt."

And they did!

We had to put up a bond of money for them to release the film. There was Stanley Hall, Graham Payn and me on the flight, and *none* of us had that amount of money that they wanted. So, I remember, we were turning our pockets out to meet the price of the bond, and we *literally turned out all our pockets,* all our travelers' checks and everything. In those days, credit cards weren't what they are now. You couldn't get any cash-out money from a credit card because they didn't exist in those days.

So, we turned out all the money and said, "That's all we've got." And they *took it* and *gave* us the receipt.

At least *we got* the film!

Showed it to Noël. He suggested one or two things to be removed. Nothing that could be changed, because the people, who had been interviewed, had *been* interviewed. They were a reality.

But, one or two things that he didn't think appropriate for the film, the inclusion that didn't really represent his work. I don't mean accurately, but in the way that he thought was correct for the period and so forth.

So, there were several things that had to come out, which was all right, because the film was running over-length in any event, and to be honest, you *didn't know* what to cut, because, to you, it was *pure gold.* You didn't want to lose *one frame* of film or one sentence. One was a bit stymied because you didn't know how to reduce it to a transmittable length.

He said, "That should go . . . that should go . . . that should go." This was up until four in the morning, because he was very much a night owl. In the end, we ended up with a very good product.

AF: How much film did you shoot altogether? How many hours?

CC: I should think . . . In *film* terms it's called a *ratio.* In a documentary you would normally shoot *twenty-to-one.* That means twenty times the amount of film you're actually going to show. Then you cut it out and you end up [with that.]

My shooting ratio for it was *three-to-one*. So, I was only going to film three times as much as what I needed to bring it down to one. Given that there might be a retake. For instance, with Lord Mountbatten, the interviews couldn't ramble on for eight minutes, or sixteen minutes each. I *had eighty-two people to interview!* If you work that out, that's about thirty *seconds* each, or *one minute* each. So, they had *very little* time to make their point. So, every point they had to make had to *have* a point, and not **waffle** on, otherwise you'd just have to cut it out.

Mountbatten, for instance, did his chat at Broadlands in the Hampshire, and at the end of it he said, "Well, what do you think of that?"

I said, "Well, very good Sir, but I think it's too long. It's seven and a half minutes." He said, "Well, how long do you want?"

I said, "Four and a half."

He said, "Right! Let's do it again!"

He was sort of a film buff, really, but a sort of raging amateur. He *loved* doing it. He was the only one, I suppose, who *wasn't* involved with Noël *professionally*. As a friend, but on the other hand, Noël has used Mountbatten and Lady Edwina's life as the basis for one of the plays taken from *"Tonight at 8:30"*— *"Hands Across the Sea"*.

So, that really was another salient point, the valid reason for him being in it. A lot of people, sadly, had to be cut out. So, when you say, "How much did I have to film in order to get it?" It was *three times* as much as I needed, but I would have cut out *nothing*.

AF: Yes, I think it should *all be* seen.

CC: I think it should be. Wonderful archival material! *"Bitter Sweet"* for instance, that's just been celebrated in London for it's revival after sixty years. That again was a very, very difficult nut to crack, because we weren't allowed to use any material *from* it!

AF: What were some of the surprises to you in doing a documentary about Noël? Were there any?

CC: The surprise came *afterwards*. I didn't think it would reach that, if you like, *international acclaim,* or recognition or significance that it did. That's fifteen years ago and it's still being *shown* all over the world.

The *other* surprise was when I did the *book.*

I didn't realize that the book would be called a *"new"* sort of biography, because I used lots of photographs, typed scripts and things to illustrate certain points. To me it was simply *transferring* the film onto paper in book form. In the middle of doing the book, I took the film over for them to see in New York. There was a sort of *buzz* of interest, *buzz* of excitement. It was almost as though you were rehearsing for a play or a musical that was going to be a big success. I wasn't conscious of the impact that it would have. In fact, when the book was published, *every single notice* was an absolute *rave* notice, and one of them, for instance, Felix Barker, who is one of the top theatre critics in England, said *"this book is the biography that everybody has been trying to write, and Charles Castle, damn him, has done it. He puts us all to the post."*

Because it was so *different* in its concept.

Not that I was *trying* to do it differently, I simply did it the way I *felt* it. It was more a *process of assembly* than anything else. It became a bestseller and just went on, and that was a big surprise to me. So the film and the book, the acclaim they both reached, I should think, have been the biggest in the twenty years I've been writing, which have been television, films, plays, books, radio drama for BBC radio, drama for BBC television, and it's just gone on and on and on.

One has become known for that particular book, and that particular film, more than any of the other output, including books about Joan Crawford, for instance, and very, very, very important people, *internationally* known people. Even today, after a long time, people remember it, and say, "Oh, I've got your book," or, "I got a signed copy." It just has become a sort of *classic* in its own way, in the way that *Noël's* works have become classics.

AF: What are the chances of the ninety-minute version being released on videocassette?

CC: I think it possibly could. The difficulty with this is that the copyrights of the feature film extracts, owned by the various film companies, are very difficult to clear. The other thing was clearing the copyright of the actual music. Because, let's say, *"Bitter Sweet"* for instance, was *sold outright* to MGM in 1929 for only five thousand pounds, *totally,* outright. Five thousand pounds then was a great deal of money, sixty years ago. So, since MGM owned the rights, they jealously guarded their material, their product. The film, of course, having been made with Jeanette MacDonald and Nelson Eddy was sold all over the world.

Now, if there were to be *any* productions, *stage* productions, it would have *killed* the *film.* So, they didn't release the rights. When television came along, they certainly weren't going to, *A, sell* the film to television, and, *B, allow any* extracts of the film to be *used.* Because, remember when television came along, from the terms of movies—it was a *disastrous threat.*

AF: Oh, it was an enemy, certainly at the beginning.

CC: Absolutely! They didn't want to know *about* television or anybody *connected* with television, because it was a direct conflict with the industry. So, simply, the answer was *'no'* and that was that.

Fortunately, the film was to be the celebration of Noël's seventieth birthday, and I got their permission to use *"I'll See You Again"* with Jeanette MacDonald and Nelson Eddy, only because it was a seventieth birthday celebration, a tribute. Otherwise, they simply didn't allow anybody—in fact, people could perform numbers from *"Bitter Sweet",* but never in costume, only on condition that they were performed in evening dress or normal wear.

With *"The Merry Widow"* they owned the rights to that as well. I remember a program I did for BBC television on *"The Merry Widow'* with Elizabeth Schwartzkopf, and again, we wanted her to do the number *"Vilja"* as a *production* number, with chorus and cast and dancing, and they *wouldn't* give permission. She could only sing *"Vilja"* in evening dress, because the television production number in costume would *conflict* with their own MGM production in costume.

Things have changed a lot and, hence, *"Bitter Sweet"* is being released for London.

AF: Well, you got to know Noël Coward through this process.

CC: Oh, yes, yes. I'd known him before, but remember, he lived all over the world. He was in Jamaica, then Switzerland, and only ever came to England for three months a year.

AF: Well, that was a legal requirement, wasn't it?

CC: That was a tax requirement. Only three months. So, when you did see him performing, then they were only on his *three-month visits,* if in fact, he came to England for three months, because if there wasn't a play to do, he *didn't* come.

But, when there was a play to do, he'd rehearse it in *Ireland,* which was *outside* the jurisdiction. Like *"Suite in Three Keys"* which was the last evening of plays he did, he rehearsed them in Ireland, *outside* the jurisdiction of the British Income Tax Authority, and they were able to have the three clear months in England, after the rehearsing, and trying out in Dublin, and *then* brought it in.

AF: Well, what was he like to know?

CC: He was a lot *easier* than you'd think. Everybody would think him as sort of *forbidding* and a taskmaster, because he was to work with *professionally.* People really trembled, because he *knew* everything about anything to do with the theatre, as we know. But, *I* didn't find him difficult in any way whatsoever. He was agreeable.

He was very, very ill at the time, as we know, because he had contracted amoebic dysentery in the Seychelle Islands. They had wrongly diagnosed the illness, so he was being treated for something completely different, while the dysentery was affecting him in any event.

Then, fortunately, Lynn Fontanne and Alfred Lunt suggested he go to *their* doctor in Chicago, which, in fact, *he did.* And he was *cured* in Chicago. But, of course, the illness had a lasting effect on him, and he was supposed to have exercised everyday, walking up to the village in Switzerland and back, but he *wouldn't* do it, because his circulation started being not so good.

As well, his bedroom was *upstairs* at Les Avants in Switzerland, with this wonderful *view.* He wouldn't go *down* the stairs, nor *up* the stairs.

The doctors said, "Well, at least, if he doesn't go for a walk in the village, he'll *have* to make those *stairs* if he wants to change and go to bed."

In fact, *he overcame that by putting an elevator in!* So, he simply went up and went down. But he only ever came down for special friends, otherwise, he was fed *in bed.*

We were very flattered because he came down for dinner at about nine o'clock, and then would stay up until four in the morning, and be very, very amusing. You see, one was seeing him in that intimate atmosphere in the last years of his life, not in the peak years of his wit and health.

I remember, for instance, he'd be up till three, four *in the morning!* There would be only three or four of us. He'd go to the piano, and, again, having *settled* because of the circulation, he *didn't move.* So, he'd just sit at the piano, and sing, and play, *not* his own music, but, in fact, Cole Porter, whom he knew very well—had known very well, and sang a lot of very unknown Cole Porter lyrics and songs that had *never* been published nor heard by anybody. He had remembered them since the twenties, and not from sheet music, only just came rambling off the piano from sheer memory. One couldn't remember the derivation. You couldn't say—because they weren't *used,* you see. I don't even think they've been used or sung or performed since one heard them sung by Noël in his own drawing room.

So, those were the special moments.

Then, of course, going through all the material—the books, the films, and the archival stuff—stuff he'd not looked at for years and years and years and years! They were simply in files in the *storeroom, packed away.* So, it was a sort of 'Aladdin's Cave' going through this and finding material that had *never* been read nor seen by people for many, many, many years.

AF: I know that when Joe Layton talked about going to Les Avants to work with Noël on *"Sail Away"*, they would work in the bedroom. They would go upstairs and he had books all over the place, but, I guess, he just pretty much worked in his bed.

CC: He did, he did. At that time he was planning the last phase of his autobiography as well. All the writing was done in bed, of course, surrounded by sheer luxury—writing in bed, having food brought to him, and changing, and new clothes brought and letters and posts being brought to him.

In fact, on the last occasion, staying there, Merle Oberon came over from America to go to Switzerland, and she stayed in London at The Savoy where she always stayed, and in fact, Noël stayed at the Savoy always—and she was going over to stay with him at the time that we were. He was very, very fond of her, indeed, and when we got there we went up to see him in his bedroom, and *that* was a special occasion when he did come down to dinner, because of *Merle* being there. In fact, he came down for breakfast, as well, which again he never did normally.

I remember at breakfast the following day, he came down quite late for breakfast, which was fine, because there was no punching a clock. There was just no sense of time.

Merle had come down as well, and she had this very long black hair. She brushed it and brushed it and brushed it obviously for hours. It was long and silky and went down really to the small of her back. She was a *health fanatic*. She traveled around with her health food. I remember to this day that she had her *own yogurt* with her, even though Switzerland is known for producing the best yogurt in the world! She had a plastic bag full of nuts, mixed nuts and things. That was her breakfast.

She asked whether she could have a bowl.

She poured all these nuts from this plastic bag in the bowl, with this yogurt, and she sat at Noël's feet, really like a very enchanting young courtesan. She was advanced in years by then, but really looked quite astonishing, no different from the way she looked in movies.

>Noël said, "You are looking quite remarkable, my dear."
>She said, "Oh, Noël darling, am I really?"
>He said, "Yes. You look like a very old fourteen."
>[Charles and Alan laugh]
>And so, that's *really* how those last years went until finally he didn't make the stairs anymore, and then . . . and then we know the rest

AF: Mike Wallace on CBS used an excerpt of your film when he did a profile.

CC: That's right; they asked me in London to use an extract from it. It was at the end of the film when he sums up his life. I had, in the interview, asked him, how he would *"sum up his life?"*

>I didn't know what he was going to reply.
>When you say, what surprises did the film bring, quite aside from the acclaim the film and the book had, was when he died.
>*After* he died—at the memorial service at Saint Paul's, the Poet Laureate, who was at that time John Betjeman, from the pulpit, said he would like to pay his tributes to Noël, and quoted from the book this very statement about Noël, summing up his life. I'll read from the book, which is the way the film ended, and it's the extract from the film you've just mentioned.
>It says, *"It was the last day of filming of Sir Noël's biography in Switzerland, and we were ready to shoot the final sequence of the film. The camera was focused on the Master, whose final comment was on his life's work."* This is Noël talking. I'd asked him to sum it up. Would he sum up his life?
>*And he said, "Sum it up? Well, now comes the terrible decision as to whether to be corny or not. The answer is one word—love. To know that you're among people whom you love, and who love you. That has made all the successes wonderful. Much more wonderful than they'd have been anyway, and I don't think there's anything more to be said after that. That's it."*

AF: How did you react right at that time when you heard him say those words?

CC: I just left the film running. I couldn't ask another question after that. It was so final. It was so touching and so—the philosophy—to sum up his life in one word—love. And I kept the film running without him saying anything, we just zoomed out, and then I faded up the music of *"I'll See You Again"* after that, with the credit titles, and that's how the film ended. In fact, that's how the book ends, on that wonderful philosophy of love.

STANLEY HALL

b. August 9, 1917   d. January 5, 1994

AF: Well, Stanley, let's talk to you a little bit. You knew Noël for quite a long time.

STANLEY HALL: When Charles Castle was filming Noël in Switzerland, and we were all with him, Charles asked him what the answer was to success, how he *valued* success, and he said, "Love", as Charles Castle quoted—to be with people you love and people who love you. That is the answer to everything.
In a curious way, this was the answer to Noël's personality. He had so many dear friends around him.
The old adage that you judge people by your friends—all the friends in his circle were absolutely dear people: Graham Payn, Joyce Carey—kind, sweet people, not at all aggressive or in any way, people who would cut across Noël. This is borne-out when be says that love was the answer to everything, because he gave love and received love. And, this is curious, because my biggest impression of Noël was people think of him as witty—and wit can be cruel—but, he wasn't cruel. I mean, his wit, curiously enough, came out of his mind before he even thought about it. I don't know whether he actually thought, "Oh, I'm surprised I said that." But, in fact, he *had.*
Wonderful quotes, which are on record . . .
Ivy St. Helier, who played Manon in the original cast of *"Bitter Sweet"* was a tiny, diminutive person. She was not more, I'm certain, than five feet. Later on in her life, when somebody said to Noël, "Poor Ivy, she's broken her leg in two places."
Noël immediately said, "I didn't know there *were* two places."
Because she was so tiny. And these were the kind of quick remarks that Noël made. They weren't cruel, they were just the facts that he thought in advance, in a way.
I'd known him since the early forties, and knew him personally. I used to go to lots of his parties. He was a wonderful host at parties, of course. Although I'd worked in lots of films,

and designed makeup and designed wigs for Noël and various people—you know, I was just another guest—and yet, he treated me as a star.

He introduced me to Lord Mountbatten and Lady Mountbatten, and other people, and gave me an enormous buildup, putting me as their *equal* in a funny way, which was *his kind of success.* He really loved people. He loved stars. He loved working with Claudette Colbert—all the stars in Hollywood. He loved Merle Oberon, whom Charles has already talked about.

It's extraordinary that somebody in his position—and he was a great, great star—*loved* other stars. He was extraordinary in that way.

I used to sit up with him until the early hours of the morning. He had such warmth and sweetness and affection I thought afterwards, "You can't associate this with *the* Noël Coward—the wit, the clever, the smart, chic person."

But, in fact, he was absolutely wonderful, and this thing about love being the answer—giving love and receiving love—was a great big part of his life, which I don't think the general public would know. It's proven by the fact that all the friends around him—his circle, or *circus,* if you like—of the people who loved Noël Coward, *all* his friends—Joyce Carey, Graham Payn—all the people in his circle were *adorable* people. They say you judge people by their friends, and you certainly could by Noël Coward's friends.

It was interesting the other night, at this marvelous opening of *"Bitter Sweet"* [by The New Sadler's Wells Opera] when you saw all the friends, curiously, in a wonderful nostalgic mood. They were all theatre friends, people who had known Noël Coward, had seen his plays, and they all rallied round, and there was a feeling of love. Hoping that he was up there looking down and appreciating everybody.

AF: You sense a real moment there, as he said, he wanted to decide whether to be corny or not. In other words, really to still be the Noël Coward of the facade, or to tell the truth, which he thought of as being corny. He told the truth, I think.

CC: Yes, yes, in essence he was saying, 'Now, do you want me to be witty? To be *zippy*? To be on *show?*'

I nodded. I was off camera, and I shook my head, I should say. Meaning, *'No, be serious'* I should think that was one time in his life he really *was*. He didn't just come off pat, because he's never said that before to anybody.

SH: The marvelous thing was that it was quoted by John Betjeman, he said, "I can't do better than quote from the last paragraph of Charles Castle's book." Which was wonderful.

This was *Noël,* actually. People only thought of him as witty and sharp and cutting, in a way. He had this *tenderness* and *sweetness,* and I'd sit up until two or three in the morning with him.

He'd sort of say, "Well you don't realize that I wrote *"I'll See You Again"* in a taxi, in a taxi queue in New York." Sweet things like that. Not starry, showy things, just—

AF: Well, what were some of the productions you worked with him on?

SH: *All the plays* he did **af**ter the war, which ended in 1946. The particular one I remember was *"The Apple Cart"* by George Bernard Shaw. And the extraordinary thing was that it could have been written by Noël. He played as if it *were* one of his own plays. *I hadn't realized the similarity in their work.* I'd already worked on *"Major Barbara"* and various other things with Bernard Shaw, and suddenly I thought, "Extraordinary! This could have been written by Noël himself."

Particularly, the middle scene in *"The Apple Cart"* with the mistress. That time Noël played it with Margaret Leighton. It was absolutely *Noël Coward* dialogue. Extraordinary.

AF: That was done for the coronation of Queen Elizabeth, wasn't it?

SH: Yes, yes, it was. I worked with him, designing his hairpieces for the film *"BOOM"* which was originally the Tennessee Williams play *"The Milk Train Doesn't Stop Here Anymore."*

AF: What did your work involve?

SH: I knew him. I knew his *head,* I knew his *face,* and it was very easy to add a little extra hair, because I knew what was expected.

Similarly, he did a film with Michael Caine, *"The Italian Job"* which he made in Dublin. Because of tax reasons, he wasn't allowed to overstay in England. I arranged to meet him at the airport, and fit him with a wig. London airport were very good. They gave us a kind of reception area. I fitted him with the wig, and *off he* went, straight to Dublin without landing in Britain, as it were.

AF: How did you get into that line of work?

SH: I started in films in the thirties, doing makeup and designing wigs, and then, in 1940, I went into the army, but I was lucky, because I joined the unit that produced and directed lots of troop shows to take around to gun sites, to entertain the troops in areas where civilians weren't allowed to go.

I mean, there were a lot of civilian artists in E.N.S.A. [The Entertainment National Service Association—the British equivalent of the USA's U.S.O.], like Evelyn Laye, of course, who was in *"Bitter Sweet"* and all those people. But, they weren't allowed to go to the secret gun sites. I enlisted a lot of stars who were actually *in* the army at that time. We split them up into six-handed units and took them 'round to all these gun sites. They were very good. Excellent. I mean, a lot of them were stars, and if they weren't, they became stars. They went over to France on D-Day and, *immediately after the invasion, entertained troops.*

Then I carried on doing designing wigs and makeup for people, and then, happily, worked with great people like Noël Coward and all the great stars, and I've carried on doing it ever since.

CC: There's an interesting side point, because when Stanley Hall knew Noël Coward all those many years ago, he'd given him two of his original oil paintings, and he still has them. At Christie's recently, there was this very famous sale of Noël

Coward's oils, about thirty of them from the Noël Coward estate, and about ten or so from private collectors, and the sale went on at Christie's.

They were all original oils and all signed by Noël and painted by him in Jamaica, in Switzerland and, to begin with, at Goldenhurst, his home here in England. So, it spanned about, let's say, thirty years of his life, and he was greatly influenced by Winston Churchill, because early on his painting was in its embryo stage of learning, and then having learned Churchill so well, and seeing Churchill's technique, which was, in a way, sort of impressionist technique Noël learned from him.

So, Hall has got these two paintings, which really are almost priceless now, because some of the pictures went for fifty thousand pounds, or seventy-five, seventy-eight thousand dollars. I went to the sale myself and wanted to bid, and I have a limit—as everybody goes to an auction with a certain limit. There were two or three there in the catalogue that had an estimated price, and I thought, "Well, that's sort of within my limit," but, of course, they were all sold for three or four times the estimated price.

AF: I looked at the bottom two or three, and I thought, "Well, I could conceivably get in that range." At the end, I decided I wasn't even going to enter a bid.

CC: No. Because you'd just be running up your own bid. The fun thing about the whole thing, which could have been like a Noël Coward first night, in fact, at the end of the very sale, the auctioneer suddenly said, *"And who will bid for this pile behind me?"* And we all looked at the auctioneer in absolute astonishment, because, remember, the auction at Christies, the actual auction room isn't very big. It only accommodates about two hundred people, but the outside anterooms had about three or four hundred people each. The people that had been to the previews of the paintings were in a separate gallery, and knew what they were going to bid for, so they were bidding through the sub-auctioneer, and you could hear their bids going through the microphones, see, and on a speaker coming through, and as well, facing the auctioneer.

On the left hand side there were the assistants, who were taking calls on the telephone from Zurich, Geneva, New York—all the telephone bids—well, obviously when he said, *"And who will bid for this pile behind me?"* Clearly, the people on the *telephones* didn't know what he was talking about. Clearly, the people in the *anterooms* behind didn't know what he was talking about, because they couldn't see.

In effect, what he was referring to was a *big theatre backdrop* that Christie's had commissioned specially for the sale. It was a wonderful scene of Jamaica with palm trees. It was about twelve feet by sixteen feet. Big backdrop, very theatrical and very impressive, because it emulated the many Jamaican scenes by Noël—these wonderful colors of blue sky and green sea and the palms.

AF: Was it what they used for the cover of the poster?

CC: It *was* the poster, in fact, yes. It said, *"Christie's Sale of Noël Coward's Paintings"* which was on a banner, a sort of flying banner.

Then he referred to this thing and said, "Well, *somebody* make me an *offer!"*

There was a sort of *stunned* silence, because nobody really knew that it was going to happen—this enormous, great *thing.*

Somebody behind me said, "A hundred pounds."

There was a sort of silence, while the penny was dropping, people thought, "Well, what's going on?"

He ran up the bid a bit. He said, "Anyone else?"

Presumably, somebody bid two, because it started going up by a hundred. And somebody else bid on, two hundred. And then I heard a bid go *three hundred!*

Then, he was just about to bring the hammer down, and some instinct in me—don't ask me what the instinct was, not having had anything else from the sale, I bid and it came to me for *four hundred.*

Suddenly everybody sat up because it was a genuine bid. Then he was about to bring the hammer down, again, and I thought, "I'm going to get it for four hundred pounds, whereas, other people were paying forty thousand dollars, seventy thousand dollars, at least I'm getting *something* for six hundred dollars. Something. A memento. Anything to do with Noël Coward, even though it wasn't painted by him, it was painted by a BBC television designer as a backdrop poster for Christie's. I think the stunned silence sort of—everybody thought, "What's going on?"

Then the fellow behind me bid up.

Then I bid up.

And when it got to a *thousand* pounds, I thought, "Goodness, me, I've got to, more or less, the point of no return. I don't think I could stop here."

I was coming up to my limit anyway, and I thought, "Well, I have, *mentally,* spent that money." Like when you go out to dinner and you say I'm going to spend so much, and you haven't spent as much as you thought, so you have another bottle of wine, to make up for what you purchased it for, so to speak.

Then, it crossed my mind, in the middle of this bidding and the whole room buzzing—as to say, it suddenly became a really *Noël Coward* thing. (He makes the sounds of people chattering in whispers.) All this kind of *buzz,* which is a kind of an exciting *buzz,* and I suppose that *spurred* me on. Their necks were craning from one end to the other! Everybody was turning around in front, seeing what this *nutter* was doing bidding for this thing, and indeed, what was he going to *do* with it?

It was twelve feet wide, sixteen feet deep, and you couldn't hang it in your drawing room, for sure. Then a great flash went across my mind, because I'm about to open an art gallery, and the gallery is in three sections, and it's to do with theatre—designs, costume designs and theatre memorabilia, and designs by very famous theatre and movie designers like your American—wonderful designer—Irene Sharaff who did *"West Side Story," "The King and I"* and so forth, and her designs will be on sale, and quite a few of Noël Coward's theatre designs.

For instance, *"After the Ball"* and *"Conversation Piece,"* they were going to go into the general sale, then it suddenly occurred to me, *literally* the week before I'd bought the shop next door to convert into another gallery, and I thought, "Well, that would be the *over spill,* because there's so much material to go into the gallery," and I suddenly thought, "Ah! That will become the *Noël Coward Gallery*. And it will be the only Noël Coward gallery in the world!" And I thought, "This is absolutely ideal! This backdrop will take up *one complete wall,* and I'll *build* the gallery *around* the backdrop!" So, that spurred me on, to go on bidding.

And then the bids went up at *two* hundred pounds per bid!

I thought, "This is getting out of hand." I won't tell you the actual figure bid that I got it for, but I did actually buy it, and afterwards they said they would roll it up, and would I "like to take it home now?"

I said, "Take it home now? It wouldn't fit in the car! It's longer than the length of the car," I said, "I have to have it collected."

I didn't really think of the practicalities of it. I just had this vision of what I was going to do with it, and the fact that I'd paid all this money for it.

Then, many of the press stopped me and said, "Why did you buy it?"

I said, "Because I'm Noël Coward's television biographer and biographer of the book, and it is a memento of the occasion. I couldn't afford those prices. I was happy to have it."

Then they said, "Well, what are you going to *do* with it when you get it home?"

Of course the answer had come in a *flash* in the middle of the bidding, and I said, "*Hang it in my new gallery,* and you must come and *see* it when it's hung."

So, that was a very, very happy ending to what could have been a sort of deflated visit to this momentous occasion of the sale of these paintings, which Noël would never have envisaged as having gone on sale, because they were done purely for his own interest. He'd *give* them periodically.

He wouldn't paint them with anybody in mind, but simply like somebody doing a tapestry as a relaxation, and having done it, to have a cushion or something made of it, and then to give it to them for their birthday as a Christmas gift or something—and so with his paintings, he was doing it purely for *his* amusement, and then as with Stanley Hall, he *gave* him one on one occasion, and then *another* on another occasion.

He'd had these for many, many years never realizing that in the fullness of time, there would be an exhibition, an auction, and in fact, they would reach the prices that they finally fetched.

AF: I understand that he didn't want to exhibit them because he wanted to have at least *one part* of his life that wouldn't be subject to criticism, because he certainly didn't appreciate what critics wrote about his works.

CC: No, he was never well received by critics, as it happened, but he was very circumspect about critics, because everything he ever did was a sellout. He was a best seller so he felt that critics, no matter what they said, wouldn't influence the public.

AF: My favorite quotation by him about criticism is, "*I can take any amount of criticism as long as it is unqualified praise.*"

SH: He said that *"Private Lives"* came into a terrible rattling from the critics. They said this: *". . . only gets by on the performances of Noël Coward and Gertrude Lawrence"*
    Noël said, '*I lost faith in critics from then on, because it's been done by everybody. Every other actor and actress since, and it's always been a great success.*' I remember after *"Waiting in the Wings"* which was put on in 1960, one of the critics at the stage door accosted him as he left, and said, **"BLAH, BLAH, BLAH!"**
    And Noël said, "You must *be from the 'Daily Express.*"
    [they laugh]
    When Noël did *"In Which We Serve"* the film that was based on Lord Mountbatten's experiences, and the film opened with the sinking of the battleship, at the beginning of the World War, and among the flotsam and jetsam floating on the water, there was a *"Daily Express"* and the headline said, 'THERE WILL BE NO WAR.'

AF: Oh, I didn't know that. I'll have to look for that.

SH: *Because of that,* Beaverbrook, who was running the *"Daily Express"* then took an *instant dislike* to Noël Coward. *Absolutely CRITICIZED everything* he did, I mean, *panned everything* he did!

CC: But, he had that wonderful, *quick wit* about the press. His wit has always been very economical, and one reporter from a newspaper went up to him and said, "Oh, Mister Coward, what have you got to say to *'The Star'?"*
 He replied, "Twinkle."

AF: Yes, with just one lone word. It's amazing. Another nice quote was one when he was informed that some actor, for whom he had no regard, had *shot* himself, suicide, blown his brains out. Coward's reply was, *"He must have been an awfully good shot."*

SH: Yes. There was a very good actor, actually, who really *was* very well known, and I won't mention his name, and he was a bit *dotty,* but he really was quite a *star* in British films, and somebody said to Noël, "Poor so and so has put his *head* in the gas oven *again"*
 And Noël said, *"Don't tell me he didn't succeed!"*
 (I mean, he did *eventually* succeed in doing it.)
 Noël was very *economical* in all those quotes.

AF: There was another one on *"The Dick Cavett Show"* where Cavett asked him, "How do you account for your success in so many fields—acting, directing, writing, songwriting, painting?"
 Noël said, "Talent!"

SH: The extraordinary thing is this came up with *"Bitter Sweet"* the other night. Actually, one of the reviews in the press was that one forgets that Noël Coward wrote the *lyrics,* wrote the *music, directed,* did *everything,* long before Lerner and Lowe and all the people who collaborated, *Noël did it on his own.* Extraordinary how he did all that on his own. It was years *later* that *collaboration* came with lyrics by somebody and music by somebody else.

CC: It had happened before. There was Gilbert and Sullivan long before. There were *always* collaborators.

SH: Two people. But Noël was the *only* one who did it on his *own.*

CC: Up to this day nobody's done that.

AF: Sondheim doesn't write his books, he writes music and lyrics, but he doesn't write his books.

SH: I remember going to the first night of the film *"In Which We Serve"* where it said, *"Script by Noël Coward, Directed by Noël Coward, Music by Noël Coward—"* and, actually, people began to *laugh,* as all the things came up before the film. The whole audience kind of chuckled because it was so funny to see all that.

    I don't think Noël Coward will ever be *replaced.* He was *exceptional* in his humble beginnings, his rise to fame in the thirties, and the way he expanded and built up from that, and wrote music, lyrics and everything else, and was witty, kind and a wonderful person.

AF: I understand he just was *not* jealous of other performers.

SH: Oh, no.

CC: Yes, he was, if one is going to be *hypercritical.* I mean, we *haven't been critical* about him *at all,* and I think the grave danger about—certainly from my point of view as a biographer—writing about anybody is about being too *gushing* and being too sort of *sycophantic* about them.

    He didn't suffer fools gladly. And when actors didn't *toe the line,* he was very, very *tough* on them! There are, actually, some actors whose careers he did practically *ruin,* because they didn't take instruction from him. They had their *own* views, their *own* feeling about *how* they should play the part, and Noël as author and director, obviously, was quite decided on *how* they should play.

    So, he certainly *did* make enemies. They are never *discussed* by people. You only get the sycophants. You only get—and they were frightened, you see, because if anybody at the time criticized Noël, they certainly would never work again.

So, those are some of the elements that never generally come up. People gush about him rightly, but that—

SH: I think they were the *weaker* people, you see, because when he was with Claudette Colbert in *"Blithe Spirit"* when he said, "I'd wring her neck if I could find it."

CC: Yes, but she never *complained* about it. No, I'm talking about many others who didn't complain—

SH: *Yes,* they didn't complain, they just *disappeared*—they just kind of—

CC: That was well known, because it was reported in the press, and she sort of laughed about it. But, I'm talking about the ones whose careers he *could* have *ruined.* People who crossed him professionally—they *couldn't* complain or put word abroad, because they'd *never work again.*
    This was very true of a very, very famous impresario we had in this country who, sadly, is no longer with us. *One of the greatest theatre impresarios,* who ran H.M. Tennant, called *Binky Beaumont.*
    If you crossed him—he employed mainly people for the Haymarket Theatre and Shaftesbury Avenue—seasoned actors. People who were *stars.* Basically, people who were *known.* People who would draw audiences into his theatres. *Nobody* crossed H.M. Tennant, because they simply would not work in the West End again.

AF: Well, I heard in fact, that Binky Beaumont's death had such an impact on Noël that it might have hastened his own death.

CC: I don't think so, in that sense, not professionally, it was purely because they were very much the same age.

AF: He was forlorn days after he'd heard—and *he* died not long after.

CC: Not long after. It wasn't any great age, by today's standards, as we know. As each year goes on longevity seems to go longer—all this wonderful health food and good living, and so forth, seems to make everybody a lot more long living, but Noël was—what? seventy-two, seventy-three, and Binky would have been about that age. I think it came as a bit of a jolt, because Binky didn't have a *long illness.* He didn't have an *accident* He hadn't had an *operation.* It was simply a heart attack.

I think it *did* shake Noël, because his friends really were popping off by degrees. Remember they were all much of the same period, much of the same time. Their successes were concurrent, and they'd worked together for so many years, and seeing them all go by the way, he became almost the lone survivor. Inevitably, philosophically he must have thought, 'Well, I'm *next* in line.'

SH: Did you see the picture of Noël's in the end room where you're staying?

AF: Yes.

SH: The sweet thing about Noël—this is typical of him—when he gave me that painting he sent me a picture of himself holding the painting, as much as to say *'this is to prove that it's mine.'*

RODERICK COOK

b. 1932   d. 1990

Interviewed on December 18, 1973

Roderick Cook created and performed in *"Oh, Coward!"* a revue of Noël Coward's work, arranged for three performers. While it was playing in San Francisco, he appeared at a session with students of the American Conservatory Theatre. What follows is an excerpt from that session.

ANONYMOUS WOMAN: I'd like to know how, when and where you met Sir Noël Coward.

RC: Holy god! It sounds like a press interview!

AW: I'm sure there must be some sort of synopsis in the PLAYBILL.

RC: Yes, a whole article. I've been told since a tot that I was, you know, the *"Noël Coward person"* and looked like him, sounded like him, and that sort of thing. Which isn't actually very true, but there is a sort of similar aura. I recognize that.
   I was in New York in 1963, and they were doing a musical called *"The Girl Who Came To Supper"* which was based on an English play, *["The Sleeping Prince"]* which was then made into a movie called *"The Prince and the Showgirl"* with Laurence Olivier and Marilyn Monroe. There's a part in that, which I would have been absolutely marvelous for. I was a sort of prissy English diplomat. Not an image I have too much trouble conveying to the masses.
   [audience chuckles]
   So, I said to my agent, "Well, can we have a go at this?"
   She said, "Oh, Darling angel,"—(she was a rather affected Hungarian lady)—"darling angel, darling angel, no, there's no point in your doing this. There will be somebody over from England."

I thought, "I don't give a shit!" I knew that Noël Coward was going to take the auditions. So, I thought, "I'd been told this all my life. I might as well get it from the horse's mouth, and either it's *true,* or it *isn't* true, and for god's sake, let's get on with it."

But, I was very devious *about auditions. Auditions are very important. We all have to go through them. I knew I was going to audition for Noël Coward. So, I did my homework.* Very *important to do homework when you're going for auditions. I* knew, *automatically, you know, that schlepping in with a pair of jeans and saying, "Hi, Noël" wasn't going to do it, you know. I re-read the bit of the autobiography that he'd written called* "Present Indicative" *and talking about* himself *auditioning when he was a young man. He would go along there, he said, w*ith his [imitating Noël perfectly] *"one good suit, pressed within an inch of its life."*

[audience laughs]

Looking very nice, and walking on there and saying, *"Good morning'* and then doing the thing, and not forgetting to say, *"Thank you"* afterwards, and great manners, and that sort of thing.

It's obvious that it's the sort of thing you don't do it for every audition—but *this,* I was doing it for *Noël Coward.* He wanted to play it this way. I wanted a job from him. Okay, *you play it that way, right?*

So, I got the appointment, read the book, got the script. The script was really *for* me, like a piece of cake. It was a fairly sort of average, sort of English light comedy. The sort of thing I'd been doing for ages and ages. That was kind of all right, but I was going to have to *sing.* If you've seen the show, you know it's a slight problem.

[audience laughs]

But again, *choice of material* is very, very important. To this day, when people come to audition for me, *what* they choose is almost as important as *how* they choose it. If I know that somebody is coming on to audition, I know they've thought about the problem. They've thought about the job, and what the show is about. It's very important. I held some marvelous auditions in New York earlier this year and people came up and very cleverly *didn't* do Noël Coward, but they did certain obscure Rogers and Hart,

Gershwin, Cole Porter, slightly recherché sort of things. Very good thinking.

So, anyway, talking of recherché, I went—this musical was set in 1911, by the way, and some years ago when I was living in England, I used to appear fairly regularly at something called the Players Theatre Club, which is a recreation of an Edwardian, Victorian music hall thing, where there is a chairman who introduces the items, and you get up and sing a song. It's one of the most frightening things that I've ever done in my entire life.

To begin with, the man comes up and he says, "And now, here it is, your own, your very own Roderick Cook!" *Bangs* the hammer down on that, and the ten seconds it takes you to get from the wings to the center stage is the longest ten seconds known to man, woman or goat, I tell you, because you've got this terrific build-up and suddenly you're *ON,* and you have to do your thing, and also encourage the audience to sing, because it is a rather sort of sing-along thing.

Once it's worked, it's marvelous, because you think, "Three minutes of lovely me! Who could ask for anything more!" But anyway, at this place I'd sung a song with a rather roguish title of *"Rhoda And Her Pagoda."*

[audience laughs]

Quite.

I knew this was the one to do, because, thinking deviously, I mean, I knew that Noël Coward was *nuts* about this sort of era of musical comedy. I thought, "The musical comedy is set in that era, also, the man I want the job from is *potty* about this sort of thing! So, what do you do?"

So, I got along there. Got into the thing. Had my suit *pressed* within an *inch* of its *life,* and waited around with everybody else, and eventually it was my turn.

I got there and the moment of truth arrived. The stage manager said, "Mr. *Robert Crook"* and I was on!

I mean, there wasn't time to correct his mispronunciation of my name. Why bother? You know? Why *bother?* So, I walked up there, through the darkened auditorium, the friendly sight of the *one* work light, you know, that *bare bulb* that *blinds* you, and *nothing* else.

Remembering my manners, I walked smart to the center stage, said, "Good morning!"

And from the darkened auditorium came the great clipped tones—

"Good morning."

I thought, "Christ! He's *there* anyway."

[audience laughs]

It would be awful if he *wasn't,* I tell you. So anyway, we read through the scene with the stage manager, and there were a couple of things in it that I thought might work, and I thought I didn't hear actual *laughs,* but I thought maybe *unrest* in the orchestra, which was *encouraging.*

Anyway, come the end of the scene, Noël's clipped tones say, *"Very good, Mr. Cook. Do you* sing?"

So, I put that towards one side and said, "I thought I would do—as this is an Edwardian musical comedy—I thought I'd do a number by Lionel Monckton."

And he went, *"Uhp!"*

Monckton is one of the great Edwardian composers.

"Which one?"

I said, "Uh, something called *'Rhoda and Her Pagoda".*

He said, *"Uhp!"* again.

And the pianist started and I sang it. I don't know whatever happened to the thing. I mean, the pianist had been playing, you know, *"I'm Losing My Mind"* or something with two blocks, and I couldn't hear him, plowed on relentlessly through this thing, got to the end of it. It's quite a short number, thank god, and came to the end of it, and I thought, "Well, I've *done* it. Here we are."

And I said, [Noël's clipped tones again], *"Thank you."*

And I walked off.

Then, all of a sudden, he says, "Mr. *Cook! Mr. Cook! Could you possibly wait for a moment?"*

I couldn't, *offhand,* think of any *pressing* engagements.

[audience laughs]

—so I thought I would be graceful enough to wait. I took the time to sort out 'Mr. *Robert Crook'* from the stage manager's list and that sort of thing.

Then, suddenly, up from the orchestra came the production stage manager, and he said, "Would you step this way?"

So, I said I would step that way, and before you could say 'Players' Guide', there I was, being introduced to—first of all, Herman Levin, who had just produced "My *Fair Lady*" and Harry Kurnitz who had written the book and—*[like a fanfare]* DA DA DA, de DA! Noël Coward!

We shook hands and *instantly* he said, *"What have you been doing lately?"*

[audience laughs]

And we enter into a conversation like old *friends!* Just like *that!* Absolutely wonderful thing about the man. Just absolutely at one's *ease.* One's slightly in awe of him and within thirty seconds you're chatting away like old friends. And that's how it all went.

Then I did the show, which was mildly boring, and didn't run very long, but in the course of that we became friends. He liked what I did, and—[comic hesitation]—I like what he did—and in the fullness of time people started doing these things of Cole Porter *revisited,* and Rogers and Hart *revisited,* and all these *revisited* people.

I thought, "Well, if they can do *that* for *those* people, *I* can do it for *Noël."*

I wrote him and said, "Dear Noël, look, stop me if you've heard it BUT"—and outlined the idea of the show.

And surprisingly enough, within a *week* I got a letter back saying, *"Dear Roddy, What a lovely idea! Send me a dummy program and we'll talk."*

At that point it was very difficult, because I had *no program* at all. I had ninety-seven totally obscure numbers written down on a rather sort of grubby list. That was it.

"Send me a dummy program . . ."

So, anyway, I sat there and glared at them, and *God* or *somebody* sat on my shoulder one afternoon, and I found the format of how to arrange it, and went on from there, and here we are today.

MARY ELLIS

b. 1897   d. 2003

Interviewed on May 2, 1989

Mary Ellis was an American-born opera, musical theatre, and stage performer. After moving to England, she became a British citizen early in her career. Then, in 1954, she worked with Noël Coward in *"After the Ball"*. The interview was recorded in her London home.

ALAN FARLEY: You recently recorded Noël Coward's *"Waiting In The Wings"* for the BBC radio.

MARY ELLIS: That's right. It's a long time ago that it was done. And it was going to be [director] Graham Gold's last production. He's retiring from the BBC. So, he chose that because he can have all his old friends, the actors and actresses in it, you know? It was like old home week. It was a little bit too much like reality. You know what I mean.

AF: Well, it is about a retirement home for actresses.

ME: I played the same part that Marie Lohr played in the original. It was especially interesting for me, because I always adored her. She played—I don't know whether you are familiar with Terrence Rattigan's *"Browning Version"?* I starred in that with Eric Portman over here, and she played the nurse in the *"Romeo and Juliet"* and she is simply marvelous in that, I'll never forget that. She had her seventieth birthday—No! Her *sixtieth* birthday! I apologize to her, wherever she is now—her sixtieth birthday, while she was with us.

AF Evelyn Laye was in the cast, also, in this recording.

ME: Yes, yes, yes, and it's the first time in all these long years that I ever met her.

AF: Isn't it amazing?

ME: Very extraordinary. But her career was sort of at its peak, and over, before I came over her, you know. I didn't get over here till 1932 and I've never been back.

AF: That's right. You were born in the United States.

ME: Yes! So, I had a great long career over there starting with the opera house, and then *"Rose Marie"* and I left that and went and played *"The Dybbuk"* at the Neighborhood Playhouse. Then I did straight plays till Cochran discovered me over here. He didn't *discover* me, he *knew* I sang and he wanted to make something of it.

AF: But you were singing at the Met when you were still in your teens.

ME: Yes, I was. In that season I was the youngest one they had there. I was the baby and they called me *'Virgin Marie'* because everybody was having affairs and flirting with each other, and I was very, sort of, *chaperoned,* and, at that age, one's terribly *prim,* you know.

AF: Well, it must have been very exciting for you.

ME: Oh, it was wonderful! You know, not long ago—it's not *quite* amusing—but, *one day* I was at a reception to do with Americans, I've forgotten where it was, and I was sitting in a big chair, sort of thinking about everything else, because I *hate* parties like that, and two elderly ladies came up to me and what they said—they acted like as though I *wasn't there!* And one said to the other, "And THIS is the original *'Rose Marie!"*
    And I thought I was being *dug up!*
    It was *terrifying! [laughs]*

AF: So, how did you get to London? You say Cochran saw you?

ME: No, I married over there. I married Basil Sydney, the English actor. And we had wonderful seasons, sort of an offshoot of the Theatre Guild. I had ten years. He taught me really so much. I mean, I just got a terrific knowledge and love of the theatre from that. The Theatre Guild sent us over in *"Strange Interlude"* and London had its first dish of long Eugene O'Neill, which I was very proud of. You see, those things I'm much prouder of than all the musicals, and yet in over sixty years in the theatre, not counting these years that I've been retired, I've only done five musicals.

AF: That's interesting, because people do think of you that way. Well, let's talk about Ivor Novello.

ME: Let's talk about Ivor. He was quite unique. Quite unique. The most generous loving and warm—and *talented.* Someday, people will realize how good his music is. But he never caught on in America. Now, I don't know why. Never.

AF: Did they try?

ME: I don't know. The productions were so big at the Drury Lane they needed *eighty* in the orchestra, and *hundred and fifty* on the stage! You've heard the records, I suppose?

AF: Yes, and I heard the program that you did for the BBC about *"The Dancing Years".*

ME: That's right, yes. Well, I'll never forget *"The Dancing Years".* So, I thought they better have it. That was actually recorded in 1977. I do a great deal of radio now.

AF: Well, now Ivor Novello wrote some of his musicals *for you,* didn't he?

ME: Three of them for me, yes. And the first one—he put Drury Lane back on its feet. I should think [wig-maker] Stanley [Hall] must have told you a little about him, because he was in on all of those. I don't think I had a wig in *any* of them. I just had *pieces* that he made for it.

AF: But when he wrote it for you did you—

ME: I worked with him all the time.

AF: *While* he was writing it?

ME: He was a very romantic person. As we *all* know—he was *not* a 'marrying gentleman.' But, he felt very romantic about 'woman.' And, he devoted his whole—I mean, I have some marvelous letters from him—I don't know who they go to after I die—about the music, and what I did for him, and things like that.

AF: It's interesting that the only collaboration he had with Noël Coward was a disaster. "*Sirocco*" wasn't it?

ME: *And* it was *frightfully* funny! It was *supposed* to be—something *else*. I never saw it. That was all long before I knew him. He came to "*Music In The Air*" which Cochran put on for me. Cochran did lovely things.

    I said, "I'll sing for you if you don't let the people in London know that I can sing." So, he just announced it as *'a play with music.'* I loved "*Music In The Air*". Don't know whether you know the score or not? It's Jerome Kern, and it's absolutely lovely. And, it was a wonderful play, anyway. It was charming.

    And then the last thing I did was Noël Coward, and that was—I mean, it certainly wasn't his best. The mixture of Noël Coward and Oscar Wilde just didn't do it.

    [chuckles]

    [Author's note: "*After the Ball*" was Noël Coward's musical version of Oscar Wilde's "*Lady Windermere's Fan*".]

AF: That's another case where you would think on the face of it, "What a great combination!"

ME: Why? What a waste! You either do an Oscar Wilde play or a Noël Coward musical, you see? And, all of us were very unhappy in it. It just didn't gel. Didn't happen.

AF: But the music—I've heard—

ME: And *then,* though I'm not *his* kind of singer, there, you see?
 He would get up and say, "No, Mary, I want you to do it this way!" and he'd start to *talk* his songs!
 I said, "Well, you're much better in this part as Miss Erlynne, and I can't sing."
 Well, I mean, it was all sort of, eh, unhappy, but I always admired him very much, and think that he's the best of what he is, I mean, at that particular thing. And he was very popular. He was quite different from Ivor. Ivor wasn't at all *social—social* in the sense of liking to hobnob and, you know. Noël always was—I mean, all his books have asterisks every second!
 Bubby or Bobbie or Nubby or Nabbie!
 And it's so, so, so, someone you *know?*
 He was an enchanting friend. I visited him one day in Switzerland, over in his lovely place, 'cause I had a little, tiny chalet *across the lake* from him in Les Avants! I used to go there.

PETER GREENWELL

Interviewed on November 20, 1995

Peter Greenwell is a songwriter, arranger, accompanist and performer, who was Noël Coward's last accompanist. He lately has assembled a show from Coward material, under the title, "*A Talent to Amuse*". The interview was recorded in London.

ALAN FARLEY: Tell us how you first met The Master and then, eventually, how this show evolved.

PETER GREENWELL: Well, it was in 1962; a big gala was being given in his honor, and Graham Payn (who, as you know, was his lifelong companion,) was a good friend of mine.
    Noël asked me if I would like to play for him, because at that point he hadn't a pianist working with him regularly. I was very thrilled. I went along to meet him at the Savoy Theatre. He was directing his musical *"Sail Away"*, which had been a big success on Broadway with Elaine Stritch, and now they were opening in London.
    So, I went along to meet him, and I should tell you I'd done my homework. I knew that he liked the *flat* keys in music, as opposed to the sharp keys, and in fact, '*E flat*' was his *favorite* key. So, we were introduced.
    He said to me, "Do you think you could manage '*Mrs. Worthington*'?"
    And I said, I thought rather brightly, "In *E-flat*'."
    "*Oh!*" he said, "*I KNEW we were destined to be lovers.*"
    [laughs]
    That was the first meeting, and that was the first example of his wonderful, wonderful razor-sharp wit. It is my own personal anecdote, which of course now, with the passage of time, I'm very thrilled about.

AF: Who put the show together? Did you work together choosing the music and all?

PG: No, no, no. He'd chosen it *himself* I regret that I didn't actually take note, but he wrote a wonderful parody of *"I'll See You Again"*. I should have made a note of it, because the reason I didn't was, he said, "You *can manage 'I'll See You Again' can't you? I might, if they're very good, do a very naughty version at the end."*

They *were* very good, of course, and he *did* a *very* naughty version. To this day, I regret that I didn't write it down, because I can't remember it. I know that he got gales and gales of laughter.

AF: He didn't write it down? He just did it?

PG: He just did it. I guess he'd written it down for himself, because that particular dialogue was for a group called the *'Gallery First Niters'* who were very powerful in Britain at that time.

I went to another one where they honored Dame Angela Lansbury, and great stars. They did a big gala evening in their honor. Noël had had one before, where he'd spoken, and this time he decided he'd sing some songs. And that was how I was lucky enough to meet him and work with him.

I remember the naughty parody of *"I'll See You Again"* was something like—

> **And, if you DARE to BOO again,**
> **UP, again**!

Something like that. It was marvelous, but I can't remember the rest of it. It was frightfully witty. The gallery had given him a terrible time over the years—you know, his play *"Sirocco"* and there was another one that they absolutely *tore to shreds,* and *shrieked* and *booed,* and carried on and behaved appallingly. Noël would never forgive them for that, but he *let them know.* He let them know, and it was my good fortune.

AF: Did he often do that? Make fun of his own numbers?

PG: Yes, yes. Well, he did, of course, the *"Let's Do It"* famous one. He did a lot of that. And he used to do—change lyrics for things like *"That Is The End Of The News"*. What's another one he changed—a topical line—oh! *"What's Going To Happen To The Tots"*. He used to introduce various things that were fashionable, you know, that adults were taking, some sort of new drug, or new pill they were taking to improve their appearance, but that was really about all.

AF: A friend of mine, to this day, is still quite offended by *"Why Must The Show Go On?"* This is someone who is a very staunch theatre fan, who thinks questioning that old axiom is *heresy*.

PG: Oh! If I may say so, I think that, for me anyway, he is the greatest entertainer—theatrical person of the twentieth century; he is the only person who *could* say it, and *has* said it, and *why not?*

AF: I agree.

PG: I mean, I think it's a wonderful, wonderful number. I just wish I could find another rhyme for *Macy's*. In London it's okay, but if I'm in the north, they think, "Well, what are they talking about?" They know about Vegas—"*. . . two shows a day at Las Vegas . . .*" BUT "*. . . the faces in Macy's . . .*"—
    There were people who said to me, "Well, what does *THAT* mean?"
    I'd say, "Well, Macy's is a big, BIG store in New York."
    If you haven't been to New York, and a lot of people in the provinces here haven't been to New York, but I can't include another rhyme that will fit, you know, without sort of wrecking it.

AF: So, you do make the odd change.

PG: Oh, yes! Oh, yes, I mean, I make a change in *"That's The End Of The News"*. I have changed it to—

> ***Poor cousin Cecil,***
> ***Got instant dismissal,***
> ***For airing his militant view***

—which you know, there were a lot of militants when I started doing the Coward numbers a few years ago. It was a very popular word. That people were being *militant,* and coming out, and saying things against the government, and their work, and everything.

Noël's line, I think, is something about—

> ***And both of her sisters Are covered in blisters***
> ***From standing about in the queues . . .***

—because he came just after the war. It was produced, as you know, in 1945 at the Piccadilly Theater, but that's a little bit sort of out-of-date now. Why would people be, you know, *covered in blisters?* The rest absolutely stands. I mean, it's a series of total disasters. He would often do little things like that himself, so, you know, I asked *permission,* of course, of course.

You know, it isn't sort of *tampering about.* It absolutely *scans,* because that was another thing that he was very keen on, if I can digress, that's something that, sort of, *does* slightly irritate me.

His marvelous parody of *"Let's Do It",* which Cole obviously gave him permission to do as a friend, the scansion is EXACTLY the same as Porter's. Sometimes, you hear people doing versions themselves and the scansion *isn't* the same. It's pulled about. And THAT is the difference in MY book, between a genius, who really cares, and someone who is just writing another lyric. *Parody and lyric—it's not the same at all.*

AF: Well, now, how did "A *Talent To Amuse"* come about—the show that you put together?

PG: Well, last year, 1994, I was in a review called, *"Noël and Cole—Let's Do It"* at the Chichester Festival. We had, incidentally, since I'm talking to you, played it at Memphis, Tennessee for a night, *two* nights. It was put together for Memphis. And then we did it at the Oxford Playhouse. From the Oxford Playhouse, *Patrick Garland,* who ran the Chichester Festival that year, had suddenly been let down with his final attraction.

He saw us on the Saturday night in Oxford and he said, "How do you feel about coming and being the fourth attraction at the Chichester Festival?"

We all said, "What a lovely idea!" That's how that happened.

Then he said to me, "I wonder if you'd do something for me, Peter."

I said, "What's that?"

He said, "Well, we have the Theatre Society, (of which there are twenty thousand members), and we have our annual, sort of, jamboree. We have a sort of meeting, you know, minutes are presented, like any straight forward board meeting, and we have a champagne lunch." And he said, "I thought it would be rather nice if you did a little cabaret for us after lunch in the smaller Minerva Theatre, (which seats just under three hundred.)"

I said, "How are you getting two thousand people in there?"

He said, "Well, they don't ALL come. A lot of them are all over the country, but there were usually two to three hundred."

So, I said, "Yes, certainly." Then, I thought, "I've done a lot of cabaret in hotels and *Pizza on the Park*, and various clubs and things," I thought, "this is an opportunity. I've been given a theatre to entertain in!"

They wanted an hour, so I put together a theatre show. In other words, I didn't just *sit* at the piano and *sing* the songs, as I would normally in cabaret. I *got up* and *moved about,* and recited some poems, and I, for the *first time in my life,* TALKED on the stage, other than introducing a song. I actually told anecdotes.

I don't know *why* I thought I could do it. I didn't even think about it. All I thought was, "I've been given this theatre."

Back in the dark ages I'd been trained as an actor, and done, you know, one or two years in rep, and it hadn't worked out, you know. I'd been put in my place.

So, I worked out this thing, and to my delight and astonishment, it was *rapturously* received, and then followed a lot of *complaints,* because, as I said, there were twenty thousand members, and three hundred people saw it.

They got a lot of letters saying, *"Why couldn't we have been told that this was going to happen?"*

So, they said to me, "Would you do it again?"

So, *I did it again!* And the same thing happened again!

So, they said, "Would you do it yet AGAIN?"

And I thought, "This is an opportunity. I think I am going to *extend* this, and I'm going to put an interval in, because, by yourself, I was finding an hour rather a long time—in fact, it was *more* than an hour. It turned out to be seventy minutes. I thought, "I've either got to make this one hour, or, I've got to make it—say, ninety minutes." And I decided, "Well, I'll try ninety minutes, because I seem to have the nucleus of something here, and maybe I've got a theatre show for myself. I mean, we spend our lives saying, 'I must get my act together! I must get an act!' and do nothing about it." Suddenly, it was forced on me to do something about it, and I DID something about it. I told you what happened. Then I thought, "Well, I'm going to extend it. I'm going to put an interval in."

Somebody said to me, "Ooo . . . do you think that's wise?"

I remember when Barbara Cook first did her one-woman show, and she did it in a block, and then she put an interval in, and she said, "I found it so difficult after the interval to get my adrenaline going again!" How true that is, I wouldn't know, but that's what I was told JUST before I was about to do it!

I thought, "Well, an artist whom I revere and admire as greatly as I do Barbara Cook," I thought, "Oh, my god! What am I doing?"

Anyway, DETERMINED that I shouldn't feel let down, I went out there and DID it! And it worked! It worked to such and extent that I had, in fact, to do *two more.* This was all in a small theatre.

Then they said, "Would you do a charity one for us?"—last February, in 1995 in the main house.

I said, "Well, that's a challenge," I thought, "it seats *fifteen hundred people* . . . why not?

Yes!"

Then, I immediately got cold feet. I thought, "I've made an absolute fool of myself! Why? Why have I said I'd do this? I mean, who's going to come? It's one thing to seat three hundred people, but fifteen hundred! Three hundred's going to look pretty daft there."

So, I got terribly afraid.

The week before the show, the box office manager telephoned me at my home and said, "Well! *You've sold fifty percent before the general bookings opened!* It's all on the subscription of the members. Fifty percent is sold out! AND—" she said, "I thought you'd like to know when we opened today, there was a queue around the box office, and it's YOU they're booking for! SO," she said, "I would think you'll sell out!"

I then became DOUBLY frightened, because I thought, "Oh, my god! I don't think I can do this! What would it be like in that huge theatre with all these people?" And I was frightened, because now they were all going to come! And that's REALLY how it all happened. It worked terribly well. People saw me, and then asked me if I would like to do this tour, which I am at present doing, which you saw last night at Watford.

AF: Is there a difference between playing for a small audience and for a big house? Do you have to do things more slowly?

PG: Yes, yes, I do. But I find, funnily enough, I find it, um, I *don't* find it *more* difficult in a big house, but I do play it a bit *slower,* and certain critical friends say, "Well, it's much better, you see, because you always play everything far too FAST."

That's what Graham always used to say to Noël when we were rehearsing, "You're not going to do it at that speed, are you? It's far too fast. Nobody will be able to understand a word!" And Noël would say to me, *"Well, WE understand it, don't we?"*

AF: Talk a bit about working with Noël, rehearsing, preparing for the shows you did with him.

PG: Oh, it was marvelous! Marvelous! I mean, he used to say, *"Do you think we're right to do this?"*

And I'd say, "Oh, yes!"

I mean, I was, what, every minute of twenty-nine, or something?—being asked by this great, GREAT man, *"Do you think we're right to do this? Let's try it a bit faster."*

Graham's absolutely right. He *did* like to take things *very fast*.

Noël said, *"Don't mess about! Don't waste people's time! Get ON with it!"*

[chuckles]

We would try things lots of different ways. Little things, I suppose, I have learnt, almost without realizing. I will remember things like Noël saying, *"No, no, no, no, no dear boy! Dear boy!* **Don't stop!** *Don't stop there! I'm not stopping off to make a point there!"*

I would say, "But it's a funny line!"

He'd say, *"It's not funny ENOUGH, and neither is the next one, but the third one's a VERY funny line! So, we'll STEP on the first two, and get a BIG'N on the third one!"*

And that's what we did!

I find now how true that is.

I'll always remember Graham telling me another story: when they were doing *"Matelot",* which is that lovely song from *"Sigh No More"*—

Noël said, *"Get on with it! Get on with it!"*

Went away.

Came back after the bit had been running for a month or two.

Graham said, *"Matelot"* isn't going as well as it used to."

Noël said, *"Well, of course it isn't. You've added one minute fifty to the running time of it."*

And you do this without THINKING, you see?"

Now, Noël NEVER did. Never, never. If anything, he took everything *faster.* And, all right, you could criticize that perhaps that you didn't get it *all,* but the *diction* was so immaculate and so perfect that you DID get it ALL.

So, poor mortals, like me, who are trying to do it at the same speed *without,* I have to say, *remotely* copying him, because that was the thing that he did *not* like, you know.

I mean, many times he said, **"Did you see so-and-so on television last night?"** or, **"Did you listen to the radio?"** or, **"Somebody's doing some of my numbers this afternoon. I must have a listen."**

He'd say, **"Why do they all always have to COPY me? Why do they always have to try and SOUND like me? Haven't**

they got personalities of their OWN? Couldn't they do it in their OWN way?"

I mean, it's amazing, really, that for years everyone has just thought, "You do a Coward *number,* you do it in a Coward *voice."*

Well, you DON'T.

They're great songs! You don't HAVE TO!

And the *nicest* compliment anyone has ever paid me was dear Maggie Courtney, you know, the lovely actress who played here with Ginger Rogers in *"Mame".* Angela Lansbury did it on Broadway.

She said, "Absolutely wonderful! You do the songs in your *own* way," and she said, "the marvelous thing about them is you sort of HUMANIZE them, because of *your* personality. Noël was so brilliant and so *brittle* and *sophisticated,* but YOUR personality is sort of *rounder*—(I think she was referring to the figure, really)—but it's rounder and it's warm and somehow the things are terribly HUMAN," and she said, "and that isn't the thing we usually think of with Coward. Particularly, of the *'Mrs. Worthington's'* and the *'Mad Dogs and Englishmen".*

Why should they be? He's making a marvelous statement. So, I think that gave me tremendous encouragement, because she saw one of the early performances. That was her comment, and she's an actress I respect.

AF: Had you ever seen him yourself in cabaret at the Cafe de Paris?

PG: Oh, yes, yes before, in the late 1950's, before I had met him, I saw him two or three times. I thought it was absolutely wonderful! Wonderful! And I saw the first night of *Marlene* when he introduced her with that marvelous poem that he wrote about her. I met her through him, when I was working.

He said to Marlene, *"You know, you should get Peter to play for you. He understands our sort of singing."*

She thought I looked too young.

What she said was, *"Well, YOU KNOW, I'm a grandmother. I KNOW I'm a grandmother. If I appear with HIM, EVERYBODY will know I'm a grandmother!"*

—which was lovely.

I think what he really meant was—we'd been doing a function and he'd said, *"'Mad Dogs' you start here, and finish there, and you don't stop in-between. You keep going! That's the secret of it. This tremendous pace that's on the Vegas record. That's the secret! You just play straight through! No stopping off. No changes of rhythm. Nothing! Just keep going."*

—Well, we got out there, and did it, and it was quite apparent to me on the first line—*In tropical climes there are certain times of day*—and I thought, "He's stopping off! He's making points! If I go straight *DA, DA, DA, DA—ta, ta, ta, ta,* I'm going to have *finished* before he's got halfway through! There'll be the most AWFUL scene!"

So, I stopped *with* him.

I think, *that's* what he meant when he said to Marlene—*"He understands our sort of singing"*—because, when we came off—

He said, *"Dear boy, I DO apologize. I'm very, very naughty. I deserve a smack."* He slapped his wrist, and he said, "I told *you* to keep going, and what did *I* do? I got out there and I did *completely the opposite* of anything we had rehearsed, and I have to say, you were *with me* ALL the way! You may not be the best MUSICIAN who has ever played for me, but you are certainly the best COMIC!"

[chuckles]

AF: I heard it from, I think, Judy Campbell, that in playing with him, that he liked to do things like that to keep actors on their toes.

PG: Yes, yes, but I don't think he did that with me on that occasion, because we'd only just done—it was about our third thing together. But, I know that he did do that sort of thing, and certainly on subsequent occasions he did things like that, or he'd turn around and he'd suddenly say—"I think we'll do *'What's Going To Happen To The Tots"*—upstage to me. *And we hadn't done it in six months!* See?

And I'd think, "Where am I? What are we doing?"

THAT he would do. He'd sometimes *change* the performance or sometimes *change* the running order, you know. But, I'd heard this with actors.

AF: How did you get started in this business?

PG: Well, I trained as an actor. I'd always been musical, since the age of four, and I'd had a formal musical education. Then I trained as an actor, because my parents insisted that I got a music degree, so that I could always have something to fall back on.

[laughs]

Then I went into the theatre and I had several small part acting jobs.

I remember my first one was a marvelous American play, *"My Sister Eileen"*—which *"Wonderful Town"* is based on. I was a Brazilian sailor! Anything LESS Brazilian, I can't imagine, but that's what I played! I went from job to job earning practically nothing, and then having long periods out of work.

Then *"The Boyfriend"* came along. It was produced in this little theatre in London called The Players Theatre. I was desperately out of work, and a friend of mine who knew The Players said to me, "Would you like to play for rehearsals? At least you can keep afloat by doing that." And so, I did. Then they said to me, would I like to go and be musical director? This is 1953.

I said, "No, no, no, no. no. I'm a *composer*. I'm *not* a musical director. I don't want to do anything like that. I want to write my *own* musicals."

So they said, "Would you like to come HERE?" Because the show is going into the West End, and as you know, it had a seven or nine year run at Wyndham's Theatre here in the West End.

AF: Really!

PG: Oh, yes. It was a huge, HUGE hit at the time, and then it came to Broadway, of course, and it was a huge hit there. I said, "Yes, alright, I'll give it a whirl."

I wrote my first musical, a 1955 musical called *"Twenty Minutes South"*, which they produced at The Players and transferred to the St. Martins Theatre here in the West End.

Then I wrote a bigger work with Peter Wildeblood called *"The Crooked Mile"* and Millicent Martin became a star overnight in that. It's very funny, because I was looking at the reviews, somebody asked me the other day if they could have some reviews, and I went through them, and the *Evening Standard* actually said I was *"England's Leonard Bernstein."*

I have to say I read it, and I thought, "Well, I wonder what happened to *him?"*

[laughter]

. . . because, I don't seem to have done quite what Mr. Bernstein did.

And that really was how I started.

Then I wrote a couple of other musicals, and produced, and then I wrote a lot of television things, then I got into pictures, and then, you know, during that time there was the *Coward period* when I worked with him. My last musical was the *"Mitford Girls"* based on the lives of the Mitford sisters, which we did at Chichester, then at the Globe Theatre here in London.

Then it was the Duchess of Devonshire who said to me—because we had to audition the show for the sisters themselves to make sure we weren't stepping out of character, or doing anything that we shouldn't be doing—she said to me, "Where do you sing as a rule?" because I used to sing the songs.

I said, "Well, I *don't."*

She said, "Well, you SHOULD!"

I thought, "I always rather *liked* the idea of doing that."

So, I spoke with some friends, who had a little restaurant in Camden Lock in North London, a very nice restaurant. I said, "Would you like me to come and do cabaret for you?"

They've got a piano there and they said, "What a good idea!"

So, I went in there for a couple of nights a week for a month, and then people saw me there, a critic on the Sunday Times saw me, that was the first thing, and gave me a wonderful write-up. That alerted the people who run *Pizza on the Park,* and they came to see me, and they said, "Would you like to appear at Pizza on the Park?" That was in July of 1985, and they asked me back again in October of 1985, and then they asked me back AGAIN in the Christmas of 1985.

Then, after that, I used to appear there once or twice a year, and then other engagements followed. That is, you know, what I've sort of roughly been doing, and that was REALLY how it all started.

AF: Well, the first time I heard of you, someone said, "You know, there is this wonderful album of *"Peter Greenwell Entertains At The Piano"* and you should look for it, but they said, "He lives in Spain now. He's not playing around much so you probably won't get a chance to hear him."

I finally *did* find the album. I loved it! Someone gave me your address, I think, in Spain, although I never wrote to you. I guess hoping someday I would have the chance to meet you.

PG: Yes! And here we are!

AF: What was it that brought you back from semi-retirement to do that show, *"Let's Do It?"*

PG: Well, what happened was lovely.

Originally an American artist, Elizabeth Welch, who is a dear, darling friend of mine, was in my show *"The Crooked Mile"*. I worked a lot with Liz. There was a big gala—I seem to spend my life doing big galas—on Shaftsbury Avenue in aid of AIDS, for *CrusAID*. She was the artist they were honoring, and everyone who took part had to sing one of her songs. Well, as she'd been in my *"Crooked Mile",* Millicent Martin and Julia McKenzie did the big song that Liz and Millie had done originally in 1959 called, *"Meet The Family"*. It was Ned Sherrin who said, "I really think *you* should appear, because you're very, very close to Liz, you know, you've been friends all these years. You've written shows for her. You've accompanied her. Why don't you do *'A Nightingale Sang in Berkeley Square"*—which was one of her big songs, because that was the stipulation—everybody had to sing one of her songs.

So, I said, "Yes," because I'd done that in my act anyway. So, that was that. I suddenly sort of came out of retirement and did that.

Everybody said, "Who's this?" Which was nice.

Later, the same year, it was 1993, the twentieth anniversary of Coward's death. They did another AIDS charity. I was asked, as I had played for him, and was his, in fact, his last accompanist, would I do something in that?

I said, "Yes, I'd love to."

They said, "Would you do *two* numbers?" I said, "Yes. I'll do *"Useless Useful Phrases"* (which a lot of people don't know, from *"Sail Away"),* and I'll do *"Mad Dogs"*—(because it's sort of to do with travel and everything else)." I did the two things. Well, I mean, the thing was an uproar! He would have been delighted.

AF: Sort of your own version of *Dad's Renaissance.*

PG: Yes, yes, absolutely! It was from *that* that David Kernan, who'd organized the thing, said, "I've *got* to do a show for Memphis, Tennessee. Would you like to come over there?"

That was really the first sort of thing that HAPPENED. We did it. I remember now, there was a wonderful review in the Memphis paper, and it says at the end, *"But ace-in-the-hole is Peter Greenwell."* It was my first sort of WONDERFUL notice, you know, overseas. I'd been noticed here, as I've said, you know, but I'd never appeared in America before. So, it was terribly exciting for me.

I've told you how all this happened, and then it all went ahead—and NOW I find my American management saying, "Could we see all the press reviews? We've got your new CD."

There's a CD out of the actual show, not just a studio recording. It's of an actual performance at the lovely Swan Theatre at Stratford-Upon-Avon, which I did in aid of the Shakespeare Library, earlier this year.

In your country, the reviews have been absolutely wonderful! Tremendously encouraging for a funny old thing that had retired! I now find myself back in the limelight! Which is lovely! I'm thoroughly enjoying it!

NORMAN HACKFORTH

b. 1908   d. 1996

Interviewed on September 21, 1990

Norman Hackforth was an accomplished composer, lyricist, arranger and accompanist; interestingly, he was in *"Twenty Questions"* for 27 years as the 'mystery voice'. He became Coward's close collaborator, accompanist, and arranger during one of the most important periods of Coward's career, from 1941—1954. He made the grueling wartime troop concert tours to the Far East and South Africa with "The Master" and helped launch his cabaret career at the Cafe de Paris in the 1950s. This interview took place in Hackie's studio behind his home, Honeysuckle Cottage, in Kent.

ALAN FARLEY: I know you worked with Noël Coward during the war. When was the *first* time you met him and worked with him?

NORMAN HACKFORTH: I met him in 1929, because I was *in* the *original* production of *"Bitter Sweet"*.

AF: Oh, you were!

NH: Yes!

AF: I didn't realize that.
  NH: I met him, well, you know, as one meets, um, meets *God,* practically, you know? He couldn't have been sweeter. He said, [clipped] *"How do you **do?**"*
  I lost touch with him, more or less, until the early days of the war, 1940. I used to play for Beatrice Lillie. I was doing a lot of troop shows with Bea. Lorne Loraine [Noël's secretary] rang me up one day and said, "Noël is doing a big concert and wondered whether you would play for him?" Bea was doing it as well.
  I said, "I'd love to! I'd be delighted!"

She said, "Would you like to go to lunch with him at the Savoy and we could talk about it?" So, I went to lunch at the Savoy, where he had a suite, because he had been *bombed out* of his studio, his London house at Gerald Road, and I did a lot of shows with him from then on!

Did that one, and then a lot more. That was the first time I'd actually worked with him. Then, I went to the middle east with a musical show for ENSA [Entertainment National Service Association] in 1942, and at the end of 1943 he was there, as well.

I met him in the *Continental Savoy Hotel* in Cairo.

He said, "What are *you* doing?"

I said, "Well, as far as I know, I'm going back to England in January."

So, he said, "Well, I'm going to South Africa. Field Marshall Spaats has invited me, and *would you* come play for me?"

I said, "Yes! I'd absolutely love to!"

So, I left for South Africa in *January 1944,* and was *supposed* to meet him ten days later, and he didn't turn up! So, I had a *wonderful* time in South Africa for about six weeks, because he was in America and couldn't get there—got side-tracked on the way. [He laughs]

AF: I was just reading from *"Future Indefinite"* that he was admonished to take a two-week rest, then after that, there were *all kinds* of delays. Bad weather and everything else. He was *hoping* you would *still* be there.

NH: I was there, all right, and having a *whale of a time!* Sort of *basking* in his reflected glory, for one thing. And he *finally* arrived, I think about in the middle of February, as far as I remember.
We got busy and did *a lot* of troop shows in hospitals around the Union. Then we started on the *grand, glamorous* concerts with the Capetown Symphony Orchestra.

He said, "We'll have the Capetown Symphony Orchestra for the *first half* of the program, because, by *then* they'll be so god-damned *bored* they'll think *I'm* wonderful."

[Laughter]

AF: His half was a long show, too, wasn't it?

NH: Oh, yes! He did the whole second half of the program. I did a solo spot in the middle to give him a rest.

AF: That was *"Scrambled Father"*.

NH: That's right, yes.

AF: What did you do?

NH: Oh, just a medley of *ALL* his songs, the ones he hadn't been singing. We did six of those concerts around. We did the first one in Capetown, Pietermaritzburg, Johannesburg, Durban, then we did one in Southern Rhodesia.

Then, he was invited to go to India by Mountbatten! India and Burma!

He asked would I 'go there?'

I said, "I'd love to."

So, then we had a *holiday* in Mombassa, and while we were in Mombassa, he had a signal from Dickie Mountbatten that said, *'would he like to go in a cruiser that was going from Mombassa to India?'*

So he went on the Navy cruiser!

You know Bert Lister, who was his manservant, general factotum, he and I stayed on and went up to Cairo, where Bert promptly developed malaria, and was shipped home.

So, I was left on my own then.

I went out to India, and did India, and Burma, and Ceylon.

I was so impressed with *South Africa* that I wanted to go back there. So, I *went* back there. He tried his best to talk me out of it, but I *wouldn't* be talked out of it. I thought it was a marvelous opportunity to start a *new* life in South Africa.

I was quite wrong!

He went back to England.

Then I had a cable from him, in February of the following year, saying,

"I'm doing a new revue. I think you'd better come back and help me over rehearsals."

That was practically a *royal command,* you know. I thought about it, and I thought I was enjoying myself so much, **why** should I go back to England where it's miserable. However, I thought, "don't be a fool, you'll wish you'd gone."

So, I did.

I did *"Sigh No More"* with him, in which he used two of my songs, which was a *tremendous* thing to happen. It was the *first time* he'd ever used *anybody else's* music apart from his own!

AF: What were those songs?

NH: A song called *"Music Hath Charms"* which Madge Elliott did. One called *"It Couldn't Matter Less"*, which finally got lost on the road, you know, as songs do. And another, a special swing arrangement I did of *"Bonny Bonny Banks of Loch Lomond".*

He said, later, that the best thing about that show was the *title.*

Which *wasn't* true, really, but it wasn't a very good show. As a matter of fact, the title song was absolutely *wonderful.* Do you know it?

AF: Yes, I do.

NH: A marvelous song! I thought it had some *good* spots! It had Cyril Ritchard and Madge Elliott, who were *dreadful,* really. *That* was the trouble. They were the *stars* of the show, you know? Heavy-handed as could be, really. They're both dead now, so I can speak freely.

[Laughter]

AF: Graham Payn was in that, too, wasn't he?

NH: Yes, Graham was in that. Then we lost touch again. I was doing various things until 1951, when again I went to the Cafe de Paris with Bea. Noël came to the first night, which was a riotous success. afterwards he came to the table and had a drink with Bea and me.

He said, "Do you think I could do this?"

I said, "Of *course* you could do it! Why don't you? Get an agent to book you into it. They'd love to have you!"

"Oh, I don't want an agent," he said, **"You** be my agent."

I was there booking him into the Cafe de Paris, which wasn't as easy as it would sound, as a matter of fact, because I said to the manager, "I have a marvelous proposition for you!"

And he said, "Oh, yes? Who?"

And I said, "Noël Coward!"

And they said, "Oh . . . I, uh . . ."

He didn't *quite* say—*'Noël WHO?'*

They said, "Well, we know he's a very, very celebrated *playwright* and *writer* and *composer* and *everything* like that, but *what's* he going to *do?*"

I said, "He's going to *sing his own songs!* You'll find they're *pretty good songs,* too!" I said, "I'll *try* to get him to see you."

He was waiting in the studio, so I brought them over to the studio. And he was, sort of, you know, a frightfully retiring boy.

They say, "Well, we'd very much like to have you at the club, but for four weeks even. Would seven hundred and fifty pounds a week be all right with you?"

Which was an **ENORMOUS** amount of money for those days! Nobody had *ever* had as much as that.

Noël said, "Well, I think that's fair enough, after all, it's such a *tiny* place."

So, they said, "all right."

He escorted them to the door and down to the car, came back—and *fell about laughing. So, then we got down to work!*

We opened about *four* weeks later! Of course, he was a *riotous* success! We did about four or five seasons there.

Then, he was booked to go to Las Vegas, and I said I *couldn't* go with him, and he was very, very disappointed.

AF: When you put together that first show, how did you decide what tunes to use?

NH: By discussion. I did a special medley of the old songs, the waltzes and the early revue songs, which was a very good medley, I don't know if you've ever heard it—

AF: Yes.

NH:—which we opened with, which absolutely got them *screaming!* I mean, by the time we got to the end of it—it ended on *"Play, Orchestra, Play"*—and they were screaming their heads off by then. Then, all the *comedy* numbers, you know? He did about an hour. They absolutely hung on his *every* word. He couldn't have been more successful. The place was jammed to the ceiling every night for four weeks.

At the end of one week they said, "Would you stay a little longer?"

He said, "No, no, no, four weeks is plenty! No, no, no, no."

At the end of the *third* week—I don't know if you've heard this story, but he was in Bond Street, and you know, he was *mad* about *pictures*. There was a gallery in Bond Street, and he saw a little Boudin picture, a seascape. He was very, very keen to have it, didn't know what it cost, umpteen thousand pounds.

So, Louie Majora, the manager of the Cafe, came in that night and said, "How about staying a little longer?"

So, he said, "Well, I might do an extra couple of weeks—"

He said, "That's wonderful! Two weeks! How much money do you want?"

Noël said, "I don't want any *money* at all! But if you can persuade the directors to buy this *picture* for me, I'll do another two weeks for you."

The picture cost a lot more than two week's salary.

So, they *bought* the picture, and they *displayed it* in the foyer with all these billings, great stickers across the billings saying—"BY SPECIAL DEMAND!"

He stayed another two weeks till the evening of his fifty-second birthday! He said in one of the books *"that was one of the happiest birthdays I've ever had."*

Then, the next year was *coronation* year. We did a special gala show for coronation. That was very funny, looking back on it, because it was terribly glamorous. The menus were printed on white satin, and the cover charge was *five* pounds. Now, isn't that extraordinary! Normally, the cover price at the Cafe was *three* pounds, but that night it was five pounds.

And Noël goes, "It'll keep them away."

It's a helluva long time ago, but that's the comparison between money values *then* and money values *now.*

AF: There were *some* critics who reviewed him in the cabaret, and said he *'... murdered his own songs.,* but obviously they were *not* accurate.

NH: *I* don't think they were right, you know.

AF: He was the *best* interpreter of his own songs.

NH: *Nobody* has ever sung his own songs *as well as he has.* Of course, *I know every* note, word and innuendo of every song. When they did *"Noël and Gertie"* last year (1989) . . . oooh . . . [whispers] . . . *terrible.*

I got so mad, because I've known *Graham* for millions of years! I know Sheridan Morley! I knew *most* of the people who were putting on the show, and I thought, "if they'd just rung me up and said, 'Look, give us an afternoon,' or, 'Can we come down and see you?" or **something.** *Nobody* could have steered them straighter than I could!

I didn't want to produce the thing, and get paid, or anything like that, but I *hated* to hear those songs *badly* done! When, with *an hour* up in the studio with a piano and the artist, I could have made them *ten times as good* as they were!

You understand about this. I mean, it was only because I cared so passionately about these songs, because most of them—I'd been **with him** when he **wrote them,** for goodness sake, and had taken the first dictation of the music, and the lyrics, and everything like that. I *can't* understand why they did that.

When I went to see the show, I was indeed invited to a matinee, and asked to come 'round afterwards, which I did, and I was absolutely charming!

[Laughter]

Simon Cadell, (whose mother is a great friend of a *friend* of mine, Celia Jennings, Paul Jennings' widow, sadly enough, with whom I'd gone,) and he said, "You know, it was awfully nice to meet Norman Hackforth, but I *do* wish he'd been able to say a little bit more what he thought about the show. He was very polite, but do you think I could ring him up or anything?"

[Laughter]

So, I said, "By *all* means! I'd *love* to hear from him!"

So, he rang me up, and we had half an hour on the telephone, and *I told him.*

He said, "This is *very* interesting, I know *exactly* what you mean. I just wish we'd done it, but now the show's coming off *anyway,* so what the hell!"

Isn't it strange about this?

AF: Yes. Well, I thought he did *"Mrs. Worthington"* quite well.

NH: [whispers] . . . no . . .

AF: You didn't—

NH: No. He was *much* too much *in tempo,* and he didn't clip it!
[Demonstrating how *"Mrs. Worthington"* ought to be sung:]

> **DON'T** put your **DAUGHT**er on the **STAGE,**
> Mrs. **WORTH**ington,
> *[half a beat]* **DON'T** put your daughter on the **STAGE.**
> *[breath]* She's a bit of an **UG**ly **DUCK**ling,
> I must **HON**estly con**FESS,**
> And the **width** of her **SEAT**
> Would **surely** de**FEAT**
> Her **chances** of suc**CESS.**

[he stops demonstrating]

It's—*clip, clip, clip!* I *didn't* want him to *imitate* Noël, any more than I was imitating Noël, but, you know . . .

[Demonstrating:]

It's a—*[takes a breath]*—**loud** voice,
To give the **WRETCHED** girl her ***due***
But **don't** you think her **bust** is too deVELoped for her ***age?***

[he stops demonstrating]

There are certain words, which you must *ac-**cen**-tuate,* and certain words that you can let go. And, where did he get that dinner jacket? It was a *bugger!* It *really* was! It was a two-handed show, for goodness sake. They *could* have gone to Halls & Curtis, paid a thousand quid, and got him a really *beautiful* dinner jacket! (I think it came from the *fifty-shilling* tailors, as far as I could see!)

[Laughter]

AF: Well, that's something that Stanley [Hall] was just saying about *"Private Lives"* that the costuming is just—it looks so *'on the cheap.'*

NH: Oh, how *awful* Well, I read the reviews, of course, over the weekend. I must say Mr. Baxter? Is that his name? [Keith Baxter] Not *my* idea of *Elyot.* He's too *old,* to start with, and he's too, sort of, *butch* altogether. He's very nearly *Victor,* you see?

I was at the *original* dress rehearsal at the Phoenix Theatre, thirty, forty, *fifty* years ago! 1930! *Sixty* years ago!! *[laughs]* You see, it was such *perfection* that! It had such a shine! I've seen umpteen productions since. I've seen John Clements and Kay Hammond, who were very good! I saw Googie Withers, and whoever-it-was, who played with her, but he is always slightly in the background, or somebody was, steering them *straight.*

It's glossy. It's hard to describe. It cannot be *heavily* played.

I'm afraid poor Joan Collins is too *old* for a start. She looks *wonderful* for her fifty-two years, or whatever she is, but you know, Amanda was *30?*

No one was ever like Gertie. No one could ever *be* like her again. She was magical! And so was Noël.

AF: Let's talk about some of the songs. The one thing I've heard from the BBC archives is your telling the story about *"Nina"*—the *first* performance of *"Nina"*—when he *forgot* the lyrics.

NH: Yes, he wrote *"Nina" that* afternoon! We were living with some dear people in Pretoria, South Africa, and he had a concert in Pretoria that night:
"I would now like to sing you a song," Noël said, "which was written only this afternoon." I knew it backwards, of course, so did *he*.
He sang,

> *Senorita Nina, from Argentina,*
> *Knew all the answers,*
> *Although her relatives and friends were perfect dancers,*
> *She swore she'd never dance a step until she died!*
> *Brrump pah—pum pum pum pum—pah!"*

Dead silence—and he *looked* at me.
Normally, as I say, I *knew every word*—I GAVE HIM THE WRONG LINE!
He says, *"No, no, no, never mind. We'll start again!"*
Although he passed it off in a lighthearted laugh and a joke, *he was livid afterwards!* **He said, "Never, never, never, *never again* will I do a *song* that isn't PROPERLY *rehearsed!*"**
We'd rehearsed for four hours all that afternoon, but it's not the same as rehearsing for a week and getting it pat.

AF: What are some of the other songs that he wrote during that period?

NH: *"I Wonder What Happened to Him?"* which was written about our escorting officer Major Mike Umfreville, who was a frightfully *nice* chap, who talks like—[grandly]—***THAT!*** He really was a jolly, pukka sahib, and very, very decent, and Noël *loved* him, you see.
And so he wrote this song about these jolly nice chaps in the Indian army, and the way they talked and everything like that, which turned out to be *"I Wonder What Happened to Him?"* 'I

wonder what became of old . . . ' And that was written in, oh I can't remember, somewhere along the line, and tried out in a show in Calcutta, where, of course, it absolutely pulled the place down.

Then there was *"Dear Uncle Harry"* which was written somewhere along the line.

Then there was a *beautiful* song, which he played to me, called *"There Will Always Be"* and it *really is* a lovely song. I'm the only person who ever knew it. Nothing ever happened to it. He said he was going to put it in a show and he didn't.

And so, in 1978 Teddy Holmes of Chappell, whether he's there—probably not now—said, "Look, would you do a piano copy of this and let us *publish* it with the *story* of how you came to hear this song?"

So, I did, and was given a *minuscule* royalty. It has never sold a copy as far as I know. I never had a check from them anyway.

AF: I just came across it in the British Library.

NH: You did? Oh!

AF: Because I'd never heard of it before. I talked to Chappell last week to find out if it was still in print. And they said, "Oh, no. It didn't last very long."

NH: It didn't *start!* *'Last very long?'!!*—my foot!

It wasn't published till 1978! Which was five years after he'd died! And it never started. I don't know what they did to it.

AF: Well, I would love to hear it.

NH: Well you *shall* hear it. We'll go out and *I'll play* it to you! In fact, I think I can even give you a copy—

AF: Okay! I'd love to have a copy, absolutely!

NH:—because it is the most beautiful song.

AF: I've read the lyrics [the lyrics appear at the end of this interview] and it's, as you said, it really does seem to express his philosophy.

NH: Absolutely, absolutely. And I thought, probably, it would catch on, but it's out of its time now, that's the trouble. Popular music is so *awful* today!

AF: Well, I think that's why programs of music of that period *are* still so popular today.

NH: You're probably right at that. You may well be right at that.

AF: I mean, I do like Stephen Sondheim,—

NH: Oh, so do I.

AF:—but even Sondheim doesn't—

NH: But poor, poor Stephen Sondheim's got the pants taken off of him over *"Into The Woods"*, which opened last night.

AF: Yes, I've seen the reviews.

NH: One song of his is being called *"Send In the Clones"*! [Laughter]

AF: Let's talk a bit about the tours. That must have been a very *strenuous* business, during the war, on those troop tours.

NH: It *was* pretty strenuous! I can't pretend it was anything else. But apart from anything else, I had polio in 1942, which wasn't a great help. I got over it and was able to walk about, but we were living on the side of a hill in Burma, which I simply *couldn't* get up.
    So, I had to be *carried* up there!
    They were *marvelous* to us! They were absolutely *wonderful,* I mean, they gave us *all* they had, which *wasn't* very much, but you know, you knew they were *so* grateful that whatever

they had was *ours*. I am talking slightly about myself now, but you must forgive me. That was one of the most moving things I've ever done, the Burma thing.

The day we were due to leave, the road had been cut, by the Japanese, a few miles away. They hadn't had any supplies for about six weeks, and they were getting pretty low. We heard that the road had been re-taken. I remember looking into the distance and seeing a convoy on the road winding its way towards us. Watching it as it came nearer, the first truck that arrived was the *beer* truck and I thought, "Well, somebody's got their priorities right for once." [Laughter]

AF: I know, on some of your tours, you trucked along a piano, and at other times you just had to do with what was there.

NH: We carried a piano most of the time, *'the little treasure'* you've heard about it.

AF: *'The little treasure'* I *have* heard about it!

NH: Yes, which was a marvelous piano. It was a little Broadwood—an English make of piano. It was quite small although it was a full keyboard, seven octaves, and it wasn't the full height of an upright, but of course it *couldn't* stay in tune. I had a key and I used to tune it *desperately!* I'm *not* a piano tuner, *god knows,* and it is one of the most difficult things you *ever*—believe me, it's *terrible!*

Particularly when you are sitting in the *back* of a *truck* with this *poor thing* All *hell's* breaking around you! It's not much fun, but still, it withstood the racket marvelously.

AF: Were there any of his tunes that were more popular with the troops than others?

NH: I can't think of anything that was really better than anything else. We only had one disaster, when we played in an open-air show, largely to colored American troops, and it was *pissing* with *rain.* They got *restless* . . . the only time I ever knew. And he behaved *beautifully.* He cut the show *short, bowed,* and walked off.

AF: You made some recordings with him, too, didn't you?

NH: I did. I made some special recordings in Calcutta, because HMV had a studio just outside Calcutta, and I got to know about this, and I said, "How would it be if we did—?" And we did. We went out there and we made six records, 78's, you know.

AF: Oh, I didn't know that. I didn't know they recorded there.

NH: They were never issued. [Ed. Note: They have since been issued Volume 4 Naxos *"Complete Recordings of Noël Coward"* 2004.]

AF: Oh . . .

NH: I've got 'em. They're great! [Laughter] They were all the songs we'd been doing, *"I Wonder What Happened to Him?"* and *"Nina from Argentina"* and the lot.

AF: Oh. 'cause I read about some of the ones I guess you made later at the Cafe de Paris.

NH: I made those, yes.

AF: You did *"Don't Make Fun of the Festival".*

NH: Yes, that's right.

AF: *"Time and Again".*

NH: *"Time and Again"* yes.

AF: *"There Are Bad Times Just Around the Corner".*

NH: That's right, yes.

AF: There was at least one more that I found in the discography . . .

NH: Well, the cabaret medley we did as well. I think that was about the lot.

AF: Actually, in *Mander and Mitchenson* there are a lot of recordings where the discography just says *'With piano accompaniment'* and it doesn't say *'by whom.'*

NH: Well, how old are they do you think?

AF: Well, they cover whole period.

NH: Because the early ones, I mean, going back to the 1930's, I wasn't playing for him. Carroll Gibbons—

AF: Carroll Gibbons was credited with some of those, but others it says *'piano accompaniment.'*

NH: Great, great, great piano player, Carroll. Marvelous! My mentor really.

AF: Didn't he lead the Savoy orchestra?

NH: Yes, he did.

AF: Among I guess other orchestras.

NH: Really, the Savoy Orpheans was the only band Carroll ever had till the day he died. He died when he was 52, poor darling, which was awful. He was a great artist. Great, great, performer.

AF: In making recordings with Coward, did he do it in one take?

NH: *He mostly did it in ONE take!* We *might* have had *two* takes. But he was an absolute perfectionist. I mean, when he got to that studio every *note* and every *line* of the lyrics was pre—rehearsed and *ready-to-go.* I mean they took a balance, and we stood up and did it.

They sometimes said, "Well, let's have another just for luck."

But, those were, of course, RPM 78's wax pressings, and if anybody made a mistake—back to the beginning, and you went again. That was the tiresome part, not like we do things today where you can just cut the tape.

AF: I imagine a technical goof would infuriate him if somebody *else* wasn't doing his or her part.

NH: Well, *no,* because he wasn't *that* sort of temperament. Unless it was sheer bloody mindedness, you know. I mean, *if* the band played a wrong note, he'd probably crack a *gag* about it and go back. He *was* an absolute *perfectionist,* but at the same time, he knew people couldn't *always* be as perfect as he could be, perhaps. He made goofs himself, *sometimes,* you know.

AF: You mentioned, talking about his songs, his inflection of every word was important. I remember seeing a tape of a kinescope of the Mary Martin special *"Together With Music".* It was the only chance I've ever really gotten to see him do his songs, you know, the use of the eyebrow, the use of his hands, everything.

NH: That was the American one.

AF: Yes.

NH: Because we did one over here at the Cafe [de Paris] in 1953, and I worked with them, and played for them both and met her. She was a darling lady and there again was a *wonderful* performer, *absolutely superb!* That was one of the greatest joys of my life.

AF: Pete Matz said that in Las Vegas they used the medley, while the medley was going on at the beginning of the show, he could see Coward casing the audience, and deciding how much he had to add, and how much he could play it safe, depending on who he saw in the audience.

NH: You met Matz, did you?

AF: Yes, in Los Angeles.

NH: Because I've never met him. So, if you see him again, tell him you met me, and say hello. He's done pretty well for himself, hasn't he? He's done a lot of film music . . .

AF: Yes, movies and things. Now he's busy all the time. He was over here a year or so ago doing an album with Samuel Ramey of Rodgers and Hammerstein.

NH: Oh, really?

AF: And before he came over he wanted to get a hold of Joan Hirst. He wanted to get her phone number. I know Graham has fond memories of their work together.
 How much did you write? How many songs have you written?

NH: [Modestly whispering] Oh, I've written a great many.

AF: *Have* you!

NH: Yes! But not very many for Noël, I'm sad to say. But he *liked* my songs. He was sweet about them. He sang *alot* of them! Jt was great!

AF: Did you write both the lyrics and the music for your songs?

NH: Yes, yes.

AF: You mentioned working with Bea Lillie; was she as difficult for you to work with as she was with Noël?

NH: Just as difficult.

AF: Just a temperamental genius?

NH: You see, poor Bea was an *extraordinary,* slightly *mad* lady, you know, really. She had a solid repertoire of songs, which she went on doing *all her life.*

We did the first season at the Cafe de Paris, which was an enormous success, and they wanted us to go *back,* and she'd *been* to America in the meantime, and she said, "I think it's time I had some *new* songs."

I said, "Marvelous. Bring some new songs back."

So, she brought these new songs back by some very good writers, written especially *for her.* We rehearsed and rehearsed and she was an *awful* rehearse-er. We'd take a studio, because I wouldn't go to her flat, because she'd never *work* in her own flat, any more than she'd work in mine. There were too many distractions. So we had a *bare* rehearsal room with a piano for two hours.

After half an hour she'd say, "What's the time, darling?"

I'd say, "It's half past two, Bea. We have another hour yet."

She'd say, "Don't you think it would be nice if we were out in the park?"

I'd say, "No, no, *come* on, get *on* with it."

So, I drove her absolutely—

We opened with these songs, and she'd **dried,** and couldn't go on! I *prompted* her, and she played it *beautifully,* and passed it off, and got laughs and things like that! So, the end of the *second* song I said to her, "What about some of the oldies?"

She said, "Yes."

We went back into the *old* routine, and pulled the place down again! They never failed. They knew every word and note of it and that's all they *wanted to hear.*

AF: As I recall, she insisted on saying, *"bar on the Picco-LO Marina"* instead of *'Picco-LA Marina.'*

NH: I didn't know that.

AF: But also, what I think is remarkable about *her* and her *recordings* of Coward's songs, is she always sang the *complete* lyric. I appreciate that, because, I try to collect in my collection as much as possible of the songs. Sometimes, because of time limitations, they didn't record all the verses, but it seems like he would record as much, and more than anyone else, and *precise*. Except for that one change, *precise lyrics.*

NH: Probably without realizing it. She was an extraordinary lady and a wonderful performer. Thank god, she died last year [Ed: 1989] at the age of 95. The end of her days must have been so awful for her, poor darling. She was ill for years in the States. You know what it *costs* to be ill in the States! It practically *bankrupted* her.

So, she came over here, and spent her declining years here, but she didn't die for *ages.*

AF: I guess the last show she did was *"High Spirits"* wasn't it?

NH: I think so, yes, yes, playing *Madame Arcati.* Which, I never saw. I last saw Noël, of course, at his 70th birthday at the Savoy Hotel. He gave a party. I was graciously invited.
[laughter]

AF: That was just before he became Sir Noël, wasn't it?

NH: Yes, I suppose it was about the same year, was it?

AF: Then, in January, he got the *knighthood.*

NH: Yes, he got the knighthood in the New Year's Honors, and I sent him a cable on that and said, *"Dear Sir Master, congratulations and about bloody time, too!"* [laughter]

AF: Do you remember times when lyrics had to be changed for recordings for censorship reasons?

NH: No. I can only think of one classic example of censorship, which I think will amuse you very much.

When he played in the show, which was *"Words and Music"* here, originally, and *"Set to Music"* when it got to New York in about 1938. It was the show that had *"Mad About The Boy"* in it. And *"Mad About The Boy"*, as you know, had *several* lyrics.

He wrote, what I think was an absolute masterpiece of a lyric of the *little businessman—frightfully important* businessman, in a black coat and striped pants, and *glasses,* and a big, *huge* office desk, dictating to his secretary.

A photograph on the desk.

She goes off, and he goes into the verse, which as I remember . . . the refrain . . . which is:

**Mad about the boy,
I know it's stupid
But I'm mad about the boy.**

That had to be cut.

It is a great lyric. The New York theatre thought it was rather '*improper*'—*isn't* that *extraordinary?*

AF: Well, that's interesting, very interesting, because there was also the story about him singing that song—he claimed he *never* sang the song. That particular lyric was never referred to.

NH: I've got a copy of it, and I've typed a note about it, and *put* it in the *songbook* to say *'this lyric'* you know, and given the story about it. It's a *brilliant lyric,* and isn't unpleasant or offensive, in any way. It's bloody funny. [Laughter] But the theater thought . . . *ooh!* . . . *Mustn't do it!*

That's how times have changed.

AF: What a shame. I'm sure that wouldn't have been cut today. Well, *"Green Carnation"* was cut from the films, from *both* films of *"Bitter Sweet"*.

NH: Was it really? Oh, of course, there *were* two films of *"Bitter Sweet"*. Anna Neagle, to start with, and what else, who else did it?

AF: Jeanette McDonald—that awful film.

NH: God, yes!

AF: But, at least, it was *included* when they did this new Sadler's Wells Opera Company revival . . .

NH: I don't understand it, you know, because . . . I suppose, Oscar Wilde was a dirty word, was he, in those days? Because, you see, the brilliance of those lyrics was, they were never *offensive*. He never wrote an *offensive* word in his life, *I* don't think. Anybody who had that tremendous wit and selectivity for words and everything like that, *couldn't be vulgar.*

AF: Well, *I* know in some of his recordings he changed 'goddamned'" to 'damn fool'.

NH: Yes, that *I* think, was to please the Americans, because Americans are very, very narrow—minded, if you'll forgive me for saying so. They *are* you know! The British will say *'goddamned'* where the Americans will say *'gosh darn.'* [Laughter]

AF: *I* remember, even in Bobby Short's recording of, *"Weary of it All"*—where the line is *"to hell with you"* and he kept changing it to *"away with you."*

NH: Ah yes, yes, it was extraordinary, yes, yes.

AF: Speaking of "I *Wonder What Happened to Him?"*—the first time he recorded it, he did use—*"Baggot, who married that faggot, he met in the Vale of Cashmere"*—*that* was changed when he recorded it.

NH: I believe it was, yes, yes. *'Faggot'* was cut out. *Extraordinary!*

AF: I'm trying to put together a book about the songs. What kind of changes there were in the lyrics and so on. I think his songs are endlessly fascinating.

NH: You're writing about his songs, more than a sort of biography about all this.

AF: Yes. That's been done pretty well, I think, but the songs have been sort of neglected, I think, unduly.

In a way, it's a dumb question to ask, *"What are your favorite Noël Coward songs?"* because you've played so many, and you realize the beauties of all of them, but *are* there any that you are *particularly* fond of?

NH: Well, I think, *"Sigh No More"* is one of the *great* songs. *"There Will Always Be",* and the song I was talking about is a marvelous tune. I think, *"If You Could Only Come With Me"* from *"Bitter Sweet"* and the whole score of *"Bitter Sweet"* had some beautiful songs.

AF: *"Kiss Me"* was one I hadn't been aware of before.

NH: Oh, *that,* of course, was a *joke* song, more or less. Sung by Ivy St. Helier as the *diseuse* in the cafe scene, with a great—sort of, you know, *overacting* going on, dressed in red and green sequins, with a—*thing* in her hair, and she was *marvelous.* She was the only one who ever played *Manon* correctly, because she *overplayed* the whole thing, which the *character* would have done. It became so real, and then of course, Carl Linden jumps over the bandstand, when his wife is set upon by the officer and kissed, and he slaps him across the face, and there's the *duel,* and he's killed, you know. He's dying on the stage in her arms, and *Manon's standing* away. As the curtain comes down, *Manon* lets out this awful sob.

AF: That was in the film, too.

NH: Was it? Actually, I'll never forget the first time I saw that, because I was engaged as a walking understudy, without appearing in the show, you see, because there's a scene in the first act—the leader of the band is in love with the society girl, which starts the whole thing going.

He's playing at her coming-out party in Mayfair. Everybody goes off and they're left on the stage together, and they have a love scene. *Lady Shayne* is the old lady who comes on and finds them in each other's arms. That starts the whole ball rolling.

I was engaged, you see, for this show.

The stage manager said, "Well, you better come and *see* it, but there *isn't* a seat to be had in the house! So you can *stand* in the *wings* and watch it."

So, I said, "That's lovely," and I watched the whole play, for the first time in my life from the wings. I stood in the wings in Act Two, when this duel scene came on, and Ivy St. Helier *sobbed*.

I was in tears.

The curtain hit the ground.

Everybody got up, and *laughed* sort of!

George kissed a chorus girl!—and like that.

I said, "How could they do this? It's awful!" I was *twenty* at the time. [he laughs]

AF: It is so moving, it really is.

NH: Wonderful, absolutely wonderful. *That, I* think, was one of the *greatest shows* he ever wrote. Jt ran for eighteen months in London, and then came off. Then we went on the road, and I played the part for a *year.*

AF: What part?

NH: *Vincent Howard,* the bandleader, with Evelyn Laye, who was wonderful, a great performer. We toured for a year, the number-one dates all around, which was lovely. Came back to London and that was it.

Now somebody tried to revive it two years ago.

AF: The New Sadler's Wells Opera.

NH: I suppose I should have been braver and gone to see it. But I simply couldn't face it you know.

AF: *I* saw it.

NH: Did you? Did you? Did you?

AF: I thought it was *okay*. The direction, I didn't care for. It was Jan Judge, who was an opera director, and I think he's in Graham's little black book. He has an unprintable adjective by him now, Tll tell you afterwards. But at least I got to hear some of the music I hadn't heard. Then they recorded it. They recorded the *full* score.

NH: *That* would have been all right.

AF: It *is* good.

NH: Except, I hate the idea of it being *over-operatic,* although, Peggy Wood, then, who played the lead, and George Metaxa, were definitely opera-style singers. *Beautiful* singers.

AF: It is the one thing that I thought *could* have been, and *should* have been revived.

NH: *I* always thought so, but it must be *cast* right, you see, that's the great thing. The leads are terribly important. Bear in mind she *starts* as the *old* lady, has a quick change back to a *girl* of eighteen, and then, sort of, *twenty-five* or so, then, the middle of her marriage, and then back to about, sort of, *fifty,* when she's a great *prima donna,* and comes to London, and Lord Shayne proposes to her in that wonderful ballroom scene! Then of course *back* to the original change!
    Well, Peggy's changes were *sensational,* absolutely!
    In the *last* change from *"Zigeuner"* to the rehash of the first scene, George Metaxa used to go up into the *dome* of what was, then, *His Majesty's Theatre,* right up on the *roof* and sing *"I'll See You Again".*
    There were no microphones. The theatre was absolutely *hushed.* This beautiful ghost voice came over, which gave *her* time to make the *change!* It was one of the most sensational things. There were no mikes at all. The whole thing was *live.* It

was simply *wonderful*. Did they make it a period piece? I'd like to think they did.

AF: Yes.

NH: Bear in mind that when it was originally done—the time was the present, you see. But of course, you couldn't have time as present today, because forty years had gone by since then and it was no good. It had to start in 1929, because that made the time scale right.

AF: I think of that last scene, too, where the young bandleader jumps on that tune and jazzes it up—

NH: He says, "What a tune! What a melody!"

AF: That is doubly sad, because that makes sense today. That could be *today*. But what he does with it just completely *massacres* it!

NH: Yes, yes.

AF: I get a little teary just thinking about it. [Laughter]

NH: Yes.

AF: Well, his other big musicals *"Operette"* and *"Conversation Piece"* never really—

NH: *"Conversation Piece"* was a marvelous show, really, and that has some lovely tunes, really.
　　"I'll Follow My Secret Heart".

AF: I think that's the one song that more opera singers have recorded than any other Coward song.

NH: Have they? [chuckles] The strange thing is, *he met Joan Sutherland,* the Australian lady? Joan Sutherland *lived* near him in

Switzerland, and became *mad* about his music, and WANTED TO SING IT ALL!

    I *heard* her singing it—[whispers]—she *couldn't* really sing it, you know, because—[grandly]—SHE WAS prRRRoducing *it AAAALL* VERRRY *OPERAAAATICALLY!*

AF: I was just talking with Stanley Hall about her, and the album that they did, and he said the one thing about it was that you couldn't understand the words.

NH: Because she was producing her beautiful voice. That's the trouble. And the words are so much a part of his songs. They belong, just as importantly as the music. And unless you can get somebody who can realize *both* at the same time, half of the music gets lost, I think.

AF: Just to go back to when he is working on a song, composing, writing a song, did he try out lyrics? Maybe change the lyrics after trying them out and seeing what they did?

NH: Oh, yes! Yes, he did! Yes! In fact, when I was working on *"After The Ball"* that **disaster** show, you know—

AF: You would serve as the Elsie April [Noël's musical transcriptionist] for that show.

NH: I wrote it down, yes, and I went out to Jamaica to finish it off. He wrote a song, which was all about Rosie O'Grady, who was a great lady of the town, and everything like that, and it *wasn't* very funny. *It was boring!*

    The next day it was *gone.* **Completely.** It became *"London At Night"*. The same tune exactly, but a quartet for four men called *"London At Night"*.

AF: Well, *that's* a good song!

NH: Wonderful song! Wonderful song! Had a terribly banal lyric to start with and he threw it out of the window you see?

AF: Well, you know, in *"The Girl Who Came To Supper"* of course, he had to pull *"Long Live The King"* after the Kennedy assassination. He added, *I* believe, *"My Family Tree"* which was just a new version of *"Countess Mitzi"*.

NH: Tell me quite honestly, how do you find his later songs?

AF: Well, *I* think some of the songs from *"Sail Away"* and *"The Girl Who Came To Supper"* are some of his *greatest* songs.

NH: *"Sail Away"* I agree with you. *I* think he rather fell apart after that. *I* think *"The Girl Who Came To Supper"*—the songs *I* heard from it, still a certain sort of cachet of Coward—*perfectly* turned lyrics, and everything like that, but *I didn't* think they were *as good* as the early ones.

AF: Well, *"Long Live The King"* he did record it on a demo record, and that's been released, and that's as witty as any of his—

NH: *That* I've never heard.

AF: Mostly the songs in that show that are good, *I* think, are the *romantic* ones. There's a wonderful one, *"Here and Now"* that's sung by Florence Henderson. Of the post war, and certainly in the sixties, *"Sail Away"* far and away, almost every song in that is, *I* think, *great,* one way or another.

NH: You see, he went into a slump after *"Sigh No More"*. He was very, very disappointed with *"Sigh No More"*. He didn't seem able to write for a while. *I* don't know why. He was only forty something. Forty-six, forty-seven, a young man, still. But he'd done an awful lot in a short time. Somehow nothing happened until he did *"Ace of Clubs"*.

It had, well, *"Juvenile Delinquents",* which is a very, very funny song, and what else?—*"Wait A Bit Joe",* and of course, *"Sail Away"*—that's where it first started, yes.

AF: And *"Chase Me, Charlie"* and *"Josephine" I* think, are marvelous.

NH: Yes, you see, they were all right. But it wasn't success, really. I enjoyed it.

AF: Well, I guess, *"Guys and Dolls"* sort of pre-empted the territory.

NH: Well, I suppose it did. It was concurrent, was it?

AF: I think so.

NH: Oh, *there* was a genius writer. Mr. Frank Loesser. *[he knocks on wood three times]* *"Guys and Dolls"* is one of my favorite shows. I've got a videocassette of it, and when I'm feeling depressed, I just run it through for the nineteenth time and enjoy every word of it. Absolutely superb. Marvelous.

AF: Someone told me once, I think it was Jose Ferrer, from *"The Girl Who Came To Supper"* that *"I'll Remember Her"* was sort of Coward's version of *"I've Grown Accustomed To Her Face"*.

NH: Oh, really, yes . . . yes . . . yes.

AF: And in a way, maybe it was. Originally he was asked to do *"My Fair Lady"* wasn't he?

NH: I *believe he was, yes!* He wouldn't have been as good as Rex [Harrison], you know, *I* don't think. He couldn't have submerged his own personality and have been as academic as Rexy was. He was absolutely wonderful. The best thing he ever did.

AF: Well, what do you do in retirement?

NH: What do I do in retirement? Absolutely nothing! [Laughter] Absolutely nothing. Enjoy my friends . . . *try* to keep in touch with things, here and there.

NORMAN HACKFORTH

AF: You mentioned your book. I didn't realize you'd written a book.

NH: I wrote a book, *"And The Next Object"* in 1975, which is fifteen years ago. Largely of course on my radio fame and celebrity, which was so boring, because I was in *"Twenty Questions"* for 27 years [as the 'mystery voice']. Became a nation-wide figure.

AF: I didn't know that.

NH: I start the book by saying one of the saddest moments in my life was when I came out from a program of *"Twenty Questions"* and an old lady stopped me as I came through the door, and said, "I must tell you, I heard you playing the piano the other day on the wireless. I never knew you played the piano, *too!*"

Wasn't that sad? [Laughter] Would you like to come up to the piano now?

AF: Yes.
    [The next part of the interview took place in Mr. Hackforth's studio.]

NH: [Singing]
Mad about the boy,
I know it's stupid but I'm mad about the boy!
And even Doctor Freud cannot explain those vexing dreams
I've had about the boy!
When I told my wife
She said, "I never heard such nonsense in my life."
Her lack of sympathy embarrassed me
And made me, frankly glad about the boy!
My doctor can't advise me
He'd help me if he could
Three times he's tried to psychoanalyze me
But it's just—no good.
People I employ,
Had the impertinence to call me Myrna Loy!

> *I rise above it, frankly, love it!*
> *'Cause I'm absolutely mad about the boy.*

AF: Marvelous! How about *"There Will Always Be"?*

NH: Well, I can't sing it, of course, but I can't sing anyway, as you may have gathered. I'll play it for you.
[singing]
> *There will always be enough in the world for me*
> *Moonlight and stars, and sea*
> *These there will always be.*
> *I shall always find, if destiny's only kind*
> *Something that's new and good and true*
> *To calm my questing mind.*
> *Though dark days may grieve me*
> *Though the fates deceive me,*
> *I'll always know, deep down inside me*
> *Love will be there to guide me*
> *There will always be*
> *This personal thing to set my spirit free*
> *This there will always be*
> *This there will always be*

AF: Great song, great song. Beautiful. Oh, thank you.

DEREK JACOBI

b. 1938

Interviewed on December 9, 1992

Derek Jacobi, actor, had been part of the cast of the pivotal revival of *"Hay Fever"* at the National Theatre, in 1964—Directed by Noël Coward, and starring Edith Evans, Maggie Smith and Lynn Redgrave, the production signaled Coward's return to popularity. Derek Jacobi was in San Francisco to perform as a narrator with the Opera. We spoke at the KALW studio.

ALAN FARLEY: The first time I saw you in London was at the unveiling of the memorial stone in Westminster Abbey for Noël Coward, in 1984.

DEREK JACOBI: Yes.

AF: That was quite a ceremony. The Queen Mother was there, Sir John Gielgud—

DJ: That's right. I read from some of his war diaries, yes. I'd worked with him at The National Theatre in the mid 1960's, when he directed *"Hay Fever"*.

AF: And you played the son?

DJ: I played *Simon* in *"Hay Fever"* yes, and he directed it, and it was a wonderful experience. He was such a generous man. I remember he took each member of the company out, *individually*, for an evening with Noël Coward.
   My turn came, and we went to the theatre. We went back to The Savoy for dinner. It was so generous, and it was wonderful to actually pick his brains. Actually, you wound him up, and he just went on, and he talked about the past and the present. It was wonderful to be with him.

AF: I spoke to someone else, not long ago, who was performing in a play, and Noël Coward came backstage afterwards, and the next thing it was *five o'clock in the morning* And it was mostly Noël Coward talking.

DJ: Yes, yes. He was a wonderful raconteur, conversationalist, wonderful.

AF: And as a director, how was he?

DJ: He was great! But the production that he did was virtually *identical* to the production that he'd done when he first wrote it in the 1920's. We had the same set—not, in fact, the *same* set, but the same *design* for the set.

Everything was in the same place—the furniture, the tables, the piano, the staircase, the French windows—*everything* was as it had been when Marie Tempest had played it originally as *Judith Bliss* [1925].

We had a wonderful cast with Dame Edith Evans, Maggie Smith, Lynn Redgrave, Robert Stephens, et cetera, and he wanted it done as it had been done then. So, a lot of the moves were the same as they'd been, and they WORKED! I mean, all these years later, *they still work!*

GEOFFREY JOHNSON

Interviewed on March 20, 1987

Geoffrey Johnson was for many years a partner in one of Broadway's most successful casting companies [Johnson-Liff Associates] responsible for casting the two musical extravaganzas *"Les Miserables"* and *"Starlight Express"*. His desire had always been to be an actor, and after graduating college, he studied at the Yale Drama School, then he spent a couple of years in New York working as an actor. He drifted into stage managing, and it is in that profession that he met Noël Coward. He began a professional relationship that lasted until the playwright's death in 1973. In fact, he is still to this day a consultant to the Noël Coward Estate. The interview was conducted in his New York office.

ALAN FARLEY: How did you first meet and begin to work with Noël Coward?

GEOFFREY JOHNSON: Well, before I was a casting director, I was a stage manager, and I stage managed some of the auditions for *"Sail Away"* which was the first time I met Noël Coward. I didn't actually stage manage the show, I stage managed his *next* show *"The Girl Who Came To Supper"* and that's how I got to know him.

AF: What was he like to work for?

GJ: Fabulous, just fabulous! He was the perfect boss, I think.

AF: How so?

GJ: Well, he *was* all those fabulous things that we know about Noël Coward, or we read about and hear about—the wit, the charm. He was a very understanding kind of person. He would go to Jamaica, and come back, and very *quickly* take care of everything that had transpired while he was gone—the same with

Switzerland, when he went off to his home in Switzerland, or to England. He was kind of a short hand boss, in a way. A wonderful, wonderful person, and also, working for him, as I did *after* I stage managed *"The Girl Who Came To Supper"* going to see him about some business matter in Jamaica, or Switzerland or England. It was the best kind of life. It was wonderful.

AF: What was he like when he was auditioning actors? Was he very kind to the actors?

GJ: Yes, he was. I think he understood actors, because he grew up *being* an actor, and he had been a *director* all his life, and so he understood an actor's *feelings* well. He was wonderful to actors. He was amusing to actors and to the rest of the people who were auditioning the actors.

AF: Did he try to put them at their ease?

GJ: Very much so.

AF: I think that is really the mark of a great person, one who realizes that you may be nervous, and tries to be very nonchalant and make you feel comfortable.

GJ: It's kind of a mark of greatness, I think. I've seen a lot of directors, a lot of actors, a lot of playwrights in the years I've been doing what I'm doing now, as a casting director, and I think the really great, or important ones, are able to put themselves in the other person's place.

AF: So, you stage managed the auditions for *"Sail Away"*?

GJ: That's right.

AF: And then stage managed *"The Girl Who Came to Supper"*.

GJ: Right.

AF: What *is* involved in that? What exactly does a stage manager do?

GJ: Well, a stage manager, of course—I was not a *production* stage manager, who is the top man on a show—I was an *assistant* stage manager. The production stage manager, the assistant stage manager, the second assistant stage manager are the people that make it all work backstage. They don't actually move the sets or change those wonderful colored lights, they give the *cues*.

They also have to deal with the actors, the temperament, the changes. A show like *"The Girl Who Came To Supper"* which had a great many changes out of town, had a long pre—Broadway tour. It opened in Boston. It was a great hit. Then it went to Toronto, then it went to Philadelphia before it opened in New York.

In that time of big pre-Broadway tours, there are an awful lot of rewrites, changes in songs, new songs put *in*, new songs taken *out*, changes in dialogue, and of course, I know you know the story about the one song that HAD to be taken out. The song about *assassination*—on the day that President Kennedy was assassinated—which was a terrible day for all of us in Philadelphia. The performance, of course, was canceled, but after that, the song *["Long Live The King, If He* Can"] could *not* stay in the show, so a new song was substituted *["My Family Tree"]*.

As assistant stage manager I had to take care of a lot of it—making sure each night that everybody had their *new* rewrites, and everybody kind of knew what they were doing. Sometimes it got pretty wild, but that often happens in shows with rewrites.

AF: It was a marvelous cast, I think.

GJ: Oh, yes! It was an incredible cast. Florence Henderson was quite wonderful in the show. Jose Ferrer was a wonderful actor, wonderful to work with. All of the stage managing experience for me was wonderful.

AF: How did you get into it?

GJ: I was initially an actor. All my life growing up I wanted to be an actor. I trained to be an actor. I went to the Yale Drama School.

After college, my mother said to me, "You can do anything you want, as long as you go to college."

So, I was an English major in college, and immediately upon graduation from University of Pennsylvania, I headed for the Yale Drama School. I was an actor in New York for two or three years, and I think kind of, by default, just *drifted* into stage managing.

I also knew that there were many people more talented than myself seeking employment in New York, and I guess I kind of thought, "Well, I'll still stay in the theatre and I'll be a stage manager." And I, fortunately, got a job outside of New York as an assistant stage manager, and when I came back to New York, I pursued that. Through the stage managing, as I said, I met one of the great ones. I met Noël Coward.

AF: After *"The Girl Who Came To Supper"* what was the nature of the work you did for Noël Coward?

GJ: Well, Noël Coward had an American corporation that dealt with "sorting out"—is the best way, I guess, of expressing it, or maybe the worst, I don't know—all the *requests*. Everyone wanted to do something of Noël Coward's. They wanted to turn *"Private Lives"* into a musical, let's say, or they wanted Noël Coward to play something on the stage, or in a film, and his corporation was dealing with all the requests that came in to do with Noël Coward, and clearing them with him, but sorting them all out. Some of them came to fruition and some of them didn't.

AF: You were actually in Jamaica when Noël Coward died.

GJ: Yes, I was.

It was kind of—well, it was an accident that I was there, really, or that I had stayed—I had *overstayed* my leave, so to speak. I was going to be there for *two* weeks, and I was *supposed* to leave on a Sunday. Cole Lesley was down there at the time, as well as Graham Payn.

Coley said to me, "Why do you have to rush back? The weather has been wonderful. Why don't you stay a few more days?"

It was very easy to be talked into those things, so I said, "fine," particularly in Jamaica, which is certainly a lovely, lovely place to be.

So, I *did* stay. I think it was the Tuesday or Wednesday that Noël died.

Then, that week following his death was quite incredible—dealing with the press and all the things that happened, that *do* happen, I suppose, in anybody's life, or in this case, *death,* because so many things have to be taken care of. But because the press was interested in the death of Noël Coward—particularly the English press—they descended on Blue Harbour like locusts.

AF: Is that one of the things you had to do, was to deal with them?

GJ: Oh, yes, I had to deal with them. I remember it was very, very *hot,* and I remember dealing with a reporter, and then going and jumping in the swimming pool to cool off, and then coming back and facing another one.

AF: You continue to have a relationship today with Graham Payn and the Noël Coward estate?

GJ: Yes. Well, I know a great deal about the Noël Coward properties. When I meet somebody, like you, I'm wondering how much I really do know, because you have such a fabulous collection, but I do have files from over the years, and often I do get calls about rather obscure things, and I can answer them. So, I'm still of some use.

AF: Are you involved in any of the productions these days?

GJ: Well, not directly involved. As a casting director, I kind of lead my own life, casting currently some rather overwhelming musicals, like *"Starlight Express"* and *"Les Miserables"*. I didn't contribute directly to *"Blithe Spirit"* [the Broadway revival that had just opened] but I did say a thing or two in the background.

AF: Let's talk a bit about that work as casting director for these huge musicals. It is quite a responsibility. I presume you work with the producers in the casting.

GJ: Oh, yes, yes working with the producers and the directors, and on a musical, first the composer and then lyricist. It's a collaborative effort and usually we *bring* actors to *them.*

AF: You do the first screening yourself?

GJ: Well, we don't always have to *screen,* because we do so many shows and we do so much of it we can often—when we know what we're dealing with—we can say, "Oh, *so and so* would be right for this." We're not always dead-on—the-nose, but we think we can bring the right people to the director without doing a lot of screening.

AF: Those two productions are open. Are you still involved in those shows?

GJ: Yes, we're retained by the producers of both of them to do replacements. Our next big New York musical is *"The Phantom of the Opera".*

AF: You seem to be getting all of the top shows.

GJ: We do some wonderful shows, and we are *very* lucky. I saw *"Phantom"* over the New Year—went to London for about four or five days—and I think it is a fabulous show. It is a beautiful show. I think it will be a great success here.

EVELYN LAYE

b. 1900   d. 1996

Interviewed on April 28, 1989

Evelyn Laye was an English actress and singer who had a long and distinguished stage career in England. She took New York by storm when she starred in Noël Coward's *"Bitter Sweet"* in 1929, produced by Charles Cochran. She was interviewed in her London home, shortly after the opening of a revival of *"Bitter Sweet"* by the New Sadlers Wells Opera.

ALAN FARLEY: I'd like to talk to you about Noël Coward, *"Bitter Sweet"* and also about Charles Cochran, because you had worked for Cochran *before "Bitter Sweet"*.

EVELYN LAYE: Oh, yes. I worked for Cochran, or, 'Cocky'—we always used to call him. When I was twenty, or twenty-one, that was my first contract I had with Charles, and of course, that went on all through my life.

I did three years for him right away, but I was also working for him when I was forty-six. So, that was some engagement, really. I mean, I didn't work for him entirely all that time, but we were very great friends.

He taught me a very great deal about what I had to be.

My diction must be perfect, and I must *mean* what I *sing*. That I *mustn't* sit down on my dress once I had put it on, particularly if I hadn't walked onto the stage, because it would make creases right across the middle of one's tummy, and that doesn't look very pretty when you're walking on a stage. That is something that I have kept up with, sometimes often, in fact, when I'd been standing at the side waiting for my cue to go on. I've always got on by the side of the place where I've got to get on, or at least ten minutes, quarter of an hour before I go on, to get into the mood. I never talk to anybody, but I don't sit *down*, either.

That was the training of Charles Cochran, and, of course, he treated everybody the same. I mean, whether they were a star, or whether they were a chorus girl or, whatever, they were all treated *exactly* the *same.* We were like one big family. He was *The Master* of it all. He knew it. *My goodness!* I owe so much to that man!

AF: Let me just read a paragraph from his autobiography where he says, **"Evelyn Laye is one of the few artists who could actually have climbed to fame on beauty alone. She seemed to me the prettiest girl I had ever seen when I first came across her in her teens. Percy Hammond, the American critic, did not exaggerate in describing her as 'the loveliest prima donna this side of heaven' when she performed in 'Bitter Sweet' in New York."**

EL: I thought that was wonderful, but I wondered *how much he'd had to drink?!*
[she laughs]

AF: There's quite a story connected with *"Bitter Sweet"* too, isn't there? You first turned *down* the opportunity to do it in London?

EL: Oh, yes! I was a very unhappy woman at that particular time, and I was *young* for my age, really. I was, what? Twenty-six? Something like that. I was *young* for my age. I was an *only* child.

Although I had been brought up in the theatre, I suppose I was a bit *spoiled* in a way, but I also had an enormous amount of *pride.*

My first husband had *looked around the corner* with one of his leading ladies. That always hurts a little bit the first time, you know. That's *life.* I was *hurt a lot.* I *hadn't* got inside me the *love of working,* as I did afterwards.

I *did,* and I *have* all my life.

I loved working for *Cochran.* He *inspired* me. He *guided* me in my *clothes,* in my *behavior* and everything. He did to all his companies. He didn't just look after me, he looked after *everybody* who was in the company.

He *gambled* like mad with shows! *Three times he went bankrupt!* It always broke our hearts when these things happened, and one wondered how one could help him.

AF: You eventually did play in the American production of *"Bitter Sweet"*.

EL: Oh, yes, I did, I did. One wet afternoon, I went to see a matinee. I was *enthralled* with it. I thought, "You *blithering idiot to turn it down! You fool! You little ass! Now you've got to get it back for New York!"*

So, I took the bull by the horns! I rang up a woman called Elsie April, who was Coward's musical advisor, and I *told her*, I said, "I wonder, have they settled on anybody for New York for *'Bitter Sweet?"*

She said, "No, they haven't."

I said, "Well, do you think you could ask them if they'd care to have me? Do you think they'd let *me* play it now?"

She said, "I don't know. I'll call you back. Where are you?"

I said, "I'm at home."

She said, "Well, I'll call you in the morning."

The phone went in half-an-hour!

She said, "Where do they send the contract?"

AF: Then you also managed to play it in London at the end of the run?

EL: Oh, yes. At the end of the run I did one or two turns on the road, and I was practically finished, but I'd also got one or two other things I was going to do.

One morning Charles Cochran rang me and said, "Boo, I'm in terrible trouble!"

(Boo is my *pet name* that everybody calls me.)

I said, "What is it?"

He said, "Well, can you come over now and play *'Bitter Sweet'* here again? Wood is very ill and she can't go on."

I said, "I don't *know.* I've one or two things fixed to do. I'll call you back and let you know." *I managed to cancel everything.*

He said to me on the phone, "Oh, darling, it'll be wonderful! Please, get on the next boat." Doesn't that sound *silly* now? It should be the next *plane!* But we didn't do that sort of thing in *those* days.

AF: This is around 1930 or 1931?

EL: That was, yes, that would be about right.

AF: You were telling me before that you sang *"Ziguener"* in a way *different* from what Coward had intended.

EL: Well, yes! He wrote it *slowly.* I had the *nerve* to ask him if I could sing it my *own* way.
    He said, "What do you mean, dear?"
    I said, "Well, I want to alter the *tempo."*
    "Oh, you do, do you?" he said.
    I said, "I *do,* Noël."
    He said, "Well, sing it to me."
    I said, "Well, I'm not quite ready at the moment. I'll be right ready in about a *week,* and *then* I'll sing it to you. If you like it, please, please let me sing it this way."
    So, the morning arrived, and I said, "Yes, Noël, I'm ready. I'll sing the *two* numbers to you I want to alter. One is *"Tell Me What Is Love?"*[Also known as *"What Is Love?"*] I want to alter that, and I want to alter *"Ziguener".*
    He said [sternly], *"Sing them to me then!"*
    So I sang, [she sings it ***slowly]*** "**. . . tell me, what is love?'** which *was* written . . .
    —into—
    [she sings it with **urgency]** **"TELL me! WHAT is LOVE!?"** *Mad!* Absolutely *mad!*
    A young girl, who didn't know what love was, and she got this enormous expression and feeling for this boy, but she *didn't know* what it was! She *didn't know* it was *love!*
    So, I sang it like that, as though she was absolutely *drunk* with love.
    And he said, *"Yes!* That is *very* interesting! Now sing the other one."
    And I sang *"Ziguener"* with much more *passion* in it than he had written.
    He said after—he was walking about the theatre—and I thought, "Oh, god! This is ghastly! *WHY did* I do this?"

He said suddenly, "That's absolutely *right* for you! **Sing them both that way!** Now, I'm going out to have a little lunch."

I think that shows great character, to be generous enough to allow me to sing it the way I wanted to, to sing them *both* the way I wanted to. There was a *magnificence* in Noël's character. I wonder what composer would allow me to do it today?

AF: *"What Is Love?'* is, I think, one of my *favorites* songs from that score that *isn't* sung as often as—

EL: Well, it *must go fast,* because she *doesn't* know what love is. She's at the party, you know, and she doesn't know what *IT is!* They're all playing hide-and-seek, which is fun, and that is when she's been *blinded-up* with a handkerchief around her. She gets hold of Karl and doesn't realize it's *him.*

AF: What was it like being the *star* of that in New York? That must have been thrilling because it was such a big hit.

EL: Oh! Well, you know, Americans are so, so generous. They didn't send me bouquets, they sent me *trees!* Truly! They sent me *trees* of roses and *coffins* of flowers! I don't think anybody sent me a *bunch* of flowers. I mean they sent—well, you see, my couch is not very small, but they were about that size! Enormous flowers! You've never seen anything like it.

AF: I was reading in, I think, Cole Lesley's book, that Noël had written that you *"knocked the spots off of Peggy Wood"* in your performance.

EL: I don't know, really, whether he did.

I remember somebody telling me that Noël had said, "Please don't accept to do anything at all. *I've* written a play for you." *["Bitter Sweet"]*

That was an odd message, thank god, but then *I turned it down,* because I was *unhappy!* Because I didn't *want* to work for *Cochran* again, because I thought that—in my *stupid, idiotic mind*—that he was one side or the other, too [of her husband's infidelity]. Oh, how *silly* can one be! I think, when you get into a bit of a bother about anything, just stand still and let the whole thing go by.

AF: Tell us what it was like last year when *"Bitter Sweet"* came back to the New Sadlers Wells Opera. What was that experience of seeing it like?

EL: It *tore* my *heart* out! It's a lovely score. *Beautiful* score. One of Noël's best, I think. His favorite, too. He loved it, and so did I

JOE LAYTON

b. 1931   d. 1994

Interviewed on February 12, 1987

Joe Layton is a Tony Award-winning choreographer and director, who worked with Noël Coward in the 1960's on *"Sail Away"* and *"The Girl Who Came to Supper"*. He enjoyed critical and public acclaim for his original ballet based on Coward's music, for the UKGB's *Royal Ballet*. He was interviewed in his Los Angeles home.

ALAN FARLEY: [reading from Noël's diary] March, 1961, your first meeting with Noël:

"On Monday morning I interviewed Joe Layton, who is the most sought after, and up and coming young choreographer on the scene at the moment. He was intelligent and I took a great liking to him. He was also available in May after he has finished with "The Sound of Music" in London. I had a television spectacular called "The Gershwin Years" run through for me, which he had choreographed and his work is brilliant. It now only depends on the terms being satisfactory, and I shall bloody well see that they are."

JOE LAYTON: Noël managed to always say the right thing at the right time.

My career was so very fast and furious up until that time. I was in the chorus, then I went into the Army, and, when I discovered that I knew what I was doing in the Army by staging shows, when I came out, I said I *wouldn't be a dancer again.* Though I did have to take a job in the Moulin Rouge in Paris to earn a fee, but, while I was there, I started choreographing for a small dance company. *I realized then that I should do that.*

I didn't like choreography. I didn't think I knew how to choreograph, but what I really wanted to do was *direct* Staging came very easy to me, but directing, that was really *it*. The choreography—*I thought I was getting away with murder in the*

Army. I was a dancer all my life, but I just was not into 'steps' so to speak. I was into *story,* but not into 'steps'.

And then, when I came quickly out of Paris, I immediately went into summer stock, where someone discovered me, and before I knew it, I had done *two* Off-Broadway shows! One of them for Richard Rodgers' daughter, and Richard Rodgers saw it and hired me for *"Sound of Music".*

So my career began with all of the greats. I was twenty-four years old and I was already working with Richard Rodgers, Noël Coward, Frank Loesser, and Jule Styne—were all my *first shows!* So, the education, along with my ambition, and courage—I mean, ignorance *is* bliss. But since I had grown up in the business, and I knew the behavior patterns, I was just one of those people who found no problem with the older generation, because there was *no such thing as an 'older generation' in the theatre.*

The reason all these people were such greats, including Noël, of course, was that they were about 'fourteen years old'. And so I felt older than most of them all the time, because their enthusiasm, and talent, and such, stemmed back from the time they discovered—just like I did early on—that they *had something,* and they wanted to *show it.*

AF: This was for the show *"Sail Away"?*

JL: Leading up to it. I digress, but at least to tell you how this all happened.

By the time I met Noël Coward, it was nothing.

I had just done a George Gershwin two hour special, when Richard Rodgers was the host; *"Sound of Music"* was already open; *"Once Upon A Mattress"* was already open; *"Greenwillow"* was already open.

I had done *THREE shows on Broadway at the same time,* so, *I* thought *I* was the cat's meow, as they say.

Nothing scared me—EXCEPT when I met Noël Coward.

Now *that* was a world! Being a *Jewish* boy, brought up in *Brooklyn,* brought up on *"Oklahoma!"* and Richard Rodgers, and that kind of *Broadway* in my life all the time—but,—*Noël Coward* was UNTOUCHABLE—his accent *alone* was enough to scare me

JOE LAYTON

to death! Thank *god I* had spent a year in Paris, and was at least a bit knowledgeable of the continent, you know, but other than that, I had not experienced too much.

Meeting *him,* and a *legend,* of course, the first thing I did was try to read everything that he had written.

At that time, don't forget, Noël Coward did not have the renaissance that he's having now. *Now,* Noël Coward is on the boards, or somewhere, at least twice a year around the world, and now his notoriety and his fame—the heralding of him is NOW.

AF: Right, that was just before.

JL: That was the lowest point. He had—just a few years prior to that—been in Las Vegas, where they said he would absolutely *die,* but they put him in the Desert Inn and *you couldn't get a seat!*

So, Noël Coward is Noël Coward.

There is *nobody* like him. His *wit* bordered on people who are very witty and are brought up in a middle class environment, *and* a theatre environment. Their humor turns to *wit.*

In other words, at first, they're funny as kids, right, and then as they get older and more *literate,* that turns into *witticisms.* So, I was able to recognize that the *basis of all the witticisms had a cutting edge,* which was not hard for me to understand.

The first meeting with him was a bit scary.

His enthusiasm and joy, as I say, was like a twelve-year-old kid with his new show called *"Sail Away" I suggested everything,* in those days. If you asked me to choreograph the cops on the corner, I'd say *'yes,'* because I wasn't stopping for anything. I had no reason to. What turned out, what actually happened was typical.

Noël Coward didn't hang around New York. I was going to be in London with *"Sound of Music"* as is stated in his book, and my wife [Evelyn Russell] was with me, and we made a trip to [Coward's chalet in] Les Avants in Switzerland. And so, the first week of pre-production, or first ten days or two weeks, was in his chalet. And when you're in the cloistered environs of creativity you find out about the person much, much faster.

What developed, because my wife was an incredible wit, and very, very well read, and knew *every* word, practically, from *every* book that he had ever written, or any play—THEY hit it off, because their humor was *so* similar. I stood in the background a lot, because *I still was panicked with him.* She not. And *they* became fast friends. Within *twenty minutes* he offered her a job right away!

She was an actress in many Broadway shows. But there was a small role, and he said, "This may be *too small* for you. *Will* you do it?"

She said, "Of course!"

And that was the end of that.

So, *she* was cast, and *I* was choreographer!

And, instead of being there for a week, we managed to be there about *three* weeks. In which time, *he wrote songs* while I was there. I developed numbers with him. We became incredibly good 'chums'—he would say. We became fast, fast friends. And, the respect for him only grew and grew, because the knowledge—I mean, I found out about his whole life, and the fact that he was very similar to me.

From five, six years old, he had the stage mother, and he learned how to dance, and learned how to sing, and did *everything*, and *worked* and *worked* and *worked!* Right away, when you start to identify whether he'd come from middle class or lower middle class in London—and I came from Brooklyn—it's the *same* person. Not his *talent,* mind you, but we come from—'cut from the same cloth,' as they say.

AF: I know he said at one point that he was certainly glad he *hadn't* been in the genteel set and gone to college and so on.

JL: He would never have been able to deal with it. He wrote from the outside looking in, also spending the time *within*. Accepting or not accepting—the wonderful thing—he was a *voyeur* in his writing, which I think is what he made fun of; his *own*—*all the classes*—he was able to look at from the outside. I think that is why his lyrics are so incredible. That's why, I think, he is one of a kind.

I don't think there will ever be, or should be, or no one will even want to be, another Noël Coward.

AF: You say he was working, writing some of the songs there?

JL: Right there. Singing them all, and playing them all.

AF: You got a chance to watch him actually do that, at work?

JL: All the time.

AF: How did he work?

JL: Well, he sat in bed, first. He never got out of bed in the morning, so that you would have the meeting upstairs, before. He only got up for lunch.

So he would get up very early.
Ready.
When you went into his suite of rooms up on top, (he lived right up on top of the chalet), there must have been five to six *hundred* books! ALL, either *being* read, or having *been* read, or *going to be* read within the month. They were all over the bed and the tables. He went to sleep reading and woke up reading. And then he had to go to work. And he'd write in this *minuscule* handwriting, which bespoke him, because he wrote like he looked and behaved, but it's, sometimes, very hard to read.

He'd write the lyric, and then hand the lyric, or read it to me, like a piece of poetry, which would be quite hysterical. It was none of my business. I was only the choreographer, but since he was directing, and writing a lot of the staging—and the big stuff he was just throwing all over to me. The small scenes, and the two people, and three people situations were his, but he was *thrilled* that I loved to stage, and didn't mind *mobs* of people. So, he would give me all the problems at hand.

The next thing I knew, he'd have the piano going and then he'd sing a verse or something that he was in the middle of. He loved to pull from his trunk, too. You know what I mean? He wrote so many songs, that he never used, he would keep pulling—

"How about *this?* How about *that?"*

And I'd say, "Well, I don't know, but, uh . . ."

He'd manage to squeeze in one or two of the old songs.

AF: The song, *"Long Live The King"* in *"The Girl Who Came To Supper"* had to be cut after the assassination of John Kennedy.

JL: Which was the opening number!

AF: He took something from way back, from *"Operette"* and re-fashioned that into a new song, *"My Family Tree"*—it came from something about the *Countess Mitzi*.

JL: I wasn't around. You see, what had happened with that one is—in Philadelphia, I got hepatitis, infectious hepatitis, and was rushed off to the hospital two weeks before it, *"The Girl Who Came To Supper"* was to go into New York.

AF: So, he had to take over directing.

JL: So, he took over. It was already finished, but it wasn't polished.
    Then, in Philadelphia, in the middle of previews, Kennedy was shot. And the opening number being *"Long Live The King"* was not quite apropos, and so, needless to say, the tone of the world was not ready for a show like that. Yet, I think it had some of the most wonderful score, and the design and the look! The show was quite wonderful. Florence Henderson was bananas. She was sensational.

AF: She was absolutely fantastic. Just hearing that original cast recording!

JL: Yes, if it was a better time and better place—in a strange way, if it *had* opened now, because we're all into spectacle—now, theatre is not small and kitchen anymore. Now we're back to *"Cats"* and *"Les Miserables"* and *"Phantom of the Opera"*—I mean, get your money's worth, it's called. If that was done now, it would have been, I think, a great success. Anyway, it had great moments to it.

AF: But, I got off track from *"Sail Away"*.

JL: So, he was writing there, and we were looking at costumes, and every time we were about to leave he'd say, *"No, stay, because Helene Pons"*—[Costume Designer for *"Sail Away"*] had arrived, and then *Oliver Smith* [Set Designer] arrived. But, instead of us leaving, he kept on having another excuse to send for the people there. So before we knew it, we were there almost a *month* getting the show ready, and at the same time *learning about him,* traveling all over Switzerland, going gambling across the water to Italy and to France. It was just unbelievable. *And talk about trial by fire!* By the time I went to rehearsal, I was shot out of a cannon. I just couldn't wait to get it on its feet.

AF: I think that show has certainly got some of his wittiest songs in it. It wasn't a complete failure, but it wasn't the big success that he had hoped for.

JL: Well, see, again, the *time*. The *time,* the *place*. Strange.
  "Sail Away" was what Noël Coward IS.
  It was light, very, very witty, and we weren't in the time for all of that. It was not meant to be. We were quite basic and the youth was entering into the picture. Noël Coward was 'old hat' in those days. It felt like he was something from the thirties that was still writing in the sixties.
  They didn't listen hard enough.
  I mean, Walter Kerr said, "There's no one in this world who writes a lyric like Noël Coward."
  But, it's a fascinating thing about *"Sail Away"* it *didn't* work on tour. You know that story? We were in terrible trouble. We had a leading lady *and* Elaine Stritch! Elaine Stritch, in those days, would have been called a *soubrette*. In other words, she was a comedienne, and carried the weight of the show, but we still had the *leading* lady and the *leading* man to sing all the gorgeous love songs, which is left over from the operetta, and left over from the Noël Coward world. It just was *not* happening.
  Then, nobody knew what to do.
  I got an idea, which was the first time—he taught me so much—the first time that there were *no rules*. Nothing HAD to be because it *was*.

All of a sudden, I just got the guts to say, "Get rid of her."

Not meaning the star, or the girl, Jean Fenn, who sang beautifully, was gorgeous to look at, perfect for the role, except the *role* wasn't perfect for the *show*. It didn't exist. It should never have been there. Since Stritch was *'landing'* just walking on stage, she *destroyed* the audience.

I said, "There's nothing quite like a funny lady to talk about, you know, a funny woman falling in love, or vice versa, with a younger man and having an affair."

Whether it went on to something, or not, was not important. The structure, by lifting her out, fell into place. One or two ballads bit the dust, but he wrote another one.

It was a Saturday, and he called Stritch down, and he asked her, what would she think if she *took over the whole show?*

And she was stunned.

The next morning, he tried it, and wrote it, and called me three hours after he started, and says, *"It works perfectly. There's not a problem at all."*

He called Jean Fenn and her manager, husband, and such, and said, *"Listen, my dear, what can I tell you?"*

And she said, "Oh, thank god!" because she was fighting a losing battle. It was upstream all the way. Very charming lady, I'll never forget . . .

We were dark on the Sunday and Monday, for some reason, I don't remember why, but Sunday and Monday—we rehearsed all day Monday, all day Tuesday—Jean Fenn was not in the show Tuesday night.

We opened without that role, and Stritch doing it, and the change in the show was death defying. It wasn't even the same show, and Jean Fenn, god bless her, was out in the audience cheering and applauding more than anyone!

He always gave me credit for it. I didn't know what I was saying, but *he* knew what I was saying. I just said, "Get rid of it." He had to do all the work.

Then it was staging *Stritch,* and putting her in other numbers, and writing a love scene, and giving her another song, and everybody who did it worked overtime, and it was unbelievable what happened.

That was the first time that I realized that I *could* take a step! One more step forward. I wasn't just a choreographer—or I still was, but again, ambition reared its ugly head, because I saw something that he gave me confidence to do.

And, oh the other thing, he—one of the great things he taught me was *simplicity.* That was during *"The Girl Who Came To Supper"* I directed and choreographed that one, and I still had a tendency to show myself off on the stage. Let me see if I can make that clearer.

What you do is you carry around with you a sign of who you are by a certain style, a certain way. I was still young enough, and it was still early enough in my career that I always made sure that I was *up there.* Subconsciously, unconsciously—but I had to put my *stamp* on it.

There was a beautiful, wonderful, poignant song called *"How Do You Do, Middle Age?"* that Jose Ferrer sang. The lyrics said it all. You could sit in a chair. You could stand still. You do everything BUT move. But not me! Oh, no! He had a *foil,* you know, a *fencing* foil, in his room, and he picked it up, and I started *doing tricks* with the foil. So, it was almost like instead of a cane, he was doing Fred Astaire with a foil. It got so overbearing! I thought it was *wonderful,* because I was labeling it with a Joe Layton handle, right?

Noël came backstage, after the first performance—it was one of the songs that was put in.

Noël said, *"WHAT are you doing to my numbers!!?"*

It was the first time I ever heard—in the middle of the stage—he SCREAMED at me!

He said, "You *are a FOOL! You are a stupid little boy! Take that bloody thing off the stage and let the man stand still! I'VE done all the work! You don't have to do anything! SIMPLICITY! Simplicity. Less is best! Less is best! You got it? Do you understand?"*

And then he stormed off stage.

I was so hurt and upset, until I realized what I had done is not learned enough what he was trying to tell me before. Follow? I was still holding on to garbage. Oh, that's the other word he used all the time with me—

"That's just garbage."

AF: That's in the song you do, too. [Editor: They recorded a special duet version of *"The Bronxville Darby and Joan"* as a present for the cast.]

JL: What? Garbage! Well, here it is! Look at that!
    [Picks up an engraved cigarette box]
    It says, *For Joe, With Love, Noël.* "Sail Away" October and on it, it says, *El Greco* which is what he used to call me.
    'Chinese cooking'—which we went in Boston— 'the Latin Quarter'—we went to see Eleanor Powell. You see, *"garbage"*—here's another *"garbage!"* So, I have this from *"Sail Away"*.
It's all tarnished now. It's a shame. But isn't that funny? He was always so wonderful with memorabilia and things. You know, when you're young, you don't think it's worth anything. Then, twenty-five, thirty years later, my god, it's just to *cherish,* because it brings back memories. It doesn't bring anything else, but *"garbage"* he used to say, *"garbage."*

AF: Later on, he talks about being unhappy with *"The Girl Who Came To Supper"* and you had 'over-directed' it. I guess that's what he's referring to.

JL: Absolutely. Oh, yes. That's what I mean. I don't even remember that. I was trying to, not impress, trying to make it the *best* I possibly could. There were so many wonderful things in it, but I wanted everything to be, you know . . . and I didn't rely on *simplicity.* So, I certainly did *learn* that from him. And now, I'm the first person to tell everybody, *"Don't do anything."* But, when you're young you don't do it that way.

AF: 'Don't just do something, *stand there.*'

JL: And I've become a great follower of that belief, because if the talent is there, and you see the person being talented, you don't have to overstate it. The only time you have to *camouflage* is if they're *lousy. That's* when you put yourself to work. So people don't get a bead on you, you know, like in a shooting gallery. *You keep moving so they can't shoot you down.*

AF: I know he and Stritch had their comings and goings.

JL: He adored her.

AF: Frustrated, but also loved her at the same time.

JL: Loved her *and* her talent. *Stritchie,* he called her. He knew how to write for her. See, there is a case again where he identified with the person, or appreciated them, he knew just what to do. He loved Florence Henderson, too. *"The Coconut Girl"* and all of that song, which is, as I said to him, that she could do something like that, and he realized after he'd worked with her awhile, that she was incredible, a great study, could do anything you wanted her to do. Very few people knew that—her talents, and how talented she really is.

AF: I can still hear her singing *"Here and Now"* that wonderful song.

JL: Gorgeous voice! And the *"Coconut Girl"* she had to learn, I'd say, seven pages. It's like a seven page number! But he sat down and wrote it *for her,* so nothing that came out of her mouth was strange to her. He did that with Stritch. I mean, *"Why Do The Wrong People Travel?"* is something Stritch *would* say from *"Sail Away"* and *"Useless Useful Phrases"*.

AF: You worked on that in London, too, didn't you?

JL: Yes, because then he didn't direct it, so, by then, I had turned director. Well, the interesting thing is because I loved him so much I had done *"Sail Away"* and then I had done *"No Strings"* for Richard Rodgers. As I say, my career was not bad with all the people I had worked for, and it opened with great success, and then the Tony nominations, and the rehearsals for *"Sail Away"* were to start, and it was the first time I was ever nominated for *both* director and choreographer!

He wanted to change his rehearsal in London so I could stay and get my award, and I said, "First of all, I don't think I'm going to win it, number one. And number two; I wouldn't do that to you."

So, I came to England and started rehearsal and found out *I had won!* In the middle of a rehearsal! That wasn't the point. The point is he was so taken by the fact that *"Sail Away"* was most important. And it was. I mean, *"No Strings"* was done. That was it. And I *came,* and I kept a *schedule,* and he never got over that. That somebody would really *do* that.

I guess he was stepped on an awful lot at times.

People, you know, a lot of phony baloney going on in that world. Well, you know, England, the superficiality was part of the culture, and he didn't know how to deal with that.

AF: Did you have any difficulty in that?

JL: No. I loved working with English people. I loved working there.

AF: Of course, you had some of the same principals in *"Sail Away"*.

JL: Yes, we had Grover Dale, who is a wonderful dancer, who came along with me for almost every show I did, because he danced my stuff better than anyone. And also, Noël loved him, and gave him a full-fledged role. I think that was it, wasn't it? I think Stritch and Grover were the only two originals. The rest were an English cast, but they were terrific to work with.

AF: It ran longer in London than in the U.S.

JL: Oh, yes. It was a great success. It ran over two years in the Savoy Theatre. Oh, of course, they would identify with it, and it was the first really *big* hit he had in quite a few years. *They fell in love with Stritch.* She never came back to America. You know that? Stritch became a star there and then proceeded to stay. Come back a little bit, then went back and became a great success on television.

JOE LAYTON

AF: What songs from *"Sail Away"* do you especially remember? Any songs you had difficulty in staging?

JL: Yes. Noël had a habit sometimes of writing songs that were a bit dated. Since I was young and very much a contemporary of the times, I had terrible trouble with *"When You Want Me"*. It was sort of a Latin type feel, but it wasn't really—it was a *Noël Coward* type Latin. That was a little bit difficult.

There was a number—I can't even remember the name of it—it was done supposedly at the Greek ruins, and it was a pas de deux between Grover and the young girl. I adored that. It was the first time I'd ever choreographed sort of a balletic—you know, taking the liberty of doing a balletic kind of number for a show, even though that's where my training was, I was sort of afraid to. I adored that.

As far as the comedy, it was the first time I realized that I *could* stage comedy with him, *his* stuff. *Loved* working with Stritch. Loved everything about Noël Coward. Everything.

When I was going to do the television special of *"Androcles and the Lion"* which Richard Rodgers wrote, the first television musicalizing of *"Androcles"*, it was Noël in the role of the Emperor. By then, Noël was already not too well. His thinking capacity, his memorization, was a little weak, because he was having hardening of the arteries and such. He came over and played the Emperor. Wonderfully funny! *Richard Rodgers' writing for Noël Coward! That* was quite a wonderful treat!

Noël always stayed in my life somehow.

But to direct him! And he was such a dear to direct. I mean, he just—You know you work in one capacity, first as a subordinate, and then, all of a sudden, a *peer*. Now, *he's* the actor and *I'm* the director. It was a great thrill. Probably the biggest thrill of my life, and to pay back as the only way I did know how, was when he was finally *knighted*. It was in later years. I was, you know, zooming along. There was no problem with my career anymore. I knew who I was, and was doing all right. I was in London doing a thing called *"Carol Channing and Her Ten Stout-Hearted Men"* Carol had never been in London, and at the Drury Lane. I fashioned this sort of revue.

AF: It's a huge place, isn't it? Drury Lane.

JL: Yes, and crazy, isn't it? A great major success.

But, I've always wanted to do a *ballet* for a ballet company. In America it was very hard, because I was known as a *Broadway Joe,* and for me to go to the ballet *after,* as opposed to *come* from the ballet—like Jerome Robbins, and those people, and Herbert Ross—I was now wanting to do a ballet, but I was already labeled as a Broadway type.

In London, *not*.

So, I sent Kenneth MacMillan, who is the Artistic Director down at the Royal Ballet, to see *"Carol Channing and Her Ten Stout-Hearted Men",* and then asked if I could do a ballet. I had an idea.

They said, "Yes."

And what it was, was Noël had just been knighted, and *I did his thirties music.* A suite of music by Hershey Kay, and he was in the ballet. It was called *"Grand Tour"* which *still* runs in the Royal Ballet, and is in the Louisville Ballet, and the Houston Ballet has it. It's around the world now. It's, well, 1970's, so it's seventeen years old by now.

The *"Grand Tour"* is about the crossing from America. First stop is in England. On *board* the ship, the *back* of the ship. And *all the people* that Noël had known were the characters in the ballet. It was a pastiche: Noël was in it, and Gertrude Lawrence, Theda Bara, Gertrude Stein and Alice B. Toklas, George Bernard Shaw, and a little old lady, which I had stolen from Somerset Maugham—one of his short stories. The little lady who goes on a ship and no one will talk to her because she's so *gauche*. Then she saves somebody's respectability by finding diamonds or something like that. Anyway, I put a little old lady sitting in the corner, who everybody sort of poo—poos. The Royal Ballet bought the concept, and I proceeded to go ahead and do the ballet, and dedicated it to him for his knighthood.

He came opening night.

It turned out to be the Queen Mother's *favorite* ballet and a great success. It ran season after season.

To see the opening night with him there, and tears in his eyes, and to have the ballet a success, took care of my saying 'thank you' to a genius.

So much of it rubbed off on me, you know. I mean, I get very—[breaks off speaking, overcome momentarily by emotion]

AF: A couple of choreographers have mentioned to me, and it intrigues me, choreographing to his music, but I didn't know that anything had been done.

JL: Yeah, uh huh. [he blows his nose loudly]

AF: Did you see *"London Morning"* the ballet that he did for the Royal Festival Ballet?

JL: The Festival Ballet? No. When I said I wanted to do a ballet, he said, *"Oh, dear, don't bother. They're going to just hate it."*

I said, "No, they're *not* going to hate it. You're not going to write it. I'm going to use all of your music."

And I only took the thirties music, from thirty to thirty-nine. Took all of that music and made the suite of music out of that. Far from a failure, it turned out to be a major success and was recorded on the BBC. Now it's in the works, still there.

AF: I'd love to see it sometime.

JL: Oh, yes. It's quite charming. Quite charming. Doreen Wells . . . a lot of famous stars from the Royal Ballet did it— Wayne Sleep. [Ed: Wayne Philip Colin Sleep OBE is a British dancer, director, choreographer, actor and panelist. He was a Principal Dancer with the Royal Ballet and has appeared as a Guest Artist with several other ballet companies. Born: July 17, 1948] And *it was the first ballet I ever did!* Subsequently, I did three others for them, but that was my treat. I got fulfilled, and it made me feel wonderful.

So, he's very much a part of my creative life, and taught me what friends are. He was a good friend. Also, he maintained an aura and an *audacity* about him that was always right, no matter where he was. He fit in every kind of environment. Nothing bothered him. He had as good a time with my mother as he had in society with Dietrich.

AF: It must have been really frustrating for him in *"Androcles"* to have a problem remembering lines, since that was always one of his rules—as a director, you had to know your lines first day of rehearsal.

JL: I'll tell you what happened. There were about three people: Brian Bedford—and I can't remember the other two actors' names—who took him under their wing—you never knew that they were there just throwing little tidbits in. He was not so bad. It was just the thing that at the drop of a hat he could probably do a three act play without thinking twice, it was just a period at the time his phlebitis was; you know the hardening of the arteries had just attacked him. He was ill all the time [September 1967]. He said 'yes.' And then he said 'no,' because he didn't feel well. But, then, because he promised he'd come and do it. So, it meant him coming to America, and rehearsing and on his feet all the time. You know, it was not the easiest time for him.

AF: Did you visit him in Jamaica as well as in Switzerland?

JL: Oh, yeah. Spent time in Jamaica. I'm just trying to think . . . Noël died, and then it wasn't but a year later, I don't remember what year he died—1974?

AF: '73.

JL: And in '75 my wife died. In 1973 she was ill, already. So, we went. We used to go visit Cole and Graham, very strange all of that, that whole world, how it happens—after that. Then she passed away. When she died, the only place I wanted to go was to retreat. I called Cole and Graham and said "could I come?"
    They were still very close, we were all very close.
    I spent about three weeks up in Les Avants. Then, the next thing I knew, it was year later.

Then, Coley died.
The same day Richard Rodgers died!
It was a very—
I was in London when it happened. I had just arrived. tch, tch, tch—all gone.
But, yes they do, people do die. Unexpectedly is when choice. You know that, don't you? *That the doctors told him.*
I tried walking him all the time. I'd go to Switzerland. Take a walk.

AF: To give up smoking.

JL: That's the one damn thing he'd never give up, because if you're a smoker, like I am, you *smoke.*
But exercise, he *refused.* To walk him down the hill and up would take you like—he walked with me a *little* bit, just to sort of, so I wouldn't keep *saying* something. But, his final days, he sat in bed. Came down for dinner. And that's the worst thing, of course. Have a smoke, and have lunch in bed, and read, and read.
And wrote.
It was like that little group was—it hurts. Noël knew. Noël made a bet with him. All that. *"Take a walk"*—
And did all of that. Took care as he wrote *"The Diaries".*
Whatever, you know . . . and uh . . . that was it.

AF: I must say, I was impressed in seeing all the books in Jamaica—although I guess, they've removed a lot of things to Switzerland just because of the humidity, and so on. Most everything there was other authors. I was just impressed by how much he read. And then you look in his diaries, the list of works referred to—pages long!

JL: He read everyone. He just read everyone. I mean, I've never seen such an avid reader. As he was writing, he was reading. That's literally—There were like three or four books *at* his bedside, *on* his bed, besides, *piled* high on either side of his bed. All thumbed down, or there were bookmarks in some that he was in the process of. And every day he'd discuss some other author. Somebody that he was reading and likes, or in his caustic wit, the ones he didn't like.

But he was always there. His presence was known. As I say, I'm not a good one for anecdotes, and I'm not—*I feel his presence*. I just think everybody should be so lucky. It rubs off, as they say. And it sure rubbed off on me.

AF: It seems to be a lot of his wit in real life, as well as in his plays, is something that sometimes can't be taken out of context.

JL: Nope.

AF: It is part of the context, and that's what makes it so funny.

JL: It's *commentary* wit. But, he has a way with putting it in the third person, and you know exactly what he's talking about.

AF: I had one question that is brought to mind by a couple of recent critical studies of Noël. They have tried to analyze what affect his homosexuality had on the way he wrote, or the fact that he was essentially closeted, but had to put on a mask.

JL: If anybody was *NOT* closeted, it was *him!*

I mean, how could you—closeted in the world that he grew up in, where it wasn't either discussible, or a topic of conversation over dinner, of course.

But, I mean, there were no qualms about—he *never pretended* to be anything else! I mean, his relationship with Graham Payn, in the early years of his life, I mean, many years of his life. And then, after that, we don't know, but that's not the point. The point is, he *never pretended.* There were no engagements to be married, and such. He was known as a homosexual, but he had the *class enough* not to be *blatant* about it, or to be *gauche* about it. And in those days you never spoke about it. I mean, you didn't speak about it twenty years ago. Why would you speak about it fifty years ago?

No. When I say 'no' I mean, what effect did it have on his writing? He *didn't* write about it. He wrote about *people*—that middle society—I mean, he really was a *voyeur*. He looked at certain people who had *superficial* character. He knew how to write of all the *superficiality* there was in that period, that middle class, upper middle class that pretended to be otherwise. Homosexual? I don't know. I mean, you can't go by me, kid.

AF: John Lahr referred to an unpublished play of his, *"Semi-Monde"* which had, I guess, some overtly homosexual characters in it, which sounds like it would be interesting. [Finally published in 1999 by Methuen in *"Noël Coward Collected Plays: Six"*]

JL: I would love to read it.

AF: The fact that that hadn't been published or produced, maybe that's what they're referring to, that he was still perhaps nervous about doing something like that, or writing about it specifically.

JL: Oh, I would think so. I would think so. I think he became—I think in the fifties, you know, after the war, and in the fifties when the *mores* change, right? He was dated. He was considered—I mean, they were into *kitchen drama*, right? The whole culture shock as far as drama and theatre was concerned. The Brandos, and the Tennessee Williamses and in this country, you were into, as he used to call it *kitchen drama,* where there would be the three people living in the sewer.

That was not Noël Coward. He didn't know how to write that. So, therefore, Noël Coward was parked away as the past. He was not happy about it in the fifties and the sixties. He wrote the way he did write.

Now, when you look back on his work, he had something to say for the generation he lived in. He represented his material, his material represented that: The culture and the times. Which every playwright does, right? Isn't it about their culture? In the fifties and sixties nobody gave a damn about the thirties. Or twenties, right? But, you look on the music that he wrote, it's like art deco. I mean, when you do a home in art deco you certainly know it's art deco.

When you hear a Noël Coward play, or hear Noël Coward music and lyrics, you know it's Noël Coward.

AF: What I've been amazed and very pleased about, is to find today the response that I've been getting from the Coward programs I do on the radio, that people just love it.

JL: But now we're in a sophisticated generation again. The young people that are now in the world, they're almost Victorian. They've gone the complete circle—and it's only getting more and more. The new generation doesn't want to know from the drugs. They're fighting all of those things, and they're being educated, supposedly, into the finer things in life, and they're finding Noël Coward. They'll find George Bernard Shaw. You find Oscar Wilde, I mean all of those people have to rear their heads again because of what they've left.

AF: And of course, I was just thinking, too, one of his last plays, *"A Song At Twilight" does* deal with the subject of homosexuality.

JL: No, I don't think he ever parked it away. I think he was a great craftsman enough to know he's not going to write something that's not going to sell. He wasn't writing for himself. He liked to produce. There's no doubt about it.

AF: The impression I get from you, too, about Noël, is what a really generous person he was, a really genuine human being.

JL: Yes. I don't even think it was questioned. You never questioned his generosity. It just existed. I think he lived hand to mouth half the time anyway, because of his generosity. Also, he loved to live well. He felt he earned that. And he did. He traveled first class. He lived first class. And he wanted first class.

He always was generous. There was always, not in money, but generosity of SPIRIT, how's that? His talent, he *gave* to me. He showed me his *talent.* He hid nothing.

He also was one of the great hosts of all time. And at the same time, he's one of the great educators of all time, because he let you know how he got there, and if you could use any of it, be his guest. So, that kind of generosity is hard to come by, huh? I was going to say 'circumspect'—no. I don't think.

*He was classy, in the sense that he didn't stand on the street corner and do any cries of **who** he was, or **what** he was, or what he **believed** in. That was nobody's business, you know?*

But as far as, if you were his friend, there was nothing that he held back. There were no secrets. He didn't have any. He told so many stories. I say I can't remember anecdotes, but I—

Marlene Dietrich was going to open at the Olympia in Paris and she came and saw, I don't know—*"Sail Away"*—and I met her, so on, and she said, "Oh! Since you're in rehearsal with *'Sail Away'* would I "come over and help her a little bit?"

She begged Noël to release me. Of course! *It was Marlene Dietrich!*

I said, "Oh, my god yes!" Everything was 'yes.'

Then, she left, and he said, *"I want you to know this is the first time I've talked to her in ten years!"* Ten years ago, Coley and I snubbed Marlene Dietrich for being a—you fill in the space—right? And we didn't talk to her for ten years. *And today WE realized, SHE never realized we didn't talk to her for ten years!"*

Typical.

She would have correspondence, obviously, but they never picked up a phone, or said 'hello' to each other or anything. And she never realized! She would talk to them and she never realized that they never talked to her. [laughter]

AF: I guess he had, pretty much, written off critics years ago.

JL: Yes. They never liked him. He is the one who told me *never* to read reviews. I used to get so terribly thrown. It was a point early in my career, because they were lauding me, thank god, because that got my career going, but if they didn't say what I wanted them to say—in other words, if they didn't see something up there I wanted them to see, but praised something *else,* or *destroyed* something, I was thrown either way.

Noël said, "Why do you read them? They'll always be that way, because you're controversial in what you do anyway.

Sometimes you're way above their heads. Sometimes you're mediocre. So whatever they say about you you're not going to like it. I stopped reading them when they called me a 'second class writer' when I was in my prime time. I was always 'second class' and so I just treated them as if *they* were 'second class' writers, and let it go at that."

And he *never* read a review—*EVER*.

He only knew at the box office. He'd get terrible reviews, and then it would run three years! So, since that day, I never read reviews, nor do I go to opening nights. *I never go to opening nights,* because I get thrown by them, *so I don't go*—my own opening nights.

AF: What is it about opening nights that throws you?

JL: Well, because the audience is so enthusiastic, and the performance usually is quite all right, and then you get terrible reviews, so you don't understand any of it. It's like you're so *thrown,* so I just stay away from opening nights. I always watch the curtain go up, and the star walk on-stage, and *then I walk out of the stage door and go* away.

I go to North Carolina, where my home is. I get in *a car* and *drive* eleven hours! By then, it's all over. They either call me and say, "Come back, it'll be here awhile," or "Don't bother, that's it."

AF: What really impressed me was the videotape of a kinescope of Noël Coward's show with Mary Martin. It was on CBS in 1955, *"Together With Music",* just the way he used his eyes, and his face, and his hands, and doing his songs.

JL: Ah! He was a master! And, also, a *craftsman.* He believed that you could do *anything* on stage. It was the *craft* that did it. He was not from the school of 'you have to feel it'—but he writes that way, too, because the superficiality is supposed to tell you where the reality is coming from.

We all live—or, I meet you now, today—I don't know you. I know that you are *conversational.* I know you're an ardent fan and *admirer,* an *historian,* very *knowledgeable,* very *nice,* but I don't *know* you.

He was able to write that kind of a person on the stage, and as you watched him, you found out who that person was. Follow? He didn't have to *say*—you didn't have to see the blood and guts. What you saw was the *facade,* and then figured out who was underneath it all. Just by the comments of other people.

Well, that's an art. That's an art of writing, and also, very theatrical.

So, to *play* that, you deal in *craft.* When he used to have to cry, he'd *stare.* He would always make sure he was staged upstage to *stare* in a light until he was blinded, and then when he turned around, he cried. He said he never had to figure out about his mother's death to call upon it. That's calling on the craft.

He said, "all the old world is that way."

And little by little, as you get older, you start to call on things. But he was not trained that way. He was trained on being a stage child star.

AF: I read a story about Noël in a play, and something wasn't working, I'm not sure if he was directing. I think he was just visiting a rehearsal, and he made a suggestion that the actors should count *"one, two, three"* at this point, and then *go from this* point, and from then on it worked perfectly. He couldn't explain *why.* He just *knew* that that's what you should do.

JL: Also, I've learned, now, being a director, mostly, and choreographing, you know shifting my world, that the actor needs **eyes.** *That's* what the director basically **is.**

Going back to his saying to me, *"Don't put yourself up there, you're there already. Put the actor up there and make them better than they are."*

That has stayed with me for all these years, and that's why I'm able to handle so many stars, because I'm able to push them *one step more* than they ever thought they were able to go, or the public thought that they were. And *you ARE* their eyes. If you learn about them, certain people will stand still for two beats, other people will get away with five beats, and as long as you know who this person is, then you're able to get the applause, or get the reaction that you want.

That's what he was in essence saying.

Stand still for three beats, because your *character,* and *you* as the *actor* will be able to handle that, and the audience will be impressed.

Here's a MASTER. He was a master **craftsman**, also, a great gent.

MOIRA LISTER

b. 1923

Interviewed on November 5, 1991

Moira Lister is an actress who has worked extensively over the years in films, television and on stage. She appeared on stage with Noël Coward in *"Present Laughter"* after World War II. The interview was conducted in her London home.

ALAN FARLEY: Tell us about working with Coward in *"Present Laughter"*.

MOIRA LISTER: That was 1949. It was the production at the Haymarket. I had just come over from South Africa at age of eighteen, and I had done a couple of plays in the West End, which both had been failures for one reason or another. It was just After the war and things were very, sort of, dicey then. Anyway, after those two plays that I did, I then went to Stratford-upon-Avon and became the star of the season that year. So, I played *Juliet, Desdemona, Olivia, Kate Hardcastle, Ann Boleyn*—ALL that! all in the one season.

So, we used to rehearse, for example, *"Cleopatra"* in the morning, and do *"Henry the Eighth"* in the afternoon and *"Romeo and Juliet"* at night. So, I mean, we would literally do three Shakespearean plays in a day. So, it was very good grounding.

So, I finished that season. I did that for a year. Then I joined the Kay Hammond and John Clements season, their first managerial venture, and I stayed with them for a year as their juvenile lead.

I was asked to go and do an audition at the Haymarket Theatre in front of Noël Coward, and I heard that it was going to be *"Present Laughter"* to play Joanna, which is a wonderful role. Of course, in those days, one didn't wear the sort of jeans and the rag-bag outfits that we wear today at auditions. Then, it was the little black dress—it was the big hat—it was the white gloves—it was the flower on the dress, and it was really *dressing for the role,* you know? ALL of which I did—ALL BORROWED, because I didn't have any money at that time at all.

So, I went to the Haymarket Theatre. I had been across to Switzerland to have a little holiday, and I'd been skiing and I was rather *brown*. So, I walked onto the stage . . .

Noël said to me, "You look very *brown*. Where have you been?"

So, I said, "Well, I've actually just come back from Switzerland."

He said, "What have you been doing there?"

I said, "I've been learning to ski for the first time."

He said, "All I can say is, I *hope* you didn't get them up your nose."

[they laugh]

So, then we did the audition, and he seemed very pleased, and then he said he would like me to go back to Ebury Street the following day and read for various friends of his that he had. So, I felt I was kind of getting warm.

Then he actually read with me at Ebury Street, and then he said, *"Yes! I would like you to do it!"*

So, of course, I walked down Ebury Street just YELLING my heart out with joy and happiness!! Oh, it was a FANTASTIC break for me! It was the first commercial theatre that I had done in the West End. But the sad thing was for me was that I was very young, you see? I was only twenty-three, and Noël was—I don't know, whatever he was then, fifty or something—and he was already very established.

I was TREMENDOUSLY in AWE of him, because he was so clever and everything he said sounded so witty, and everything *I* said just sounded so BANAL, so I just ended up not saying ANYTHING. I regret, in a way, that I wasn't OLDER when I worked with him for the first time. But then, of course, I got to KNOW him and appreciated him much more.

That play ran for two years!

On the opening night at The Haymarket, Noël sent for me, and I thought, "Oh, God! I've done something terrible now! I'm going to be sacked! Or he's going to tell me how awful I am."

So, I went to his room, absolutely *shaking.*

He said to me, "Now, Moira, I've been very, very pleased with you, and I'd like to make a little present for the opening night."

I said, "Oh, no, please, you don't have to. I mean, it is such an honor to work with you. Please, don't."

"No, no, no," he said, "I absolutely *insist!"* He went up to his dressing table and took a little bottle of perfume—I still have it—and it was HALF full of perfume, and he HANDED it to me with a MAGNANIMOUS gesture and said, "This is for *you!* I have used the *other* half."

[She laughs]

If he had given me DIAMONDS I couldn't have been more flattered!

When we got on the stage for the opening night—it's a very frightening thing when you have to HIT somebody across the face, and I was REQUIRED to do that in the play. So, of course, I was worrying about it, and I sort of—I was worrying about it, and I sort of TENSED UP, and got a bit nervous, you see, and when I came to hit him, I hit him MUCH TOO hard! I gave him a really HEFTY swipe across the jaw.

And I could see his eyes STEEL up, you know, and we went on with the scene, and when the curtain came down, he TURNED on me like a viper and he said, *"If you ever do that to me again"* he said, "I *will hit you straight back in front of the audience!"*

I said, "I'm terribly sorry for it!"

Next night, I came in—I'd been up all night worrying about it . . . frightened all day . . . came to the theatre that night, and we came to the scene again, and, of course, I was MORE frightened and MORE tense, and I hit him even *HARDER* still, the second time!

But this time I didn't take the curtain call. *I RAN!* When the curtain came down, I RAN up to my dressing room!

I was terrified the THIRD day to go into the theatre, in case I found a little note just saying "DON'T COME BACK!" But, bless his heart, there was a little poesy of forget-me-nots on my dressing table, with a little note saying, "You're FORGIVEN! But DON'T DO IT AGAIN!"

He was wonderful to work with.

He was very difficult to work with.

Of course, he used to say, "I'm going to do everything I can to make you *laugh,* but," he said, *"if* you laugh, I shall be *very* angry."

So, he would say things under his breath, you know, like in the famous Albert Hall scene, when we came to do the kiss, you know? Just as he got close to me he'd say, "Breathe *out.* I've had garlic for lunch."

All sorts of little funny things that he used to do. One of the most amusing was when we were on the stage one night. We had this scene together, and the doorbell rings, and his wife, in the play, who was played by Joyce Carey, is supposed to come into the room, right?

So, we'd played our scene.

The doorbell rang.

He went to open the door, and though the stage management had *rung* the bell, they *hadn't checked* that Joyce Carey was THERE at the door!

So, he opened the door and there was NOBODY there! His brain was so fast. He closed the door, turned to me and he said, *"Silly little boys ringing bells and running away."* And then he turned to me and said, *"Now, Joanna,"* he said, *"YOU come from South Africa, don't you?"*

I said, "Yes."

He said, "Very well. *Teach me Zulu."*

[they laugh]

From the time that it took Joyce Carey to get down from the third floor, down to the stage, I was teaching him "ZOOMBA ZOOMBA" and "HUMP-AH-LUPA CHYWAN VA KORZAN FAR—TOOCH-I-MON!"

So, of course, Joyce came in and HE said, *"ZAG-A-VOR-AN-BA-FOOTAH!"*

[she laughs again]

And that *face* was an absolute PICTURE! She didn't know where to put herself or what had been going on!

So, he was full of nonsense like that.

AF: Judy Campbell said that, while of course everything was set, and you worked by the book, yet he improvised to keep people on their toes.

ML: Yes, he did! But it was mostly little sort of asides that kept you on your toes.

Judy's quite interesting. I don't know quite what happened there, because when they tried out the play, Judy played my part, but she didn't come to the Haymarket with it. She didn't come into the West End with it. That was just two or three weeks, it seemed. Then, I played for the whole of the two year run. Noël played it for six months and then he left.

AF: For HIM that's a LONG time.

ML: A LONG time. So, I had various leading men. Hugh Sinclair was one of them. Noël had been away for six months. We didn't even know he was back in the country. Hugh Sinclair was playing his role and it was a matinee, and Hugh had LOST his VOICE. He was struggling, you know—*[hoarse whisper]—trying to do the role with this terribly strained voice.*

Noël happened to be in the theatre! He'd come in and he sat there listening to the First Act, and he couldn't STAND it anymore. He came backstage. He went into Hugh's dressing room. He said, *"Get those clothes off! I'll play the Second Act!"*

Imagine the audience!

Having SEEN Hugh Sinclair playing the FIRST ACT, and Noël Coward playing the SECOND act!? It made NONSENSE of the play, but he just could not sit still.

He said, *"I can't stand you. You're ruining my LINES! You're ruining the PLAY! Get OFF! Give me those clothes!"*

[they laugh]

AF: You also took part in the cabaret that Stanley Hall put together, a tribute to Coward, *"Curtain Up on Coward"*.

ML: Yes, yes.

AF: Where you sang some of his songs.

ML: That's right. I had two boys with me, and we did a lot of his numbers, and then we sort of did the dance routines, and things. It was GREAT FUN, I must say.

AF: Had you been familiar with his songs before that?

ML: I starred in *"Cowardy Custard"*. I also did some of the numbers in cabaret that I had done in *"Cowardy Custard"* again.
   "Cowardy Custard" was a great challenge, I must say. It was beautifully done! Freddie Carpenter directed it and we did it all in black and white. It really was beautifully done. But, I think I had something like *twenty-two* numbers to do. They are very DEMANDING, his numbers. You know, you can't *sit back* on them AT ALL. Like, *"I've Been To A Marvelous Party"* and all those sort of numbers, they take a lot of precision concentration—the *words,* and the getting them across.

AF: The *words* are so important.

ML: TERRIBLY important! And you can't fluff around with them at all.
   Also, the *MUSIC* is not all that easy, either!
   I remember Noël saying to me, "There are very few people who can actually speak my dialogue. Happily, *you* are one of them."
   So, I was very flattered. But it's true, because since doing that, I've done *"Hay Fever"* which I absolutely adored doing. I've played *"Private Lives"* and I've played *"The Marquise"* which I also ADORE! So, I'm really very familiar with playing his work.
   I LOVED directing! I directed *"Present Laughter"* and I got a great kick out of that. I thought I would hate it. I thought I would hate NOT being UP THERE, and doing it MYSELF, but—

AF: What compensated for that?

ML: Well, the compensation was that I felt that I could *give* the other actors an enormous amount. Having played with Noël, having had the sort of ultimate production, *being* in it, and all the casting of that was so superb—and *I could still hear the laughs and the lines the WAY they were DELIVERED in those days.* I was able to impart that, which was a rare thing for a company to have—somebody direct it who had actually worked WITH Noël and being IN the original production! So, I got a huge kick out of that, I really did. Had the most wonderful set!

I helped design the clothes, too, because the clothes that I had were designed by Molyneaux. They were simply beautiful of that period. Just wonderful 1950's clothes. So, we did it in '50's, and I helped to design, because I remembered what my clothes were like [in the original production]. So, I had a very good designer, who designed the clothes very much with that feeling.

AF: I was thinking back—of course, *"Present Laughter"* was written, and then it wasn't produced because of the war, and that's why the opening was delayed until *after* the war.

ML: That's right.

AF: So, it was written much earlier, but wasn't produced till then. It certainly requires a great star in the part.

ML: Oh, absolutely.

AF: At least someone who can play the Coward part.

ML: Yes.

AF: Although, it's not completely autobiographical, there is a large amount of autobiography, I think, in the part.

ML: Yes, there is, yes. And his personality and his sort of marvelous thespian quality comes out in his character. He's dealing with these people—

AF: That young playwright, *Roland Maule*—

ML: *Roland Maule*—

AF: That's an interesting part. I've seen it played, overplayed and played very, very well. How was it played in the original?

ML: Well, the original was played—the WHOLE of the original, funnily enough, was played very much for TRUTH. Noël himself—(and I had quite a lot of trouble with the leading man that I had, to direct), to stop them CARICATURING the character and Noël—Noël played it very strict. He played himself with his *wicked eye* and his wonderful appreciation of comedy, but he wasn't over—the top. He wasn't *playing the great actor* and all that. He was sending himself up, very delicately and very lightly, and it was just wonderful!

    That is the danger is that they all think, "Oh, *Noël Coward*, and we must *camp* it around." *And this is absolutely the WRONG attitude.*

AF: Exactly. That's terrible. I've seen some productions like that, too.

ML: Oh, I'm sure you have. So have I.

AF: Playing *"Fallen Angels"* as slapstick! I mean, it isn't slapstick. If you play it as it's *written*—

ML: *As is written, is superb.* The same thing, you see, applies to *"Hay Fever"*.

AF: Yes.

ML: You can go WAY over the top with that, too. But if you play it absolutely for what it's worth, and the TRUTH of it, and really get through—and the interesting thing, I find—I don't know if you'll agree with me—but *I don't think Noël's work translates to the small screen.* Have you *ever* seen *anything* really satisfying of his work on television? On film it works, but television—I find the small screen does something to EMACIATE it.

AF: The only thing I've found interesting on the small screen—but this is because they were adaptations of *short stories*—were *"Me and the Girls"* I think, and *"Star Quality"* I thought, worked well when they transposed those to television.

ML: I didn't see either of those. Where were those done? In America?

AF: They were done here in England, and then we saw them in America.

ML: They weren't part of the Joan Collins run?

AF: No. This was a couple of years—

ML: She's going to do *"Private Lives"* over there.

AF: Yes, in San Francisco. I've seen her play it over here. People will say she's too old, but *Amanda* and *Elyot* don't have to be thirty, or thirty-five, just because Noël and Gertie played them at that age.

ML: *Yes,* it's not a question of *age*. It's a question of—

AF: Style.

ML:—she has her *own* wonderful, inimitable style, which is the rich, slightly brassy thing, but that goes AGAINST that character altogether. They were very, frightfully English, wonderfully etched characters. You can't hit them on the head with a hammer. Both Noël and Gertie, and particularly Gertie, had that wonderful light, delicate touch.

AF: *Evanescence.*

ML: *Flip. Evanescence.* Funnily enough, the little girl who plays—

AF: Sara Crowe. Oh, she stole the show!

ML: Perfect! And the first time ever. Because *Sybil* is the *most boring* part in the world. But she just hit that right quality, which that part requires, you see. You can't play her DULL, because then, she becomes dull. I must say all credit to Joan that she let her stay!
    [*with laughter bubbling up as she speaks*]
    I'd have asked her to LEAVE on the FIRST NIGHT, *frankly!!* If that had been the competition and I couldn't stand up to it!! *Ah, ha, ha ha!*

AF: How did you play *Amanda?*

ML: Well, I just played her the way, hopefully, the way Noël wrote it—with, I hope—a wonderful kind of *delicacy,* but *also* the sense of humor, and the wonderful *badinage* between the two of them. The tremendous understanding they had of each other, because they were so similar, they kind of SPARKED each other off. The wonderful starting of the quarrels, sort of *delicately,* and *then* they get out of control until they *GO!*
    It's an amazing exercise in CONTROL, actually, so that you don't go over the top. Just play it as a wonderful comedic role, but with tremendous reality.

AF: It's a play that, I think, is ageless.
    People were saying, when his plays were first done, "Oh, well, it's ephemeral. It won't last." But there are *perennial* truths in that play.

ML: Yes. I certainly think *"Present Laughter"* is ageless. I think *"Present Laughter"* is one of his BEST plays, because it's a very WHOLE play. Having done it again, I think it still has an enormous amount to offer, PROVIDING you get the right man, and, obviously, it's not too easy to do that anymore.

AF: In fact, I have seen a production of *"Design For Living"* which was a disaster, because everything was underlined and overdone. *Over-the-top* is the word for that.

ML: When Maggie Smith did *"Private Lives"* here, she was WAY over-the-top, and they tore her to shreds. Now, she's going to do *"Hay Fever"* I hear.

AF: *"Hay Fever"* got a rave review from Frank Rich of the *New York Times,* which, in *itself,* is an accomplishment. And Roger Peters, whom I met last year when I was here, worked and worked at Graham to finally get the rights to film *"Hay Fever"*. Got the rights. Had Maggie Smith lined up and Lindsay Anderson to direct the film and hasn't been able to raise the money!

ML: You're KIDDING! REALLY?! That is AMAZING! I did *"Hay Fever* all over the Far East, and Hong Kong, with Derek Nimmo. You know, he does these Far East tours. I ADORED playing that part! It was such FUN!

AF: [recalling a line from *"Hay Fever"*:]
  "It's so bad for your skin to leave things about on it."

ML: Yes! [laughs]

AF: It's one of my favorite lines. [laughs]

ML: One thing that AMAZED me—I mean, I got a HUGE laugh when I did the *'Wellington boots'* business—and Penelope Keith [in a West End production] CUT that business altogether! It was gone!
  I thought, *"You're raving mad, girl! That's one of the best laughs in the play!"*—when she makes the boy put the boots on for her, you know, the lover! She CUT it! I couldn't believe it! Not easy to play Coward, you know, it really isn't easy.

AF: One of the most interesting castings I saw was in a production of *"Hay Fever"* at the *Shaw Festival* in Canada, and they cast a black actor as *Sandy Tyrell.*

ML: Oh, oh.

AF: Yes.

ML: Oh! Ah. ha, ha ha! That puts a whole new light on it! Goodness me!

AF: It worked very well!

ML: Really?! Fascinating!

AF: Yes, as it turned out, because they said, well, at the last minute they *had* to make a change. I don't know whose idea it was.

ML: *"Look Who's Coming To Dinner"*—by Noël Coward! Ha, ha, ha ha ha!

AF: They only had to change one or two words. Very little they had to change.

ML: Fascinating.

AF: Yes. They said the only objections they had were from some AMERICANS in the audience.

ML: [laughs] Ahh, how lovely. So, do they do much Coward in San Francisco?

AF: Not as much as I'd like. The American Conservatory Theatre, which is now celebrating its 25th year, used to do more. They've done *"Tonight at 8:30"*. They've done *"Private Lives"* a couple of times. They've done *"Hay Fever"* In the last five years or six years they have done ZERO Coward. And it's been run by a man who proclaims himself to be a Coward aficionado. In fact, the year

After he took over, they had announced *"Present Laughter"* and then they cancelled it, and substituted a play which had a smaller cast, because they were in financial problems. And they haven't done Coward since.

ML: Good lord. Well, tell them I'll come and direct *"Present Laughter"* for them.

AF: I'd love to see it. I don't know how long it's been since it's been done in San Francisco. Maybe it was when Noël Coward was there, because I think he alternated it with *"Nude With Violin".*

ML: *"Present Laughter"* did he? I was supposed to go to Broadway with the last plays he did, you know, that Lily Palmer did?

AF: The *"Suite In Three Keys"*?

ML: Yes. I was supposed to play the Lily Palmer part, because she didn't want to go to New York, and then, of course, Noël got ill. It's never actually been done on Broadway—has it?—to my knowledge.

AF: I saw two of those three plays done by Hume Cronyn and Jessica Tandy. They did two of them. *"Noël Coward in Two Keys"* it was called. I think they did *"Come Into The Garden Maude"* and *"A Song At Twilight"* because it was the full-length one.

ML: That's a GOOD play! Noël wasn't right in it, and he wasn't well, either. With a very good, sort of, all around strong actor playing that part, it could work terribly well, that play. You need a very full-blooded kind of man, and Noël was a little too light for it, but also, he was ill at the time, and didn't do it justice.

AF: Do you have any particular favorites of his songs?

ML: Well, I love the numbers that I did. I love *"A Talent To Amuse"* [*"If Love Were All"*] I think that is a lovely number, I adore it. It always makes me cry when I sing it. I love, of course, the 'point' numbers, *"Mrs. Worthington"*—*"I've Been To A Marvelous Party"*—*"A Bar On The Piccola Marina"*—and all those lovely numbers are great fun. And all the wonderful Cockney ones are fun, too. I LOVE doing *"Three Juvenile Delinquents"*. That was one of my favorites.

AF: I love that, too. Just recently I saw it referred to as sort of a precursor of *"Officer Krupke"* from *"West Side Story"* I hadn't thought about that connection, but it is sort of the same kind of thing—very impertinent juvenile delinquents.

ML: And, of course, *"Let's Do It"* is lovely, because we were able to—one is ALLOWED to put in the topical jokes. So, we were allowed to do *"Princess Anne on her horse—DOES IT!"* [they laugh]

AF: Have you done Coward in South Africa?

ML: I did *"Hay Fever"* on television there. I wasn't happy with it. *I just don't think Coward works well on television.* I did it to try and see what COULD be made to work, but it just—I don't know what it is. It's the medium that you can't see everybody together—or—the interplay gets lost. I don't know what it is, but it just simply falls flat. It just doesn't seem to have the spark on television. Whether the camera gets in too close, whether it needs this sort of ebullience that it has on a stage. I just can't put my finger on it, but I just haven't seen ONE Coward television that I really thought worked.

It would be interesting, as you say, if they are going to do *"Hay Fever"* on film, on *proper* film.

AF: *"Brief Encounter"* certainly works as a film.

ML: Yes, but that was WRITTEN as a film, wasn't it? That's different when it's written as a film The others were written for stage.

AF: Without Coward to do the adaptation—

ML: Well, there you go, or the direction, there you see. I must tell you one lovely Christmas story, as we're getting near Christmas.

At Christmas time when I get amusing cards, I always put the special ones up on the mantelpiece there, and, as you know, Noël Coward, every year, used to send to his chums a sort of nonsense card, with himself in various different moods, and costumes and so on.

One Christmas it was the wonderful eagle wings that we had in *"Cowardy Custard"* The other one was himself, superimposed, sitting on his own lap! Silly, fun cards.

Well, this particular year, (and I'm talking a long time ago, now, because the children were small,) he sent a card of himself as a little boy of fourteen! A *genuine* picture of himself, with a little white collar—and, as you know, in the profession we call him *'The Master'* and in England a little boy is called *'master* until he reaches majority—so, he had the picture on the front of the card.

And then, you open the card, and all it said was—

"Happy Christmas
Master Noël Coward"

—which was very sweet, so we all laughed.

So, I put it on my mantelpiece, and I was having a children's party.

Those were the days when we had rather *grand* nannies. This room was *filled with children,* and two or three rather *grand* nannies, with their little wards.

I saw this particular nanny going up to the mantelpiece to look at who the cards had come from, to see if *she* was in the *right kind* of house, or, whether she'd *demeaned* herself for the afternoon, to come to my house.

So, I thought I'd go and chat her up a bit. I took Noël Coward's card, with *himself* as the boy of fourteen on the cover, and I said, *"There* you are, Nanny. *There's* somebody you *know."*

She looked at the little boy's face, and she said, "Yes, the face is *very* familiar. Could it be Lord Perth's son?"

I said, "No, Nanny. Try again."

She said, "Well, I *do know* the face. Could it be Lord Abercrombie's son?"

I said, "No." I knew she wasn't going to get it. So, I said, "No, Nanny. YOU open it, and see who it's from."

She opened it and read, *"Happy Christmas, Master Noël Coward."* She said, "Well, I *thought* I knew the face, *but*, all I can say is, I hope he grows up to be as clever as his *FATHER.*"

[laughter]

I told that to Noël and he absolutely fell off his chair! He repeated it to EVERYBODY from then on.

The other lovely one, was on the first night of *"Sail Away"*.

I went with Noël. He very sweetly asked me to go and watch. I was sitting in the box with him, and Judy Garland, was in the box with me, too. It was a wonderful night! Princess Margaret was sitting in the stalls. It was the time when darling Elaine Stritch was still a little bit on the bottle, you see?

So, Noël said to her, "On pain of death, *don't* you have one *sniff* of gin, or whatever you're on, before the performance!" He said, "This is your BIG night, now don't you DARE ruin it!" She said, "NO, no no! Of course not!"

And she was wonderful! It was a wonderful first night, and she didn't miss a trick. She was simply wonderful!

But what he *FORGOT* to say was, "As *soon as the curtain comes down, don't hit the bottle then, either, because you want to meet Princess Margaret—right."*

Curtain came down.

Stritch went *straight* to her dressing room, and I think, half a bottle of gin went down in one gulp.

So, we were all waiting in the royal anteroom for her to come through with Princess Margaret and Judy Garland and everything. As you know, Princess Margaret is a little bit, sort of, *snooty* sometimes. So, we waited and we *waited*, and we WAITED, and I think she was sort of finishing the *other* half of the gin bottle before she arrived.

Anyway, the doors *flew open,* and Stritch, who's all of *six-foot-two*—Princess Margaret is all of *five-foot-one*—came into the room and saw Princess Margaret standing there—

Stritch opened her arms WIDE and said, "GOD, I'VE BEEN WANTING TO MEET YOU FOR YEARS!"

Went *up* to Princess Margaret, *took her* in her arms! *Clasped* her to her bosom!

She looked *down* at this tiny, little head that she was clasping to her bosom, and she said to her, "JESUS, YOU'RE SMALL!"

[laughter]

Princess Margaret's face is an *absolute picture,* because she has an absolute *phobia* about being small, and she married a small man, and she's *so* grateful her son *isn't* small—and all that! . . . so . . . it was *wonderful,* you see?

AF: What Coward plays would you like to do that you *haven't* had a chance to do?

ML: Oh, gosh! I wonder now. I'd *love* to do *"Hay Fever"* again. I adored doing that. I'd love to do it in the West End, actually.

AF: Well, I'll come back to see you.

ML: I would really adore to do that. I really felt I was able to bring something to that. What are the other ones? I don't know what other ones there are that I would be right for, now, because he didn't write too many for the 'older lady,' should I say? As you say, any of them can be played by any age, really.

AF: Which would you like to direct?

ML: Oh, I would love to direct *any* of them. *"Happy Breed"* or *"Private Lives"* or any of them. I would absolutely adore to direct.

PETER MATZ

b. 1928   d. 2002

Interviewed on May 23, 1986

Peter Matz was a composer, arranger and musical director for films, Broadway and television. Marlene Dietrich recommended him to Noël Coward to be his musical accompanist, when he was just twenty-six years old, and was beginning to make a name. He accompanied Coward in Las Vegas in 1955, and was the Musical Director for *"Sail Away"* in New York. For eleven years, he was the Musical Director for the weekly television comedy/variety classic, *"The Carol Burnett Show"* and was one of the most prolific and sought-after composers of film and television scores. This interview was recorded in his Beverly Hills office.

ALAN FARLEY: This is from Cole Lesley's book:
"The last big difficulty to be overcome was that no American work permit could be obtained for Norman Hackforth. Where on earth would Noël find another accompanist as sympathetic? He interviewed eight people, none of whom were good enough, and then one evening the telephone rang. This time his savior was Marlene, who had been loyally working away on his behalf. She was calling from the airport and her plane for London was already boarding; had he got a pencil ready, quick, Pete Matz, this is his number, ring him at once and grab him.

Pete came round the next day. He seemed absurdly young, only twenty-six, dark and intelligent, with a great sense of dehydrated humour, and Noël knew in his bones that he was exactly what was needed.

When Noël showed him the old arrangements he had been using at the Cafe, Pete said, not contemptuously but matter-of-factly, 'You're not going to use these are you?'

Noël lied quickly, 'Of course not, but who could make new ones in the time?'

Quite calmly Pete said, 'I will.'

Noël had no way as yet of knowing how brilliant a musician Pete was. Later we discovered from experience that for instance there was no need for labored conversation at the breakfast table; instead of Agatha Christie, Pete read silently from a Mozart score propped against the toast-rack. Pete flew out to Hollywood a few days later and I flew from Jamaica to join Noël in Clifton Webb's house in North Rexford Drive.

Pete had made brilliant new orchestrations for Noël; often musically witty, always highly imaginative in their own right, yet they never obtruded on Noël's singing. They sound as fresh today on the record *"Noël Coward at Las Vegas"* as they did then, and so does Noël. He had never been in better vocal form thanks to Alfred Dixon, [vocal coach] and his own strength of purpose, and the record is the best, the most truly representative, he ever made."

PETER MATZ: That's very, very flattering.

He called me and said, "Would you like to go to Las Vegas?"

And I said, "Sure!"—not having any idea what it was about. I had done some work for Marlene just before the famous *transparent dress* at the Sahara Hotel. I'd worked on that nightclub act. I guess that was why I was fresh in her mind.

AF: How did you get to that point at twenty-six, working in Las Vegas? What were your roots in show business?

PM: Oh, boy, such a crazy prelude to that.

My education was basically at UCLA. I went to the *engineering* school. I was going to be an engineer! Music was a *sideline*. I played in a band. A high school band. Then, by the time I got to college I was playing in dance bands. Finished engineering and said, "That's not it."

I went to Europe and got into music seriously, and realized that there was a music industry, which I never really had thought about before. So, I started in the very early fifties when I was living in Europe, accompanying singers and playing with jazz bands, and I had a good feel for that. I came back here just to get into the music business and to continue studying. I decided that I really wanted to study music seriously. Since my folks were living here, this was the place to do it. So, I came to L.A.

An enormous break came my way—Kay Thompson and the Williams Brothers.

That act was on the road, and their accompanist got sick, and I was on a list of guys to call, and that happened, in Las Vegas, strangely enough. She was one of a long list of great teachers that I happened to have the chance to "earn while you learn"—to work for. She knows and knew more music than any three people we'll ever meet. And *in addition* to giving me this job, she became a teacher. So, I learned a tremendous amount from her.

While I was with her, I became aware of what the musical theatre was. Somehow, that light hadn't gone on yet.

I said, "I *must* go to *New York.* Must get to New York and get in the theatre."

So, when the act with the Williams Brothers folded, she then went out as a single, and took me with her to New York, and I *stayed.* Just started working around as a rehearsal pianist for choreographers and people like that. People who put acts together, and working as a rehearsal pianist on Broadway shows. One door opened to another. I worked on—the real line was—from Kay Thompson, to the choreographer, Herb Ross, to—

"*House of Flowers*", the Broadway show. It was my *first* job on a Broadway show.

The composer, Harold Arlen—His friend, Marlene Dietrich—Her nightclub act—To Noël Coward. *That* was the line.

He *came to the house* to audition *me,* which I thought was nice.

The truth was, that *I didn't really know what that meant.* I knew Noël Coward, the playwright, but I had *no idea* about his *songs* or the *style* of English Music Hall comedy. This was completely new to me.

Somehow . . . I guess, he sensed that.

He came into the apartment—it was a *terrible* apartment—and he took a kind of disdainful look around, and he said, "Well, do you know the *'Trolley Song?"*

I said, "Yes, I do know the *'Trolley Song"*. (My piano playing was pretty *up* then. I was practicing *a lot*. I was playing a lot of piano in those days, so I wasn't uncomfortable.)

He said, "Can you play in the key of 'B?"

I don't know if you know anything about music, but some keys are *very* difficult to play, and you seldom play in the key of 'B—all *sharps,* and that kind of thing.

So, I said, "Well, it's kind of weird, but I'll play it in 'B."

And he said, "Very fast."

So, I said, "How fast?"

He said, "About *this* fast," and he started singing in that great funny voice, "In *my high starched collar, in my high top boots*—"

A Judy Garland song!

Flying through the song!

So, *I CAUGHT UP* with him on the piano!

I was playing along, and he sort of looked down at the keyboard, and then he asked me to play one or two other things, which were sort of American film type songs, or show tunes, which I knew.

And then he said, "Can you be in Los Angeles tomorrow?"

I said, "Yeah, I guess so."

And he said, *"Fine*. I'll be at Clifton Webb's house. We'll start rehearsing."

It turned out we had ten days, or some ridiculous amount of time. No time at all. My folks were living in L.A. at the time. So, I flew from New York, and went to my folks' house, and met him at Clifton's house, who I didn't know. He was a movie star, you know.

Noël started teaching me, not only his songs, but also this whole *style* of playing. He was so wonderful and so brilliant. I don't know if he ever thought of himself as a teacher. He could have. He was a great director. He made me learn, very forcefully, that this was about *comedy.*

And a couple times he screamed, *"Don't play when I'm making a joke!"*

You know, things like that. I gradually saw that this was a whole *other* kind of music. I had just been playing jazz and show tunes. So, there was that. I didn't really realize what a learning process that was. That was terrific.

Then, at night, I was working on the *orchestrations,* because he *didn't* really *have* orchestrations! He had just played this act at the *Cafe de Paris,* where they had five or six musicians. Norman Hackforth was playing the piano. They had a drummer, and a bass player, one saxophone or something.

I'll never forget—there was one little shred of paper, music paper, like this, with one staff, maybe two—and it said "saxophone."

There were a few notes written on it, and somebody had written

"HARRY, DON'T PLAY THIS."

[laughing] . . . so, I didn't know *what* that meant, but I said, "God, there's *no time!* We'll need at *least—"* as I began to see what the shape of the act was, and where there would be *tempo,* and then there would be a song *out* of tempo, for *comedy.* Then, maybe something *rhythmic*—I began to get a picture of where we would need the orchestra. What it really boiled down to was—I mean, that's *very flattering* in the book, but I didn't really *do* that—what it boiled down to was *introductions.*

The orchestra would play an *introduction,* and get the thing *started,* and then mostly it would be just the *piano* and the *drum* and the *bass, maybe.* And *then* the orchestra would play, maybe an *interlude,* and then an *ending.* I didn't really do a full-blown thing.

They did sound good. It was a good band in Las Vegas. The truth is, I was too young and too dumb to be frightened by this. I didn't realize how important it all was. And, of course, the truth is, that it was a tremendously important thing in his life, and in a sense, in the whole cabaret scene there. I didn't know.

It was a job in *Vegas* and it was great!

AF: It was recorded. How many sessions were recorded? How many shows were recorded? Do you remember?

PM: I don't really remember. I seem to recall it was three nights. When everybody realized what was happening—*I think a lot of people thought that this would not be successful.*

This wonderful story, which a friend of mine just told me last week—

The man who booked Noël was a man named Joe Glaser.

AF: Yes, he's in *"The Diaries"*.

PM: Right. Joe Glaser, a friend of mine reminded me—Joe was an agent at, I guess, GAC or Associated Booking, or one of those places—and *somehow he knew* in London, when he went to see Noël, that this would be a *terrific* thing in *Vegas!*

It really was a *strange* booking.

But, Joe, later, *after* the success, was real tickled that his roster used to read: **Count Basie—Noël Coward**—you know, the alphabetical thing.

Anyhow, when the rest of the world saw that this engagement was a triumph, then *Columbia Records* got interested. I think Joe had something to do with that, too, bringing *Columbia* in. And Goddard Lieberson himself, who was one of the top guys and later the head of *Columbia, he* came to Vegas!

Of course, sociologically speaking, Goddard was on Coward's *level*. He was a man of learning and a man of culture, so he knew what was going on.

The album itself—they brought in equipment. I think it was three nights—two shows a night, so they probably taped, or actually recorded six shows. Is that possible? Something like that.

AF: I think he mentions, at one point, what the shows were. There was a supper show, and then a dinner show, which was at midnight. I was just in the record store the other day getting some out-of-print records, and they said they could sell as many copies of that album today as ever.

PM: It's amazing. That album has remained, and the picture from the cover has remained a classic moment. [Editor's note: Noël standing unruffled, bemused, in tuxedo in the Nevada desert, holding a teacup and saucer, under a blazing sun.]

AF: This is from Noël's *"Diaries"*:

"Peter Matz has arrived and we have been rehearsing. He is quick, intelligent, and a fine pianist."

That's May 29. And this is, I guess, now during the engagement.

PM: That was at Clifton Webb's house.

AF: In Beverly Hills. Now, in Las Vegas:

"Pete Matz, at the age of twenty-six, knows more about the range of various instruments and the potentialities of different combinations, than anyone of any age I have ever met in England."

Amazing.

PM: That's nice, yeah. Actually, of course, he did work with a guy who is a marvelous, marvelous orchestrator and composer, Wally Stott. Wally Stott is now Angela Morley, who is one of the leading composers of film music out in California. So, it's not that there was any shortage of people in England, I think Noël was just being nice.
One thing is true, though, he hadn't had experience with the combination that the orchestra was in Las Vegas. It really was kind of a hot *dance* band, a typical Las Vegas *show* band with *saxophones* and many *trumpets* and *trombones.* That was kind of *new* to him. He was more used to the operetta type music, so my facility with that combination probably surprised him. And, of course, it's a high-energy combination, that nightclub band thing.

AF: Here is something else from Cole Lesley's book about Las Vegas:

"On the day of Noël's opening, to his consternation, Carlton Hayes, the orchestra leader, went down with the Las Vegas virus, exactly as Marlene had predicted, 'everybody' would. Pete remained cucumber-cool, told Noël that he would take charge of the orchestra, and he was not to worry.

But Noël was very anxious, indeed.

Pete at the piano would be upstage right, with the orchestra way behind Noël, and Noël downstage center, alone. He had never before performed without being able to catch somebody's eye—his accompanist's or the conductor's. They got through the afternoon rehearsal with no trouble; neither Noël nor Pete once faltered, and I could comfort Noël by telling him truthfully the arrangement looked ten times more effective visually.

The two shows at night were known as the 'dinner' show at eight-thirty, and the 'supper' show which started at midnight. Noël was preceded by forty-five minutes of first—class entertainment, including a chorus line of lovely girls (one of whom, Janet Morrison, Pete fell for and later married), and which ended with a backdrop looking as unlike the facade of the *Cafe de Paris* as it possibly could, although a sign stated firmly that that was what it was, with *NOËL COWARD* flashing on and off in electric lights.

The stage was then pumped knee-high with *Nujol* mist to represent a pea-soup London fog, sending diners in the front tables into *paroxysms of coughing,* and the entire company rendered a song which, Noël swore, consisted of the most heavenly lyrics he had ever heard, starting, *'So, this is London, Land of Romance."*

PM: [imitating Noël] *"London is not a land!"* he would say. [laughter]

He was furious at that. It was so funny.

AF: [reading]

"Then Noël came down the steps to the strains of *"I'll See You Again"* and started to sing."

[stops reading]

Some of the songs—most of these had been sung before, although, *"Alice"* I guess, at least, he hadn't recorded *"Alice Is At It Again"* before this recording. And the same for "A *Bar On The Piccola Marina"* But *"Let's Do It"* I guess, had been done many times. Did he change the verses of *"Let's Do It"* in the performance there?

PM: Yes, I think he did *a lot* of new writing, rewriting, updating some of those lyrics, which he felt people might be familiar with. *"Let's Do It"* was one, and I know he wrote some new words for *"Senorita Nina from Argentina"*.

    He changed the medley around. We spent a lot of time reworking that from the *Cafe de Paris* medley. I think it was stronger the way we ended up with it.

AF: About *"Mad Dogs And Englishmen"*—I think it was Cole Porter who said after a performance, it was the first time he'd **"ever heard a song sung in one breath."**

PM: Oh, yes!

AF: Because of the speed.

PM: Relentless. I don't think I could play it *now* the way I used to do it, but I, at least, *did.* It's very exciting.

AF: Do you have a particular favorite, or favorites among his songs?

PM: Well, the things that were *fun.* I mean, *"Uncle Harry"* and *"Mad Dogs"* and those things were such fun to do, because they were like *athletic* experiences. I mean, you never knew *when* he was going to STOP! How the *laugh* was going to be. Then, *catch up,* and all that stuff. It's very exciting.

    Just as far as the heart and the sweetness—his love songs are just wonderful. I love all his love songs. I like most of his music.

AF: Then later that year there was the TV special with Mary Martin, then the following year the recording session in New York.

PM: Right.

AF: And you were involved in all of those?

PM: I was. The TV special with Mary was *live.* It was an hour and a half—***LIVE!*** Unbelievable in these days of videotape to think of that.

AF: And I read that the three of you rehearsed daily for two months.

PM: We rehearsed a lot. We rehearsed in New York, to begin with, and Mary rehearsed separately. I went down to Jamaica, which was wonderful. We did a lot of work there. Except, there is an interesting sidelight to that.

He liked to write in the *mornings.* As I remember, the schedule. we would be in *separate* places. He would be in his *study,* and I would be in my little guest area that I was staying in. I would write on a desk in there in the morning, when the sun was very hot. He would be writing over in his place. Then we would all meet for lunch. Then we would rehearse *all* afternoon, rehearse *part* of the evening, and that would be it.

The next morning, I would come back to what I had written the day before. and it was almost.

Everything ***ran!***

Electrographic pencil lead *ran* on the paper! It became real *soggy.* It was so *damp* down there—the paper—the lead—I had to get a *different* kind of lead!

It's a *fascinating* piece of information. [laughs]

AF: Was it comfortable working in Jamaica, aside from the fact of the wet paper?

PM: I remember the Jamaica trip as really being *fun.*

I had a violent crush on Mary, so I was trying to get to her in the swimming pool.

By then I was a little more experienced about what the work was. Not only from having worked with *him* in Vegas, but then, when we came back from Vegas, and I started working with *other* people. It seemed that my eyes were a little more *open* than they had been. So, I was a little more attuned to the work process, by the time we got to Jamaica.

I remember being just in awe of the level of the work that was going on. The *quality* of the rehearsal, and *that feeling* that—a *dangerous feeling* in terms of your *EGO,* but the truth is, that it was a feeling that something kind of. *historical* was happening here.

It was very important stuff. So it was *very* exciting. It was great fun.

The food was wonderful. He had a wonderful staff of people running his house. The weather was gorgeous.

As I say, we would work separately in the mornings. Then have dinner and rehearse a little bit more in the evening, but by then, we would start *drinking.* And the evenings were *a lot* of fun. There was a lot of laughing and yelling, and that's when the arguments would start. Richard [Halliday, Mary's husband] and Noël would argue about—*'should it be chiffon or should it be gauze?'*

Mary and I would usually discreetly go for a walk at that point, or *something* at that point. So, it was fun. Anyhow, that was very intense rehearsing and wonderful.

Mary. I had never met her before and what a treat that was!

AF: Well, they had had, I guess, you'd say, sort of a falling out when they did *"Pacific 1860"* in London, and this was sort of patching things up, I guess, in a way.

PM: I don't think they ever really—I know they had serious disagreements on it. Noël and Richard Halliday, Mary's late husband, used to scream at each other an awful lot.

AF: I seem to recall that one of the arguments in *"Pacific 1860"* was about a hat, or a bow, or something like that.

PM: I'm sure it was. The thing on *"Together With Music"* that made a major argument that I remember was—

Richard had an idea about *big columns of fabric,* chiffon, or something that should be shaped like columns. It's a very attractive *idea,* when you think about it, except there's no way to hold them rigid. They are just going to *blow* and *sway* and everything.

And he said, "Well, we'll *weight* them."

And they started *arguing* about *what* could be put on the bottom—chains or whatever.

That was really so—it was about *who was going to be boss,* is what the argument was about. But Mary and Noël *never* fought.

She was wonderful. She was just great.

And the material for the show evolved there, and we rehearsed *a lot*. And then she rehearsed separately, when she came back with her accompanist. This guy named Johnny Lesko, who is still in New York. Wonderful conductor, accompanist. The two of us played pianos, and the overall musical director was a man named Tutti Camarata, who, *thank god,* was there, because he was *experienced,* and could get through a *live* hour and a half.

In those days, I don't think I could have done that.

AF: I read in two places, that when Mary arrived, she had some objections to *"Together With Music"* and Noël *rewrote* it to make it more *romantic* for her. He was writing that it was *"bloody hell"* to do, but he agreed with her, in the end, that it was *better.*

PM: That's right. I'd forgotten that.

AF: Which is one of the numbers that was written for the show, as well as *"Ninety Minutes Is A Long, Long Time".*

PM: Long, long time! [laughs] And then some things that, let's see, *"The Tots"*—*"What's Going To Happen To The Children?"*—wasn't that new for that show? Or was that something he'd written before and rewrote?

AF: He had written the original in 1927, but he did it at Las Vegas and called it a new song, because he wrote new *American lyrics* for Las Vegas, and then they did it on the TV special, too.

PM: They did argue about her determination to sing in her *soprano* voice. They argued about *that.* Of course, he gave in and let her do *"Un Bel Di"* from Puccini's *"Madam Butterfly"*.

AF: You mean, that the *skit* they did on that, was based on *fact?*

PM: *Exactly.* He took the *argument* and made it into an *event!*

AF: In Mander and Mitchenson's *"Theatrical Companion To Coward"* they have a run-down, an outline of the script of the show, including a couple of numbers, which were *not in* the final show. I presume it was because things were running a little bit late, and they had to cut a couple of things? For instance, a version of *"Tit Willow"* from Gilbert & Sullivan's *"The Mikado"*.

PM: Right.

AF: It sounds *great.* And then *DRG* has issued a nice disc of the *complete* show.

PM: I didn't even know that.

AF: I also came across a videotape of the broadcast recently. Coward said, about the television special, that at first they weren't using the camera the way he thought—they weren't giving him enough *close ups*—he objected to that, and proposed them doing a *kinescope* [a film recording of the television picture, used before the advent of videotape] of a run-through *so he could take a look at it.* This was *a revelation* to them. It seems like a normal thing for him to do—

PM:—to take a look at it—

AF:—*before* they do it.

PM: I'm sure that there was a lot of behind-the-scenes stuff going on that I was not aware of. I was very naive about the whole process of television in those days. That was probably the first thing I was involved in. I had, yet, a lot to learn about stuff that we now take for granted.

AF: What did you observe of him as a lyricist and composer, or was all his work done away in his study?

PM: No, I *saw* him at work. He was very comfortable working in front of people.

He was extremely prolific. He was just natural, I mean, he *spoke* the written word. He loved the language. So, he'd just sit down, take out a pen, cross his legs, and away he would go. He just was very prolific.

Musically, he was not as *literate* as he was *verbally*. He was not ever formally trained, musically. He *could* play the piano. He played *okay*. He played nice. He didn't play wrong notes or anything, but he was limited harmonically, and he didn't know how to read or write music, so he'd have to get someone to transcribe what he composed.

Like all of us who compose anything, you reach a point where you start *repeating*. There are certain things that you fall into that are frequently called *style,* but they really are the demonstration of the *limitation* of what you *know* about music. So, he tended after a point, to *repeat* certain harmonic things and certain melodic things.

Yet, he wasn't closed off to modern music.

I mean he would listen to whatever was coming up. And the same thing was true musically. If something was needed, he'd sit down and compose a few bars and say, *"Did you get that? Somebody write that down. That'll do for the transition"—'* or something. He was quite comfortable doing that.

AF: I would like to read you a bit from *"The Diaries"* about the recording session in 1956.

PM: Was that the New York album? That was not so good.

AF: [reading from *"The Diaries"* Sunday, November 4, 1956:]

> *"On Friday I finished off my recordings, fairly triumphantly. Pete [Matz] had assembled a brilliant rhythm section consisting of piano, double bass, trumpet, guitar and drums, each instrumentalist an expert. The result was, to me, exciting and I sang well. We did 'Time And Again,' 'Twentieth Century Blues,' 'Sail Away,' 'Half Caste Woman' and 'Marvelous Party'. We also did our experimental remake of the medley, but this didn't come off. Altogether, however, it was a very successful session and the finished record should be good."*

But, *how* do you choose the songs, and how to put them together in a medley, so cleverly moving from one to the next?

PM: That's something either you *know* how to do, or, I don't know.

Look, years later *"The Carol Burnett Show"* existed on *medleys!* We used to do *endless—fifteen or twenty minute* medleys of the *film* songs, or *composer* songs, or whatever. It's something that I think I have a knack for.

And, I think the *Streisand* medley of the animals in her second television show—remember that? Her second television show, which was *"Color Me Barbra"*—we had a big circus sequence. There was a *huge* medley. It had to be *fourteen minutes!*

That, I did.

That, I constructed of songs in which she was able to come face to face with an *anteater* and sing—*"Look at that face, just look at it . . ."*

And her dog, Sadie—*"that face, that face, that fabulous face . . ."*

And with a *penguin* standing there—*"Sam, you made the pants too long . . ."*

Either you have a *feel* for those kinds of things, or you don't. I think that's the best medley I ever wrote. Probably the New York Coward medley wasn't too good. I bet that it was because the songs were already used up. That we had used all the good ones. I don't remember.

I remember that he was fairly well satisfied with it. Of course, it didn't have the *heat* that the Las Vegas album had. We had talked at one time about having an audience in the studio, and

I don't remember if it was *Columbia* or who, that said it wouldn't be *practical,* but there's something that I felt was missing from that second album. I have to go back and listen to it to see if I'm right. He actually, probably, was in better voice, mechanically, but there is nothing like *performance,* you know? It's hard to generate, unless you're really a *recording* artist, *then* you can generate that.

AF: Then, a couple of years later, you had a falling out over a ballet. It was the ballet *London Morning* [1958].

PM: That's right. He wanted me to work on that, and by now I was already working in television, and starting to have a lot of activity. Also, I started to make some money. The falling out was basically about the fee, the money. He felt that our relationship was such that I should still be working on the same basis as I was before, which was rather a small scale.

AF: That isn't mentioned.

PM: I don't want to say anything about that, but the fact is that I was doing pretty well in TV by then, and to stop and do Noël's project would have been a serious financial drop. I was already married, and had one small kid, and you know how all those things are. I think, to be really honest, also, I didn't have the *passion* about doing this work that he wanted. I didn't think it was, actually, all so wonderful.

It looked, to me, like a very hard job to go to London, and I *wasn't sure* if there were music copyists, and we *weren't sure* how long the suite should be, and *who* was going to play rehearsal piano? *I* might have to play rehearsal piano for the dancers, and it didn't look too good.

I kept trying to say, "Well, could we iron this out? Can we find out about this?" It was very loose, and I finally had to say, "Noël, I don't think I can do it."

He was very upset. It seemed to him that I was being *disloyal.* And, in a way, I guess I *was.*

AF: But then, you worked again on *"Sail Away"*.

PM: Then *"Sail Away"* came up, and he came back to me and said that he wanted me to work on that, and it was a tremendous opportunity for me. It was the *first* job I did in the theatre as *music director!* I had had jobs as rehearsal pianist, and dance music arranger, and that kind of thing, but it really represented my *whole reason* for having gone to New York to begin with. I came off the road working with bands and with acts because I was *fascinated* with the musical theatre, and I wanted to learn that medium.

Part of what you have to do if you're going to learn about musical theatre is *conduct, orchestrate* and *do* that. And here it was!

So, I was thrilled that he asked me to do that. It was a wonderful learning experience. The show was not what we had hoped. I guess it did all right. It's sort of remembered, isn't it?

AF: Yes. I think it's got some of his wittiest lyrics in it.

PM: It wasn't a hit, though. Why do you think it didn't hit?

AF: I don't know, really.

PM: Kind of old fashioned, I guess.

AF: I think he said at one point, or someone said, that it was just because it was sort of making fun of Americans, and maybe Americans just didn't want to go see it.

PM: I don't think it was that. The making fun of Americans was very good humored. I think he was writing—it's strange—
I think if that show were done today it would be very successful. I think it was too close to its own time, *just* past being old fashioned, you know? Not far *enough* away to be campy, or really satirical.

AF: The one song, when I first heard it, that stuck out was *"Beatnik Love Affair"*. I don't know, something—just using the term *'beatnik'* to me sort of *dated* it, I guess, but the more I listened to it, the more I *like* that, too.

PM: It's a charming song.

AF: The whole score is.

PM: I always think of it, when somebody says, *'Why didn't you think it worked?'* I always think—there's one moment when the hero, I guess, is on the bridge of the boat with the girl, and there's a pause, and in what was in the era of *"Vortex"* or in the era of *"Hay Fever"*—a romantic moment—which is—

The man says to the woman, *"Cigarette?"*

[laughter]

You know? To do that, nowadays, *is* kind of funny. And here was this moment where the guy offered her a *cigarette,* and it was *supposed* to be *seductive!* Well, *come on,* you know? *Cigarettes ain't sexual weapons anymore.* But, I think, maybe Noël—of course, *Joe*—it was very *Joe Layton,* who took over directing the show, and started choreographing.

Joe was very open with Noël about saying, *"This is dated. We have to update this."*

AF: I guess there were some major changes made. Cutting out characters—

PM: Oh, boy! Incredible *chaos* on the road. Maybe that was it. Maybe we never really had time to settle. But it was fun.

AF: What was Elaine Stritch like to work with?

PM: Wonderful! Brilliant, wonderful, *funny,* brilliant! One of the best working actors I've ever known in my life. I had a chance to work with her again, recently. There have been three shows. Mrs. Danny Kaye—*Sylvia Fine Kaye,* does a show called, *"Musical Comedy Tonight".* There was *"Musical Comedy Tonight" I, II and III* on public television. And on the third one, which was just a little while ago, Elaine did a Rodgers and Hart song called *"To Keep My Love Alive".*

I hadn't seen Elaine for, god, fifteen years or something. Just the little rehearsal that we had working up that song, and seeing how she approached it, and what she went through! In fact, I wrote *two* orchestrations of the song.

The first one I wrote, and we rehearsed the *day* before the show!

She said, "It's *not* right. It *doesn't* work."

I said, "Wait a minute we can *fix*—"

She said, "It's not about *fixing*. This is *wrong"*

And she was absolutely right. I came back here, and it was late, and I said, "She's right! God damn it, she's right!"

And I *fixed* this, and rewrote, and a new orchestration came in the next morning, and she said, "Now, *that,* I can work with that!"

She's meticulous. Every word counts. And at the end of it she gave a *performance.* Elaine is absolutely *electric.* She's just wonderful and I love her and have great respect for her, and of course, on *"Sail Away"* the *ongoing love/hate?* There was *not* hate.

It was all love—

—but there was a lot of war between her and Noël. Was really *hilarious! And* it was just wonderful! He was impatient with her, but he realized her talent. It was wonderful. It was really exciting. She *gave* so much. She taught everybody so much. She's just a dynamite woman.

AF: About the solo album, [reading:]

"My first day recording the solo album was disastrous—

PM: Which was this?

AF: From *"Sail Away".*

PM: Right, right.

AF: [reading:]

"Pete was exhausted and the orchestra was cumbersome and slow. Fortunately, my voice was in good condition. The next day was a bit better because we used only a rhythm section;

also, I had delivered a few sharp words. The third day was good, and when we had done the numbers we were scheduled to do, I insisted on re-recording all the ones we had done on Monday. The result, after much exhaustive work, is one of the best records I have ever made. It really is good, and will, I am sure, help the show enormously."

PM: What happened to that record? Was it released?

AF: Yes, on *Capital*.

PM: And what did it say? *"Noël Coward Sings 'Sail Away"* or something like that? [It was reissued on CD by EMI in 1999: *"Noël Coward Sings His New Broadway Hit 'Sail Away"*.]

I was just looking at the list of songs from *"Sail Away".* There are some lovely songs in there. *"Where Shall I Find Him"* is a lovely song. *"Later Than Spring"* is a lovely song.

I remember that *"Go Slow, Johnny"* came in very late. That came in at the end of the Philadelphia run, I think. And it was very much an attempt by Noël to write a more *modern* song, a more *contemporary* song. He asked me to orchestrate it, rather than Irwin Kostal, who had been orchestrating the songs in the show. I had orchestrated all the dance numbers, but he asked me to orchestrate this, and *I did a blatant Nelson Riddle imitation,* on this song, he thought was *just right.*

"Don't Turn Away From Love" is nice. *"When You Want Me"* was late, I believe, near the end of the out-of-town. A lot of stuff came in from out-of-town. Interesting. I have to look up that *Capital* record.

AF: You mentioned that, in doing that show, *overnight* you would do a new orchestration. How do you work so fast?

PM: I'm *very fast* now, *after years of doing weekly television.* I did weekly television for Carol Burnett, and for about six years before that, in New York, I did a *terrible* country western show with Jimmy Dean as the star, which was my basic training. Then I did a show called *"Hullabaloo"* which was a rock and roll show on NBC.

For several years, I was one of the arrangers on the Perry Como show. Then I was the musical director of a show called *"The Kraft Music Hall"* which was an hour of almost total music, three times a month, three weeks out of four. I started picking up speed.

Then I started learning about television writing, which is different than film writing, or record writing. You really do write for the orchestra in a different way when you're writing for television. In a lot of ways it's more economical. You write *less* than you would for a film recording, or for a record, or for live performance, simply because the television environment *doesn't accept as much sound.* You have to be more *economical* in what the orchestra is saying, because *it doesn't come out* You just don't get it. You learn to trust your first thought, and I just did develop a lot of speed.

Then, *"The Carol Burnett Show"* once a week—a lot of music. The first few years I did that show I had help. I had people come in and work with me. As we got near the end I was doing it all myself.

So, it's a mechanical thing.

This is no great talent, orchestration, given you can hear the idea in your *head,* and you *know* what is going to be played. Then there is a great range of just mechanical speed that you can develop by repetition. It's really like accounting or any other numerical thing. I've gotten to the point where I'm *very* fast at it now.

So, Elaine's thing was not so much *how will I get it done in this amount of time?* but, *will I be able to figure out what it needs to be to work for her?* Once the idea's there, it was very easy in terms of time.

So, going back to the era that I was working with Noël, that was very much an *'earn while you learn'* situation. I was learning a lot through those years. *Always* learning from him. Just to be working on a project, *watching him rehearse*—what I said before, about Stritch, he didn't waste a moment. *Everything* was absolutely calculated to make the line *work,* or to get the joke pay-off three lines *later,* or whatever the situation was. He was brilliant at that.

AF: In seeing a videotape of him, too, you can see how he was insisting that there be *close ups,* so that you could see his face, because there was so much in his *face.*

PM: *Of course!* He would tip off! That was interesting in Las Vegas. I first began to be aware of this in Las Vegas—that he would USE the opening medley!

He came down the stairs—and he *used* that walk down the stairs to *case* the audience! He would come down to the mic—

—The audience would be quite different for each show. Some nights there would be guys in shirtsleeves, gamblers, *whatever,* people in on a *tour* from *Reno.* Some nights there would be some people in *black tie* who would come up, as a group, from *Hollywood.*

So, he would *USE* those opening songs, which were really just a rehash of some of his old songs—*"Zigeuner"* and those things—*a little memory jog—was what he was doing—WHILE* he was singing those, he was *casing* the audience.

That would determine, to a great extent, *HOW he played* the comedy songs. I began to see *how,* if it was a *square* audience, an audience that perhaps didn't understand the form that he was working in, he would **lift an eyebrow three lines earlier,** *to let you know* that a little *'funny'* was coming here, *'now be on your toes!'*

If it were a *friendlier,* you know, a *Hollywood* or *show business* audience, he would play it absolutely *deadpan . . .*

. . . but, *tiny . . . tiny* things, to *tip off* the jokes, and to MAKE YOU COMFORTABLE laughing. It was brilliant!

There's a whole theory of comedy performance there.

So, if you wanted to *watch,* you could really learn a lot from him.

AF: Did you sense that he was ever tired of any of the songs? Tired of having to sing *"Mad Dogs and Englishmen"* for instance?

PM: No! I don't think he *ever* tired of the material, because he had that wonderful thing that a real, true actor has at every performance, is a *fresh performance.*

What he *did* very definitely get tired of was *Las Vegas.* He got tired of the *environment* there. He got a little tired of some of the audiences that he had to play, because some of the audiences were.

One night, I remember we went across the street to the Thunderbird [Casino] between shows. There was, like an hour and a half gap between the two shows. We went across the street and performed for a private party, a convention of some kind of *elderly women.* I don't know what it was—*Hadassah,* or *Daughters of the American Revolution,* or *something*—almost *all women* in the audience. Almost all *elderly*—*flower dresses!*

They didn't have any idea what he was doing!

He was annoyed that the booking had been made. God knows what he *made!* He probably made many thousands of dollars for that little jaunt across the road, but he was annoyed with that. I think, he thought that was a little bit of a sellout. He was *impatient* with the audiences sometimes. Impatient with the whole *Las Vegas* nonsense.

Not the material though. I think he loved his material.

AF: I was wondering, because it was so *successful,* why he never went back? I guess that's the reason?

PM: I wonder. I don't know. He had talked about it. Of course, they were talking astronomical figures in those Days. I think he was more excited about what happened in terms of how this seemed to *open* the Broadway doors again. I didn't realize at the time what he had been through in terms of his *'semi-retirement.'*

You know that line?—**"What do you think about your comeback?"**

[Noël said,] "I wasn't aware that I had been away!"

But, in fact, he *had* been away. the Vegas success and notoriety enabled him to start again in the theatre thing, and I think that is what he was mainly interested in.

AF: Did you get to spend much time with him aside from just working? Did you socialize?

PM: Not an awful lot. Most of the social time was connected with the work. He did spend several evenings with us. He liked my ex-wife, Janet. They got along great. She was a feisty woman and they used to *argue* about all kinds of things. Friendly arguments, but he *loved* to tear into anything. *Politics,* whatever, he would love to talk about that.

So, we had a little apartment there. In fact, it was the same apartment there, for a while, where he had come to audition me, on East 61st Street. He did come several times there, and we had a visit in Bermuda with him, once, which was wonderful. Delightful time.

Then when we went to England, on one trip we spent some time. He was in a play that I can't remember. It would have been in '68?

AF: *"Suite In Three Keys".* It was *"Come In From The Garden, Maude" "Shadows of the Evening"* and *"A Song At Twilight"*— *three* plays.

PM: *That's* it! We went backstage and saw him, and then met him a night or two later and had dinner. Another day, we met him for lunch, *so it was very warm.* Of course, then I was out *here.* I came out here in '71. His trips back and forth to this country—he usually stayed in New York.

Again, you're left with that thing—*God, I wish I'd made one more trip to see him* because, I really was *very fond* of him. That brief illness and then his passing were very sad for us. My current wife [Marilynn Lovell] also knew him, strangely enough. She was a performer in an earlier part of her life. She's now a psychotherapist, but she *was* a performer, and she was in the company of *"Hello Dolly!"* that Mary Martin was in, that went to London. They were there almost two years. So, during that time she knew Noël, because—Noël and Mary of course had a long bond. So, we all sort of know each other, and there is *a lot of affection there.*

He bequeathed me a *baton.* Wonderful, *silver* baton, that *folds* up into a little case. The orchestra he went to conduct up north in England gave it to him. Where would it have been?

Liverpool, I guess. *The Liverpool Symphony.* A guest performance many years before I knew him. He had come to guest conduct one of his suites from one of his shows, and they presented him with this baton. He *willed* that to me, which I thought was quite wonderful. So we have that.

AF: I know you do TV specials from time to time. What else do you do these days?

PM: Well, the main thing that I like to do now is compose scores for film. I do quite a bit of that. I just mentioned to you, the score to "As *Is* which I just finished today, before we met. I'm pleased with that. That will be on the air soon. The last thing I did was a television movie with Katherine Hepburn called *"Mrs. Delafield Wants To Marry"* which was a lot of fun to do, because it was a period piece in a way.

I still do a lot of *arranging* jobs, and I just did a whole new *rearrangement* of the Gershwins' *"Girl Crazy"* which the *Seattle Rep* is doing. We hope it will become a road company. So, in truth, I wear many hats and enjoy all of them.

AF: Well, I really appreciate your giving us time to talk to us.

PM: It's a pleasure to be part of this.

JOE MITCHENSON

b. 1911

Interviewed on October 13, 1987

Joe Mitchenson, together with his partner, Raymond Mander, created one of the most extensive collections of theatre memorabilia in England. They published several volumes based on their collection, including their *"Theatrical Companion"* to Bernard Shaw, Somerset Maugham, and Noël Coward. The interview was conducted in Kent, at the mansion at Grace Park, at The Mander and Mitchenson Collection, which was just in the process of moving into this new location.

ALAN FARLEY: I first became familiar with the names *Mander and Mitchenson* with your *"Theatrical Companion to Coward"* which is, I think, probably the most comprehensive one-volume sourcebook on Noël Coward that exists! It's fantastic! It took me several years, but I finally tracked down a copy for myself. It's proved to be eminently valuable.

JOE MITCHENSON: I think it has proved tremendously valuable all over the place, because Coward is most certainly very much still alive. One never thinks of him having died, and with the plays being done all over this country, and overseas, America—everywhere. I think it has proved invaluable, because, as I say, *nowadays people want to know all the data.*

It proved to be a very difficult book to get published. We had little headaches over that, because Noël was out of the country when we submitted one of our other *"Companions"*. I think we'd done the Shaw, and Maugham volumes by then. Things got wrong, and letters got wrong. They delivered wrong addresses and things happened, until *at last* one day, the phone went, and a voice said—

"It's Noël Coward here. I wonder if you'd come and have drinks with me at five o'clock on Friday the tenth to discuss this book."

Our publishers had been very annoyed 'cause they couldn't get an answer out of him. It was just one of those unfortunate things. And these sorts of things often blackened somebody's name that doesn't deserve to be blackened. It can be a muddle and a mistake, which sorted itself out eventually.

Our publisher was very bright, and when Coward landed in England from one of his trips from overseas, I think, from America, he had one of his staff give him a copy of the *"Companion to Shaw"* for him to see. Of course, he was so delighted and honored, and Shaw is, of course, *a GOD for Noël*. You know Noël admired Shaw's work tremendously.

AF: Well, Shaw helped Coward, too, didn't he?

JM: Yes. He helped him. As you know, Noël played impeccably in Shaw's *"The Apple Cart"* revival.

AF: When did you first meet him?

JM: I only met him on the day we *'went to drinks at five o'clock.'*

AF: What was that like?

JM: *Very* pleasant. It was extremely nice. It was an ENORMOUS couch we sat on! The *three of us*! We were sort of *tight* and Noël had drinks prepared, and I think we all had very *large* drinks here, because we wanted to *talk,* and we don't have to keep on having another little sip. So, one was given a very lavish gin and tonic, I think, and then we got *talking.*

Of course, he found that we were *theatre,* as well, and we talked about his early beginnings, his childhood appearances, and all sorts of things, long before we got 'round to *the book.* It was a very lovely and interesting conversation.

Eventually, Graham arrived, and Joyce Carey arrived. They were off to Goldenhurst for the weekend. They came to collect him.

I remember Joyce coming in with a great *tray of eggs!*

Whenever you're in Noël's company—he was highly civilized. You *never* knew where you were *going,* or, if you're with any of the entourage, they might suddenly be saying to you, *'Oh, we're going to The Caprice after this at Noël's expense.'*

Everything was laid on beautifully. Noël's household was wonderfully geared.

AF: In putting together the book, did you get materials from him?

JM: Yes, of course we did! Lorne Loraine was alive then, and with her assistant, Joan Hirst, as her secretary, we worked days *in,* and days *out,* in the offices *looking things up!* There were lots of nice treasures and things that turned up, that one hadn't even known about.

AF: One of the things I regret is that it stopped at 1957. It could have continued.

JM: Yes. Well, we've published, I think, *twenty* books, and although you sometimes get reprints quickly on—they've sold out—if they've sold tremendously *quickly* and *well,* then you get reprints. Nothing's more difficult about ten or twelve years *later* than to come along and to get anyone interested in keeping these up-to-date. They just don't *see.* They're on to the next thing! *Publishers!* I think it's a great *pity* these books *aren't* carried on! [Ed: In 2000, Oberon Books published an updated version of the *"Companion"* edited by Barry Day and Sheridan Morley.]

AF: Well, what *is* the extent of your collection of Noël Coward materials here at *"The Mander and Mitchenson Collection"?*

JM: In the office, everything is very carefully filed.

Under the PLAYS—taking the plays of Noël Coward and the pictorial scenes from the plays, under whatever theatre they were played at. So, if you are looking for *"This Happy Breed"* in pictures, you go to the *Haymarket Theatre,* and enter the date, and find ALL the materials there. That's done right through the files, so that's quite a lengthy process.

But, then there are what we call the *'PERSONAL FILES.'* Just pictures of him overseas, anywhere he might be, concerts, odd things, the more offstage element is kept under *'HIMSELF'*.

AF: Noël Coward was a very *civilized* person to be with.

JM: It was marvelous to *hear*—remarks that he would make about people coming out of a theatre! or going back to the dressing room.
Then you'd suddenly think, "Well, they're not invented! He really does say them!"

AF: Just on the spur of the moment?

JM: On the spur of the moment.
I remember when he was faced with going 'round to see John Neville—I'm sure Johnny won't mind my saying it now—but it was *such* a very *bad* evening in the theatre, that. It was a *really* bad evening, but Noël is a *very* brave man, and he would face *even* going back to see people, *even* if he didn't approve.
I'll always remember him getting into Johnny Neville's room, and I was in there previously, because I'm an old friend, and Noël appeared and said, "Really! I never knew you could sing! And on *note,* too!!" and retired.
But he'd got his word in, you know. [He laughs.]

AF: Are you still acquiring material?

JM: Oh, yes, yes indeed. Never a day goes by without *something* being collected, like *tonight's* first night programme! We hope some of us will be at the theatre. I hardly missed *anything* at one time, so a programme automatically goes into the collection after I've finished with it, and of course, some of the managements automatically send their stuff to us.

AF: It would seem just by the sheer amount of theatre that is produced in London, that the volume of material would be just overwhelming.

JM: It *is* overwhelming, and it gets *more*. Even this house, if you've seen our other house, which was quite *smallish* compared to this, but—*ALL THIS* that you've wandered 'round, and been through *rooms—was at the smaller house!* We can hardly believe that we've, you know, *spread* here, but true we've got a lot of rooms downstairs to be finished off, and then it will eat up quite a lot *more*.

AF: Is the collection computerized at all?

JM: Not really, no. I know that Colin [Mabberly, the *Collection's* curator] has attempted that, but the poor chap, he's had so much on his plate with everything going, that he hasn't been able to get really far with that. In fact, it seems to want another, even *younger*, generation to start that.

AF: How about microfilm? Do you use microfilm?

JM: No, we don't at the moment, no.

AF: I'm just thinking of some of the things that might be used to—

JM: Yes, yes, yes it would be—definitely. We had a certain amount of slides and things, an enormous collection of photography, things in photography. We're very lucky there.

AF: Your rooms are right here as part of this building?

JM: Yes, they are, yes, *this* part of the building. I don't know whether you've been through the sitting room back there. I call it the GOG AND MAGOG ROOM, because—*Noël christened Raymond and I* GOG AND MAGOG' *years ago!*

AF: What was that reference?

JM: Because Noël said, "I can't *slavishly* follow in Somerset Maugham's language and call you *'Mr. Mander'* and *'Mr. Mitchenson.'* I've got to call you something *else,* and I'm *christening* you! *From now on*—**GOG AND MAGOG!** And now, pick it out! Which *name* you want for each of you!"

And the next time we met him, he said,
"NOW! *Which* is GOG and *which* is MAGOG?!"

AF: And which are you?

JM: [chuckling] And which are you?—Quite! I'M *GOG*! Yes! No! MAGOG! I beg your pardon, yes. In that order, we always were Mander and Mitchenson, yes.

He had names for most of his friends. I think, particularly, that by the time you *got a NAME,* that meant you were *'in the household'* as it were. YOU *were part of the family.*

AF: This, it's just like living in a museum here.

JM: Yes, it is . . . Well, that's what I've *always wanted,* and not for this place.

It is very difficult for security, and all sorts of things to think of. But, one is trying to think of it as like coming into a *house* that is a *theatre house,* more than a *museum.* I've loathed the word *museum.* I always have, from a little boy. I wanted something like that when you've come through 'GOG AND MAGOG' as you must have done just now. I'd love to keep it like that, but I realize how difficult it is.

AF: It's really very comfortable, and the location here is *gorgeous.*

JM: Oh, it's *beautiful* because there is a wonderful view from *every* window—of *countryside* and that *golf course,* which extends all around the house. It is a lovely outlook, a beautiful outlook. I did my first broadcast in the *library* from the window! I said, "I *must* do it from looking out of this gorgeous window." I used to come and live here weekends and things. You've noticed the golf course out there?

[Looking out the window]

I always think, dear Ethel Merman said once, and she told me this herself, when she was over on a trip. It was a time that there was a big musical called *"Blitz"* on in London, you may have heard of it, and—

AF: I remember Noël Coward writing something about it—*"It was even louder than the real thing and twice as long."*

JM: Yes, quite! *I was with him that night,* and there were *quite a few* remarks of that nature made, but I think Ethel Merman's one was so marvelous, because *there was all this SCENERY moving, and doing everything* on the stage, you know? THIS UP! and THAT *down!*
 And she *looked* at it!
 "Well?" they asked, was she "interested in doing it in New York?'
 She said, *"Well,* it would be a case of either *ME,* or the *SCENERY*—but not *BOTH* of us!"

AF: Well, you must have seen just literally *thousands* of shows over your lifetime.

JM: Yes! *I have indeed! I* went to the theatre very early, when I was at the age of about *five!* Regularly! Every week! First of all, to the *London Coliseum,* which in those days was variety and music hall, and that I spent *every week* at it, I think. Once a week I went *there!*

AF: It would be hard to pick out two or three events out of that?

JM: Oh, yes, there are lots of things you could pick out, but there's so many to pick from, aren't there? There are great actresses and people like Dame Irene Rambert, who I thought was the most marvelous comedy actress I've ever seen. I saw Edith Evans very early, and people like that. They were tremendous.

AF: I noticed that Lord Olivier is your 'Honorary President.'

JM: Dear Larry is our president, yes.

I did have a surprise meeting with him on New Year's Eve. I was taken to a small party with June Havoc, from your side of the world. She said we were *'going to have a dinner out of town, but it was far too far for me to traipse on my bad leg!'*

And so, she rang, and she said we were *'going to a little dinner party at eight.'*

And while she was in the bedroom, sort of getting rid of her wraps and things, (I'd left mine in the car), I went into the sitting room, and the first person I saw among six other people was *Larry*.

AF: What a pleasant surprise.

JM: It was a lovely surprise. And at that moment to hear him say, "Oh, Joe, come and sit over here by me! Oh, no! You *can't* sit by me, there's this beautiful *girl* here!"

Which turned out in the end to be his nurse!

He was delightful. He was being well looked after. He was in a splendid mood and full of jokes, all his *doubtful* jokes that he loves to tell.

AF: Well, I appreciate your taking the time to talk with us today. It's really been quite a great pleasure.

JM: Well, it's been a surprise to me to meet you today, and I've thoroughly enjoyed talking to you. Now I wish you best of luck with any of your enterprises.

AF: Thank you.

SHERIDAN MORLEY

b. 1941

Interviewed April 3, 1984

Sheridan Morley is a journalist, author and broadcaster, who was the first biographer of Noël Coward, and has for many years served as an adviser to the Coward Estate. He was interviewed in London in his office at *"Punch"* the day after a memorial stone to Coward was unveiled in Westminster Abbey.

ALAN FARLEY: I guess you must be one of the few authors, if not the only author, whose book title, "A *Talent to Amuse"* is now enshrined in Westminster Abbey.

SHERIDAN MORLEY: Well, I was very pleased to see that. I am very proud, indeed! I, in fact, took that title out of a song he wrote in about 1930, in a show called *"Bitter Sweet"*.

The full quote is: *"For I believe that since my life began, the most I've had is just a talent to amuse."*

It seemed to me to sum up an awful lot of what was important about Coward. I have faint feelings of schizophrenia about it, though, because although it does summarize an awful lot of what matters about Coward, it's easy, in a way, to rather dismiss him. He had actually much *more* than *just* a talent to amuse. He had a talent to *entertain*.

AF: I think he felt that, too.

SM: Although he, himself, approved my title. We talked about what I should call it. The book was not an *authorized* biography, although he was very good about it.

He said he would *"like to see a couple of chapters, and,"* he said, *"if* you get those right, I will then *let* you do the rest, but I will *not* interfere, and I will *not* ask to see a final manuscript."

So it wasn't a kind of *'approved'* biography, although it was written with *his blessing.* And luckily, he then *liked* it very much, and it coincided with his great return to popularity, after the years in which he'd been a tax exile living in Jamaica.

The late 1960's were a tremendous kind of return to fame and fortune and popularity. He then got the knighthood and he became *Sir Noël.*

We thought of calling it just *"Noël"* and that seemed a bit lazy. We thought of calling it *"The Master",* because he was always known as *The Master,* but even in those days that had become a bit of a cliché. Then, when I found this song, I said, "Look, can I use it?"

And he said, "Yes, go ahead and use it!" because it did seem to be, in a way, evocative, certainly of the kind of music he wrote, and of those *kind* of shows.

But it's marvelous, now, to see the stone in Westminster Abbey, which, in fact, was something that had been fought for, for a long time by Graham Payn, and one or two others, and to see that we have all come full cycle.

When I began writing about him in the middle sixties, I actually couldn't find a publisher. People said, "Well, look he's not really very fashionable."

It was then the hay-day of the *Royal Court Theatre* and John Osborne and the *'angry young men'* and the swinging sixties. Somehow, Noël seemed like Fred Astaire—a *relic* from a lost world of *cigarette holders,* and *silk dressing gowns,* and *piano cabarets.* Nobody wanted to know. Then, gradually, the whole thing came *back!*

Now, *there* he is, quite rightly, I think, in Westminster Abbey!

Of all the writers of the century, Coward was the most *prolific,* and, in a way, the most *interesting.*

He was not *just* a playwright, or *just* an actor. He also wrote *three hundred* songs—[Ed: Thanks to Barry Day in *"The Complete Lyrics of Noël Coward"* 1998, we now know he wrote over five hundred songs.]

He made *movies.* He wrote *poems, short stories,* and *painted* a lot of pictures.

He was a man of extraordinary versatility. That was the marvelous thing about writing about him.

I did a couple of other books after my biography. I did a big picture book with Graham Payn and Cole Lesley called *"Noël Coward and His Friends"*. Then a couple of years ago we did *"The Noël Coward Diaries"*, which I edited with Graham. Since then, I've done a book about Gertrude Lawrence, [*"A Bright Particular Star"*] for whom, of course, he wrote *"Private Lives"* and who was his lifelong partner.

Now, in fact, I have a show called *"Noël and Gertie"* which plays in dinner theatres around America. It's been in Toronto for a year, and it's playing over here in summer theatres. It's really *an anthology* of their *letters,* and *diaries,* and *poems,* and *plays,* and *everything* he wrote—either *for* her, or *about* her.

So, I do seem to have spent the last fifteen years—when I'm not here working at *"Punch"* as the drama critic—dealing with Coward, really.

My son was his last godchild, so, we did become *great* friends in the last few years of his life, after my book came out. I now help Graham Payn look after the Coward Estate. So, I do feel, in a way, very *attached* to him. He was a wonderfully funny man, and for me, as a journalist, to have that as your first book—I mean, to have Coward, and at a time when there *hadn't* been a book about him, in fact, spoils you.

I've done fifteen other books, ranging from Oscar Wilde to Sibyl Thorndike, and I've just published in America a book about the English in California, called, *"Tales From The Hollywood Raj"* which *Viking* has published.

Although I've done a lot of other books, in a way, they all go back to *Coward. Coward* is where I *started. Coward* is what fascinated me *originally* as a writer, and that *kind* of England that *he* stood for.

I've just now been commissioned to do the authorized life of David Niven, by his family. There again, there is a great *connection.* I think, in people like Coward and Niven there was a kind of *'lost England.'* A kind of rather clenched, very *elegant,* very tight lipped—a sense of *dignity* and stature—a sense, particularly when they went abroad—in Niven's case to Hollywood—in Coward's case, to Jamaica and America—a sense of standing for an England that, somehow, had *gone,* but that *still mattered* abroad.

Standing, almost like an ambassador.

I think that is important. I think that what Coward stood for was a *kind of England* that really had *gone,* by the end of he war.

After all, as a child of Victorians, he grew up in that world. He grew up in *not at all* a glamorous world. He had *no money* as a child. It wasn't the world he then wrote about and became a part of—the world of cocktail parties and glamour. He came, in fact, from South London. His mother ran a *boarding house.* His father was an *unsuccessful* piano salesman. There was no money. *He was put on the stage to make the family income.*

So, there was no sense of aristocracy in his past. There was a real kind of middle class English *determination* to *survive.* That's *really* what got him through.

I find the other books I've done, the Niven book I'm starting now, and *"Tales From The Hollywood Raj"* have all been about Englishmen *abroad,* and about that sense of a *lost world* that somehow you perpetuate by plays or films or songs, but you do it from *abroad.*

When Noël came back, at the end of his life to England, he was often very depressed by the England he found, because it *wasn't* actually the England of the *"Stately Homes"* or the *"Mad Dogs"* or *any* of the things he'd written about. It *wasn't* the England of *"Private Lives".*

I think there were things in his life that he never really got over.

He *never* got over the death of Gertrude Lawrence, who had been his childhood friend, for whom, he had written *"Private Lives"* and *"Tonight at 8:30"* and *"Brief Encounter"* And then, to find that she died of cancer, on Broadway, during the run of the *"King and I"*—she was only 53, I think. He *never* really got over it. He *never* understood that she wasn't always going to be there.

And he said at the very end of his life, he said to me,

"I used to look—in *'Private Lives'*—across the stage at her, in that long, white, silk dress, and she would take my breath away."

Now, *there* is something very interesting about that, about that partnership.

People think of him as a kind of *lonely, single* figure. He wasn't. He was really half of that Gertrude Lawrence partnership.

You have to understand about HER, to understand about HIM.

AF: What attracted you to Noël in the very first place as a subject for your first book?

SM: Well, I'd always had the records. I'd grown up in the theatre. My father is an actor, Robert Morley, although he actually never knew Noël, but, my *grandmother,* who was an actress called Gladys Cooper, *had* worked with him, way back in the *twenties,* when they were both starting out in the theatre.

And so, I think when I was child, *I'd once met him with her,* but I'd never known him at all.

Then I went through Oxford in the late fifties, early sixties—and I think precisely because Coward was so *un*fashionable, because the world had gone so far *away* from *him,* I did get *fascinated* by that other world, that world of 1930's elegance and rather clenched sexuality.

Imagine the same thing that happened to thousands of moviegoers when they first discover Fred Astaire or Ginger Rogers! There is the sense that they're being *let in to a world of which we know nothing!*

Because it *can't happen* now.'

You *can't have* people dancing like that on pianos.

You *can't have* people sounding like Coward.'

The sheer un-'fashionability' of him fascinated me!

And, *by the* way, he did seem to stand for a *'lost England.'* Then I began to *read* him, and realized there was a *great deal more* to Coward than just the echo of those very, very English songs sung at Las Vegas.

So, I realized that, in fact, he was a very major dramatist.

Then I went to interview Harold Pinter, at the very beginning of his career, and we were talking about *"The Caretaker"* which could not SEEM to be *further away* from Coward. It was an *extraordinary* difference in *every kind of social and theatrical writing!*

Pinter, to my *amazement,* said to me, "The thing about *'The Caretaker'* is that it wasn't till I saw *'Private Lives'* that I understood—

A character could stand on a stage and SAY one thing, and the audience would KNOW he actually meant something ELSE!

When they are in *'Private Lives'* talking about the *'flatness of Norfolk'* and *'the Taj Mahal by moonlight'* and *'the potency of cheap music'*—what these two characters on that balcony in the south of France are REALLY saying is *'Let's go back to bed. Let's go back to the marriage. Let's get back together."*

"*Now,*" Pinter said, "when I *realized* that an audience *knew* that, even though they *weren't* being *told* it, I realized I could write on *TWO LEVELS"*

And that seemed to me *fascinating.*

So, then, I went back to Coward. I went through all the plays, and I realized this extraordinary *range* of talent, and I began writing about him.

"The London Times" were the first people to send me to interview him when he'd come over here to direct *"Hay Fever"* at the National Theatre with Lynn Redgrave and Edith Evans and a marvelous cast—Maggie Smith.

"The London Times" who I've always written profiles for, asked would I go and do an interview at the Savoy Hotel, where he was staying? This must have been about 1964.

I think I expected to meet a rather embittered, old man, living in a kind of Somerset "Maugham-esque" twilight, because the press had been vitriolic about his later work. His songs had stopped being played on the radio. England had gone so far away from him. He did seem to be an absolute leftover from a lost age. I thought I'd find this rather cross gentleman. Instead, I found this wonderfully *blithe* spirit, *leaping* around the Savoy Hotel!

Amazingly *young* for his—what was then—his 65 years.

I began to write rather *patronizingly* about him saying—

"The old man is still very much around, and still has got some good jokes in him, and there are still some good songs . . ."

—and all that. I think it was the first kind of *good* piece he'd seen in print about himself for a long time.

217

He *wrote* to me and we became, sort of, not friends, but *correspondents.* We used to write to each other.

Then he suddenly said, "Do you want to do a book?"

I'd never done a book. At that time, I was working as a newscaster in television. I was terrified of the idea of the book. I'd never done more than a thousand words in print. I began really trying to avoid the whole thing by making conditions.

I said, "Look, it must be a critical book. It mustn't be a fan book. It mustn't be a kind of 'as told to' book. It must be a really critical study." Rather hoping he would not then want it, and I could get out ofthe whole thing.

But, to my terror, he said, "Yes," he would *like* that!

So, I then began work on this, and I worked on it for about three years. I went 'round to hundreds of people who'd worked with him and just collected all these *stories,* and the *memories,* and put them together.

Then, I did get more and more fascinated. He then became *godfather* to my son, and so, *he then became a friend.* For the last five years of his life I did see him a great deal.

AF: When you edited *"The Diaries"* with Graham Payn. What did that involve? What was left out? I'm not saying there are some big secrets that were not published in *"The Diaries".*

SM: No, there aren't. We left out a certain amount, because, in fact, *"The Diaries"* run to something like a *million* words, and we only had room for about half that.

So, we did *cut* a lot of rather *boring* details:

"Got up, cleaned teeth,
Went to the airport, plane late,
Rotten meal in flight, arrived late at Heathrow."

We cut a lot of travel stuff. We just left in really what interested us.

Now, Graham had, of course, been Noël's greatest friend for nearly half a century [actually, 27 years]. So, what fascinated him were, I think, the sort of *private* details. What fascinated me were the *public* things, like first nights, and *rows* with critics, or *rows* with actors, or *backstage dramas* on Broadway. Between us we had two rather different attitudes, which is a good thing for editors of a diary. We approached it, therefore, from two different sides.

We simply had to work for about two years mainly on the *footnotes explaining who people were.* A lot of people, after all, don't know 1930's figures very well anymore, so we had to do *a lot of explaining* of whom Noël was talking about, and with whom he met.

Then, we cut inevitably more and more as we got closer to the end, because we found that we had to fit the whole thing in. I suppose we lost about forty percent of the total, but there were certainly no great secrets there. There were certainly no great scandals that we *didn't* put in.

Occasionally we had to be careful, because the editors are liable for reputations. So, when Noël would accuse somebody of being alcoholic onstage, we had to be a bit careful, in case they were alive and would sue. But, apart from that, very minor, occasional trimming of a few words, just to save law suits, we didn't actually have anything to hide.

I don't think that anybody going through the *complete* diaries, (which do run to about four hundred thousand words), would think there's anything important that we left out.

AF: At times, one gets the feeling that he did write *knowing* that this was going to be published.

SM: Towards the end he did, yes. When he started *"The Diaries"*—after all, they only *start* in the war, so you haven't got a complete life. I mean *"The Diaries"* only start in 1942.

Before that he had written a volume of autobiography called *"Present Indicative"* which covers his childhood and how he made his name. The curious thing about Coward is that by the time *"The Diaries"* start in the war, although he's only as old as the century, so he's only forty-two himself in 1942, he's *done most of the best work.*

Most of the great plays—*"Private Lives"*, *"Hay Fever"*, *"Tonight At 8:30"*, *"Cavalcade"*—most of the *great* songs—*"Dance Little Lady"*, *"Poor Little Rich Girl"*, *"Room With A View"*, *"Mrs. Worthington"*, *"Mad Dogs"*—ALL stem from the twenties and thirties.

The *only* major work he did in the last half of his life, really, I suppose you'd say, *"In Which We Serve"*—the wartime film. *"Blithe Spirit,"* of course. Then the Broadway musicals like *"Sail Away"* and *"Girl Who Came To Supper"*. But, in fact, the fifties and sixties were not very prolific times for him. He was mainly in cabaret in Vegas, or in the Cafe de Paris here in London.

So, the 'great years' were actually before *"The Diaries"* start.

I think, you're right, by the time you get to the fifties and sixties, when he's suddenly a man of a lot of leisure! He's suddenly kind of retired, living in Switzerland—he has time to write.

"The Diaries" do become, not just journals of *whom* he met, and *where* he went—but they become much more *essays*.

He began writing, not every day, but every week. That makes a great difference. If you write every day you obviously put *"got up, cleaned teeth, met so and so, had lunch"* If you write once a week you *forget* all the boring bits of the week. What you do is a kind of weekly letter to *yourself* That's what *"The Diaries"* then become. They become essays, really, about *England.*

He writes about America. He writes about the Kennedys. He writes about Marilyn Monroe. He writes about things he's read in the papers. He writes about *all kinds* of issues that would *not* normally have concerned him when he was in the midst of rehearsal in London or New York.

AF: It's interesting that he writes a number of times about the issue of homosexuality and the change in the laws here that didn't happen; then when they *did,* but he never really talks about his *own.*

SM: I don't think there was any great secret there. He indeed was homosexual for most of his life, but it wasn't, in his case, tremendously character forming, or significant, or influential part of his life. He wasn't the kind of gay like Tennessee Williams, who actually it *does* affect. It does affect the work. It affects the life.

Noël had a very Victorian sense of sexuality, sex being *not* one of the most important things in life. Noël was a very puritanical man. He was a man absolutely in the old English Victorian virtues: *the virtues of hard work,* the virtues of keeping yourself *in trim,* not *giving in* to sex, emotion, alcohol, worry, paranoia—the old disciplines which are absolutely enshrined in Noël's family background, in his suburban London childhood, and in the kind of England he believed in—like Mountbatten, indeed, like Niven to some extent, like *all* of those men who went *abroad* and *stood for England.*

He believed in an absolute discipline.

Noël's life, really, was *work.* Noël worked eight, ten, twelve, fifteen hours a day. *Noël would do, literally, ten or twelve hours on the typewriter every day.* Now, a life like that didn't leave much *time* for sex. Of course, there were one or two very happy and long-lasting affairs. But they were not, I think, in his life, of such importance that you'd expect to find them either in *"The Diaries"* or, indeed, in the plays.

He wasn't the kind of writer who *used* himself as an autobiography. He did *use* jokes he'd overheard. Jokes he'd, indeed, made up. He *used* friends in his plays. He *used* London life. But homosexuality wasn't, I think, anything that he himself regarded as of tremendous importance, either to himself or to his work. He got rather bored with the *'coming out of closets'* that went on towards the end of his life among his colleagues, friends and contemporaries. He didn't really understand why there was this fascination with sex. It wasn't something he ever shared.

There was a wonderful quote somewhere—

He said, "Sex has been important to me, but when the time comes that I can go to bed with an apple and a good book, I certainly shall."

[Ed: he is paraphrasing a line from *"Present Laughter"*]

And then, one thought that the *apple* and the good *book* were actually rather more important than the *sex.* I think that's not unique among his generation, that didn't allow their sexuality to condition themselves, or their work, or their *lives.*

He *didn't give in* to passionate affairs.

AF: I'm wondering if there's going to be a book of letters published at some point? There must be a lot of letters.

SM: The short answer is, no. We looked at that and thought about it very hard. Oddly enough, *there aren't a lot of letters.*

Noël was one of the very early *'telephones.'*

Noël, unfortunately, coincided in his career with the coming of the telephone. So, from about the middle twenties, Noël was one of the first to *leap* on to the phone as a way of communicating. Therefore, his letters tend to be fairly abrupt. They are usually thank you notes for presents, or first night telegrams. He did not actually put much of himself—because he was doing *"The Diaries"*, and because he had done not only the first autobiography *"Present Indicative"* but also the wartime one *"Future Indefinite"*—he didn't put much of himself into his letters.

I once did ask to see what there was. I wrote to a number of friends and said, "Send me your Coward letters." When I went through them, they were surprisingly thin. There really isn't enough there for a book. I think there are one or two letters that would be fun to have in print, but not nearly enough to make a whole volume.

AF: Hadn't his mother saved all of his letters?

SM: Mother saved his *childhood* letters, but they're *very* childhood letters, they really are. I don't think you'd do much service to the Coward memory by printing a few old schoolboy letters.

Also, I think there is a limit.

I mean *I've* done a biography. Cole Lesley has done a marvelous biography called *"Remembered Laughter"*. We've now done *"The Diaries"*. We've done the *album of photographs.*

I *would* quite like to do *"The Films of Noël Coward"* which, I think, no one has yet done, which is rather important. [Ed: Barry Day's book, *"Coward On Film"* pub. 2005]

He went through *sixty years* of filming!

He started with Lillian Gish in 1917 for D. W. Griffith [Ed: *"Hearts of the World"*] in the silent movies. He went right through

"In Which We Serve" and the major wartime movies. Then, of course, he wrote *"Brief Encounter"*.

Then, you get the films in the sixties when he's the *guest* star, like in *"Our Man In Havana"* and *"Italian Job"* and the film with the Burtons, *"Boom!"* So, there's a lot of film work there, which I think needs to be looked at, and perhaps catalogued properly.

AF: Is there any archive maintained?

SM: Oh, yes! There are two or three. First of all, in *Switzerland,* where Graham Payn still lives in Noël's last home. There is a huge library and a vast file of press cuttings and records.

In *London* there is a marvelous office run by Joan Hirst, who was his secretary, which again, keeps a lot of archives for journalists who want information.

Then in *Jamaica,* where he died, the *Jamaican National Trust* kept his home there, as a kind of writer's retreat. There too, there are some papers and letters and books, but unfortunately the Jamaican climate, being very damp, means that we had to move all the stuff out of there, because the books literally do start to crumble. The damp does get to them.

So, *most* of the material is in Switzerland.

[Ed: Joan Hirst passed away in 2002. In 1999 an archive was established at The University of Birmingham, England, where the Coward papers will be collected. Some have already been acquired from the office of the late Joan Hirst.]

AF: There is a play that he mentioned in the last bit of the diary, *"Age Will Not Wither Us"* that he was working on. Had he finished some scenes or an act?

SM: I don't think he ever got much further than a few scenes with that. He left behind one or two fragments, and indeed, one or two unpublished plays, but they're not tremendously strong, and I don't think there's a case for dredging them up, simply because they happen to be by him.

If you look after someone's estate, you have a duty to preserve it, not only at its best, but also to make sure that the things that he in his lifetime didn't publish, *don't* simply get thrown up into print because he happens to be dead. [Ed: Barry Day's book, *"The Unknown Noël"* pub. 2001, published the fragment as *"Age Cannot Wither"*]

AF: I was just reading part of *"The Diaries"* this morning. I understand that when Lorn *Loraine* was dying from cancer, Noël said he hoped that he would go to bed when it was his time, and I guess he really did.

SM: He did. In fact, in Jamaica, when he was with Graham Payn and Cole Lesley, he left them at night and said, *"Good night, my darlings"* and went to bed, and died, virtually, in his sleep.

It was a wonderful way to go.

It was sadly early. He was only seventy-three, but he had been ill for a while, and it was, indeed, a wonderful way to go.

AF: Noël's knighthood, at the age of seventy, came with a resurgence of interest in his work, and there was a ceremony at Westminster Abbey, the other day which was marvelous.

SM: I thought it was very moving to see that huge abbey used as a kind of orchestra hall for his songs, and to hear that marvelous romantic 1930's music welling up from that great auditorium.

Then, of course, on Sunday at Drury Lane Theatre, we had a kind of sing-along with a lot of people doing his songs. One is always amazed by how many of those songs actually do survive, and how strong they are—either how *jokey,* or how *evocative,* or how *symbolic* of a kind of England that he wrote about.

I think *a lot* of his autobiography is actually *not* in *"The Diaries"* but in the *songs.*

I think a lot of those songs—songs like *"I Travel Alone"* and *"I Am No Good At Love"*—those are songs that, I think, summarize an awful lot about Coward—the sense of *loneliness;* a sense of *isolation;* a sense of *fascination* with travel—*"Sail*

Away"—a sense of *constant exploration* and *inquiry.* And, also, I think, a sense of *detachment*

He was an observer.

He was very like Maugham in that sense. He was a *'man of his time,'* but also he stood back and saw that the *kind* of England that he most *loved* and most understood, was actually *doomed*—I think, by the war, and by the coming of the fifties and the *change.* Travel to him was *boats,* and not planes.

Somehow, the whole world that he *believed in—changed.* It just ceased to be economically feasible.

SHERIDAN MORLEY

b. 1941 December 23, 1989

Interviewed December 1989

Sheridan Morley is a journalist, author and broadcaster, who was the first biographer of Noël Coward, and has for many years served as an adviser to the Coward Estate. He was interviewed in his London home.

ALAN FARLEY: I'm here with Sheridan Morley, who is the deviser *of "Noël and Gertie"*. It has just opened in the West End. It's a show about Noël Coward and Gertrude Lawrence, which has a long history, doesn't it?

SHERIDAN MORLEY: Well, it does, Alan, yes, it goes back about ten years. I wrote a book about Noël Coward, in fact, the *first* biography, way back in 1969, called *"A Talent To Amuse"*—at his own invitation. I then got to know him very well. Towards the end of his life, he became a great friend of mine, and my son, who is now twenty-three, became his last godchild. I rather carefully didn't get to know him too well *while* I was writing the book. I wanted it to be a critical biography and not a fan book. So, I didn't really become a friend until *after* the book had been published.

Then we began talking, particularly about the influence of Gertrude Lawrence, who was, to me, a very shadowy figure, because she had, of course, been living in America since 1940, and she had died in 1952. So, she was largely unknown to my generation. I'm now forty-nine. Very few people in this country, under sixty, ever saw her live, and she'd only made a couple of quite bad films. So, she was very much the unknown quantity in the Coward pattern.

But Noël kept talking to me about her, and saying that, "You'll never understand my work till you understand about *her*, because we were children together in the first world war. We went through the 1920's together."

Although we know he was extremely gay, Gertie was in many ways the mother, the sister, the friend, the partner, the lover he never had. If you look closely at his work, you'll find that nearly all his best plays and best songs are about the *impossibility* of love. They are about people unable to live together—unable to live apart. *"Private Lives"*—*"Blithe Spirit"*—where she's a ghost, *"Design for Living"* where you have a triangle—and I think all of that, in a way, has to do with Gertie.

She was the unattainable love of his life.

All the great songs, all the great plays from *"Private Lives"* to *"Brief Encounter"*, which became a film for Celia Johnson, were in fact written for <u>Gertie</u>.

At the end of his life, which was—what?—twenty years after her death, and forty years after *"Private Lives"*

Noël said to me—

"You know, every night and every morning I go to sleep and I wake up thinking about her in that white Molyneaux dress, on that balcony in the south of France for 'Private Lives' and she would simply take my breath away."

So, I began to get more and more fascinated by her, and I began to realize that you had to approach Coward through *her*. She was the *key* to a lot of *mystery* about Coward.

Then, **at his urging,** I wrote a book about her ten years ago, called *"A Bright Particular Star"*. Then having had these two books written, I looked at them and thought, "There's something *more* here. There's a kind of stage show."

So, I began about ten years ago putting together—originally, a sort of *concert* for charity and Sunday nights, and arts festivals—a mixture of letters, and diaries, and songs, either written *for* Gertie, or *about* Gertie, by Noël, or sung by them both, or acted by them both.

Over the years, I refined it, *and* refined it, and organized it, and changed it like a jigsaw puzzle—played with it, and took pieces out, and put them back in other orders. It's like an old fashioned revue, in a way. It has jokes, songs, dances, sketches, scenes, parodies and *bits of everything*—it's like a *collage*. I began readjusting it, shaping it and changing it.

Then, about two years ago, Patricia Hodge was very keen to play it, and we began doing it with her in very small spaces like the Donmar Warehouse.

She was the one who said, "Look, I really think there is a West End show here."

We began, therefore, again revising it. Simon Cadell, who had played it some ten years ago for me, came back to it. We have now, to our great delight, got a West End success! We've had some of the best reviews this week I've ever seen. I am a critic, myself. *I couldn't have written better reviews than I have got for this show!* Quite rightly *they* have, because it's really more *their* show than *mine* now. *They're* the ones who do it every night. I feel that my child has grown up, in a way.

I watch them doing it and think, "Well, it's no longer quite my baby," but I do still feel very proud of it. Like my children suddenly getting cars and going off on their own, I feel this show now takes on a life of its own, away from me. I'm just thrilled to have been its parent.

AF: Well, I think you've done a marvelous job, too, of putting this collage together. I mean, it isn't like a collage at all, it's really quite seamless. To me, the resonances that you get from certain extracts and songs that one didn't think of—in connection with Gertrude Lawrence—just work marvelously well.

SM: Well, I have tried, of course, to not make it too abrupt, and not make the transitions—from play, to song, to scene, to letter, to diary, to poem—too jerky.

There *are* wonderful keys to their partnership. If you look at *"Brief Encounter"* which is, of course, the film that became world famous, really was written for Gertie as a play [Editor: *"Still Life"* from *"Tonight at 8:30"*] Again, it's about two people, who can't live apart, can't live together. So, we used that almost through the whole second half as a kind of metaphor for their real lives.

I have, of course, *cheated-in* songs from other shows, songs that were not written precisely for what we use them for. When, for instance, Gertie goes to America, she sings, *"Sail Away"*—which was a song Noël, in fact, wrote for himself and for Graham Payn to sing. It was never written for Gertie, but it summarizes what Gertie did at that moment. She *sailed away* from Noël. She left him. I think Noël was never quite the same after her death.

There was a moment, in about 1950, when she commissioned Rogers and Hammerstein to write *"The King and I"* as a musical! She had *seen* the movie, *"Anna and the King of Siam"* with Rex Harrison and Irene Dunne, and she had *asked* Richard Rodgers and Oscar to make it into a musical.

In fact, it was the *only* time in their lives they actually did a *commissioned* job. They *never* ever worked for anybody else but themselves, but *they took her commission,* took her money, went away and wrote *"The King and I".*

Gertie, then, *went* to Noël with it and said, *"You've got to play the king!"*

Noël said [politely], "No, I really don't like *long runs,* and it will clearly be a *huge hit.* I *don't* like singing *other* people's music."

He suggested a young cabaret guitarist he'd seen, called Yul Brynner, and ***that's*** how Brynner ***got*** the job!

During the run on Broadway, Gertie's health got worse and *worse.* Rogers and Hammerstein wrote to Noël and said, "Look, you're her great friend. Can you persuade her to leave the cast, because she really *isn't* very well, and her voice is getting very croaky."

Noël wrote to her and said, "Look, you know . . . do be careful."

But she said, "I've never given up before. I will not give up now."

She had one great dream. Her dream was to come back to London for the Coronation Summer of 1953, and play *"The King and I"* at Drury Lane, and she was sure that if she left the show on Broadway, she would *not* get that chance.

So, she clung to the show, *and clung to the show,* even though she was in ill health.

Then one afternoon in September 1952, Noël was on a racecourse here in England, at a place called Folkstone. In those days you could back horses, not just on the track you were on, but *other* tracks around the country, and there was a horse called

'Bittersweet' running in the north of England. So, of course, Noël *had to* back it, and, as he was leaving Folkstone races that night, he bought the evening paper to check whether the horse had won, and he turned to the "Stop Press" and saw—

GERTRUDE LAWRENCE

It absolutely *floored* him.
He went home. The London Times rang and asked him to write the obituary. He said, through the tears, he "could *hardly* write."
He finally wrote,

"No one I have ever known, however gifted, however brilliant, has contributed quite what she did to my work. Her quality was to me unique and her magic imperishable."

And that seems to me very central to any understanding of Coward.
They had an *extraordinary* friendship. Obviously, it finished very sadly, and although he lived on for twenty more years, he never again really wrote a great song or a great play, because the inspiration had gone with her.
But—they had a very *funny* time when she finally married Richard Aldrich, who ran the theatre on Cape Cod. She, therefore, *left* Noël, *left* England, *left* the West End and settled in America.
Noël sent her a wire, which read,

"Dear Missus 'A'
HOORAY! HOORAY!
At last you are deflowered!
On this, as every other day,
I love you,
Noël Coward"

Then, years later, he tried to cable her for an opening night, and he wanted to **sign** the cable, **"Mayor LaGuardia"**—*who was, then, the mayor of New York*—Fiorello.

And the Operator said, "Is your name *REALLY Mayor LaGuardia?"*

Noël said, "Well, uh, *NO*."

The Operator said, "In *THAT* case, you may *NOT SIGN* the cable *'Mayor LaGuardia'*. [pause] What is you *REAL* name?"

He said, "Noël Coward."

[pause]

The Operator said, "Is it *REALLY Noël Coward?"*

He said, *"Yes!"*

[pause]

She said, "Then you *MAY* sign it *'Mayor LaGuardia."*

Which, I thought, was lovely!

AF: You've been doing a lot besides this—your biographies of David Niven, and James Mason—you're working now on the biography of Sir John Gielgud. [Pub. 2002]

SM: That's right, Alan, I've been asked by Sir John to write the authorized biography, which I regard as a major task, because, obviously, John, rather like Noël, *IS* the history of the English theatre in this century. They, in fact, began together. John was Noël's understudy in *"The Vortex"*, which *made* Noël's name, way back in 1924.

So, to some extent, I've covered that ground before, but in a very different way with Noël, who, obviously, *wasn't* a Shakespearean actor. And, although it is a great honor to be asked by John to write his book, it is also rather daunting, because you feel you are dealing with the *last of the giants,* now that Olivier has gone, *and* Redgrave, *and* Richardson. Gielgud is the *last* of that extraordinary generation of Shakespearean giants. We shall never again—I mean, our lifetime has been so *lucky.* Yes, there was Garrick, and Irving, and Keane, but they were a hundred years apart. We had these *four great knights* in the *same* generation!

AF: I came across your compilation on CD, *"The Compact Coward"* which I was very pleased to see transferring some of those recordings to CD now.

SM: That's right. It suddenly occurred to me that there was now a whole young audience of record buyers, who only had CDs in this country. CDs have taken off in a very big way over here, as you know. And it seemed to me they were missing out on the old Coward—what we called 'LP's'—the old twelve inch "long playing' records, which I've always had, rather scratched. It seemed to me we had to bring Coward to a *new* audience, who were into CD players.

So, we put, indeed, *twenty* of his best tracks from cassette and from long playing record onto CD. We hope very much to do some more.

AF: Also, then, you put out the book of paintings, too, after the auction.

SM: That's right! That was an extraordinary time, because Graham, (who as you know was Noël's executor, heir and great friend), always had this collection of Coward paintings.

As the years went by, he said, "Really and truly, they should be more publicly available than they are—simply in his house in Switzerland."

So, I said, "We'll offer them to a museum or to a gallery."

We offered them to a number of English museums, who were very kind of off-putting and said, "Well, they're *not really very good* paintings, and although they *are* by Noël Coward, we don't quite see what to *do* with them. They're not really great art."

Finally, after we had offered them to all kinds of people who *turned them down,* I said to Graham, "Why not simply sell them and give the money to charity?"

So, we invited Christie's, the big auction house, to come over and value them. Christie's understandably said, "Well, we don't know quite *how* to value these, because they're not great *paintings,* but they are by an interesting *man"* The only parallel is Winston Churchill, who, of course, painted landscapes a great deal. Again, they weren't great paintings, but they were by Churchill, so they sold quite well.

So, Christie's said, "On the evidence of the Churchill sales, we think we can probably estimate *ten thousand pounds* per canvas."

We had thirty of them, so we thought, "Well, that's *three hundred thousand* pounds—very nice for charity—and fine!"

So, we had the auction, and the bidding started.

Every single painting went for *THREE TIMES* the estimate! We finished up with a **MILLION POUNDS!**

And THEN—because they were bought by private collectors—I realized they were AGAIN going to *vanish* into Swiss banks, or whatever. So, before they actually got handed over to the purchasers, I got them all photographed, and we put them together into a book called, *"Out In The Midday Sun"* which Phaidon have published in England, and it's available in the States, I think quite recently. That really is a collection of just Noël's paintings.

As Noël said, "My **'TOUCH and GAU—guin period'.**"

The paintings are landscapes, basically, of Jamaica, where he lived and died, and which he loved very much.

AF: Your regular positions include doing theatre criticism and broadcasting.

SM: Yes, I do, like you, a lot of radio, over here, about the theatre and the cinema. I review and interview and I have a column in the *"Herald Tribune"* which is a theatre column. I am the drama critic there, and have been for fifteen years, and I'm just taking over as the television critic *of "The Times"* which starts in January. So, I'm starting at the age of fifty a whole new life of television viewing, which may, or may *not* be a good thing. I shall report back to you in a year or two's time on how *that* works!

AF: Also, I see your *"Theatre Quiz"* in theatre programmes everywhere.

SM: That I've done for years. I began it as a book, actually. I've always been kind of intrigued by quizzes and trivia quizzes, even before Trivial Pursuit ever appeared, I was into all that.

AF: In your work with Methuen [publishers] trying to organize the Coward *oeuvre,* what is currently available, and what plans are there for bringing more of Coward's work forward?

SM: Well, we've now got *ALL* the plays into five volumes called *"Play Parade* and we've now got the *complete* set of plays. We've done the *short stories,* we've done the *poems,* the *lyrics,* I think we have now nearly got *everything* into print, but the trouble is that some go out of print, and we have to get them back *in,* in a kind of uniform edition.

The *plan* is to have the *full* Methuen set, and you can then buy the lyrics, the plays, the songs, the poems, the short stories, in the same red binding, and you can have a shelf of Coward.

NED SHERRIN

b. 1931

Interviewed January 13, 1993

Ned Sherrin is a writer, director, performer, and broadcaster, who has published numerous books of show business anecdotes, and studies of the works of songwriters. He was interviewed in his London home.

ALAN FARLEY: I'm trying to find out what I can about Noël's songs—when they were written, what each one was written for, and anything about them.

NED SHERRIN: Cyril Ritchard, who played my part in *"Side By Side by Sondheim"* in Chicago, told me the one about the *three nuns,* which I'm sure you know, in *"I Wonder What Happened to Him?"*

Whatever became of old Keeling?
I hear that he got back from France And frightened three nuns in a train in Darjeeling By stripping and waving his lance!

Cyril said to Coward, "I really think this is very, very *offensive,* because, uh, you know, I have an aunt who ***is*** a nun." Coward—who *wasn't* going to *change* it, said, "Alright! I'll make it *FOUR* nuns!"

[they laugh]

There was Coward's one about going 'round to see Cyril.

Cyril was playing *"Private Lives"* in New York just after the war. Coward thought it was *terrible*—the *performance,* the *production*—but he *also* realized that it was bringing him income, because it was quite a success. He *didn't* want to upset Cyril, so he went 'round.

Noël was transfixed by Cyril's new toupee!

Cyril eventually said, "What do you think of my new piece?" Coward said, "Oh, *my god!* Is *that* what it is? I thought it was a yachting cap."

[laughs]

235

But *Cyril was triumphant,* because when he was doing *"Sigh No More"* his voice gave out from doing all those numbers. He was not too pleased to hear that the *understudy* was not going on, but that The Master was coming on **himself,** to play.

Noël learnt it all very quickly.

Cyril had always *complained* that the role was *too taxing for the voice.* He was *thrilled* to hear that—(Coward took over on Thursday)—by Saturday night *HiS* voice had given out! So, Cyril had to *come back* on Monday, because The Master's voice had *gone,* too! He was *triumphant* about that! They were obviously, in a sort of a love/hate relationship.

AF: What is your familiarity with the songs?

NS: Oh, I mean, I've heard them all the time. I *grew up* hearing them.

I thought that Roderick Cook's compilation, *"Oh, Coward!"* was the best! Whereas, the one in *"Cowardy Custard"* seemed to me to be sort of overblown. Roderick's is so elegant and sharp, and economical. That wonderful way of doing *"Marvelous Party"* as though he had a terrible hangover, and he couldn't crack his face at all, was wonderful.

I did a *disastrous* version! I *directed* a disastrous version of *"Cowardy Custard"* simply using the material in Connecticut at Goodspeed, with Millicent Martin and Jeremy Brett. But, we always *filled* the theatre at *Goodspeed!*—it seems NOTHING will keep the audience away.

They were immensely *puzzled* by it all.

There was one wonderful woman at one interval, I heard, saying to her friend, "Now, just **who *was*** this *Noël Coward guy?* Was he the one who collaborated with Hitler during the war?"

I mean, she'd got it *wrong* every way! She thought he was P. G. Wodehouse. She thought that P. G. Wodehouse literally had—you know, I mean, EVERYTHING was wrong about it.

I don't think that that bit of Connecticut was absolutely ready for that show—but we didn't do it very successfully anyway.

AF: It hasn't really played the States, except perhaps for that.

NS: *"Oh, Coward!"* constantly, is played all over. That was the only attempt at doing *"Cowardy Custard"* there. They just tried doing *"Noël and Gertie"* haven't they, off-Broadway? Who did that there? I don't know, because Patricia Hodge [Editor: and Simon Cadell] did it wonderfully here. She's the natural successor.

AF: I saw her here in it. Excellent. Did you know Coward?

NS: I used to meet him off and on. He was a friend of my friend, Caryl Brahms, with whom I've collaborated a lot, and they were near contemporaries. A couple of years between. But he was interesting. He always seemed to have a tremendous interest in anybody sort of big and exotic, and a tremendous interest in anybody who had absolutely no credentials at all. You know, I mean, somebody terribly small he would find fascinating. I was somewhere away in—between on the downside. One time I engaged his attention was at a party, and I'd been doing a lot of research on Marie Lloyd, because Caryl and I were going to do a great English music hall stuff, and although she didn't die until 1922, and he'd seen her, he didn't know much about her. I sort of awakened an interest in him because I'd been doing a lot of research about her, and he lapped it up. That's the only time I sort of felt that one had engaged his attention at all.

AF: Do you have any particular favorites among his songs?

NS: I think, on the whole, I like all the **patter** *songs,* better.
   I'm very fond of *"A Little Eggy Something On A Tray"* [from *"After The Ball"*], which I gather that Irene Browne insisted on having, because she didn't have a song in the show, and she suddenly realized—because she had been in *"No, No, Nannette"* a *hundred years before*—she suddenly realized, belatedly, that people who *had songs* were getting *applause* at the end of them. So, she'd better *have* one.
   There's a wonderful story of her in the tour of *"After The Ball"* . . . .
   Patricia Cree was playing Lady Agatha, the little girl who marries *Mr. Hopper,* Graham Payn's part, who goes off with her.

Patricia got *ALL* the notices out-of-town, and Irene was *furious* about that!

Irene wasn't getting ANY notices.

I think they were at the Bristol Hippodrome when Pat Cree *delivered herself* into Irene's hands, really, by being *late for an entrance!* . . . .

Irene is playing her mother. So, Irene was left onstage with no one to talk to—*a cardinal sin in the theatre.* The girl eventually arrived and they played the scene.

But, at the END of the scene, *she bore down on her* in the wings! Vanessa Lee, who was playing the good girl, sensing trouble, *zoomed in on the two of them,* and said, "Oh, Irene! *Do* be kind to the poor girl! *Look at her!* She's THIN as a MATCH!"

Irene said, "Precisely! She should be STRUCK and *thrown* AWAY!"

[they laugh]

Which is good enough for Coward or Wilde, really, isn't it?

AF: Yes.

NS: There are too many. I do on the whole like the patter songs better than the other stuff.

I think he wrote more *absolute rubbish* than most people of the same distinction. Mind you, if you look through the scores of *anybody,* there's a lot of *rubbish,* but there's a *huge* amount of rubbish—but then, *marvelous* things. I'm very keen on the one that Graham sang in *"Waiting In The Wings".*

AF: *"Come The Wild, Wild Weather"*?

NS: Yes, yes. It's a very pretty song. I did a series over here that PBS did, *"Song by Song"* where Gemma Craven sang that, and Cleo Laine sang lots of nice things, as well. David Kernan and Ian Carmichael did a very good sort of duet of *"I Wonder What Happened To Him?"* which is another favorite.

The extraordinary thing, I think, is the 'attack' that you see on that two-handed show that he did with Mary Martin [*"Together With Music"*]. It's just extraordinary, the 'attack' and the *not stopping-off for a laugh,* you know. I've sat through so many performers trying to WRING *a laugh* out of various things, and failing dismally. Whereas, he seems to just do it *effortlessly* by plowing on, and having *confidence* in the material, or he wouldn't be performing it.

What's the one that he gave Graham? *"I Like America"* isn't it?—which Graham always had trouble getting any reaction from. He thought it was a *terrible* song. Noël finally put it into a program of his *own,* and found *exactly* the same. That it really *doesn't* work.

Did you see him *live?*

AF: No, I didn't.

NS: I saw also the *last,* the three plays, [*"Suite in Three Keys"*], which was rather sad, because, plainly, that's when the memory went, and he *was* so meticulous about knowing every word of the script, first of all.

Have you seen Peter O'Toole? O'Toole's a most enormous fan of Noël's. He's in a play I just directed. He has ACRES of Coward stories.

AF: Oh, really?

NS: Wonderful story about Peter O'Toole going to Switzerland and staying.

Noël said, "Oh, *at last* I have my music *properly* sung! It's absolutely ravishing!"—and he brought out that AWFUL Joan Sutherland recording, and *put it on!* He said, *"THIS* is the sort of voice that I really *need* for my music!" (Plainly, Coley and Graham had heard it countless times, and didn't entirely approve.)

Peter listened to about three tracks and finally said, **"It's CRAP, Noël!"**

Whereupon, Noël *STAMPED* on the record and *THREW* it into the bin, because he realized that he'd been kidding himself that this was any good!

When we started doing *"Jeffrey Barnard Is Unwell"*, Peter had just been about to mount a production of *"Present Laughter"*. Noël is his great idol—so, Peter goes through a script—*as Coward did*—**marking the laughs with a red pencil**—'*There WILL be a laugh HERE!*'—and if there *isn't*, he wants to know *why!* So, he's absolutely the most enthusiastic Coward devotee *I* know. Coward and Shaw are his two gods, apart from Shakespeare.

AF: Well, let me ask you a little bit about *you*.

NS: What about me?

AF: How you got into this business.

NS: I was doing revues at Oxford and the BBC televised one. The leading lady was also the assistant stage manager, (from the local repertory company, The Oxford Playhouse), who was Margaret Smith, in those days—now, *Dame* Maggie. It was televised, and it went awfully well. I then finished my finals, and went on to take bar exams, which took about another six months.

I was walking down The Strand the day after I'd been called to the bar, and I met a man who'd been the stage manager, or studio manager of the broadcast on the BBC, and he said, "What are you doing?"

I said, "I'm a barrister."

He said, "Oh. Well, we're starting commercial television next week. Why don't you come and join us?"

So, we had lunch, and *I* went back and saw his boss, who said, "What are you doing?" I said, "I'm a barrister."

He said, "Oh! I'm afraid we can only offer you a producer's job."

So, *I started* as a *producer!* I joined on the Monday, and we started transmissions on the Thursday, I think. So, I went straight in as a producer! They quite soon found out that *I didn't know anything* about it.

So, I *couldn't* be a producer, but I was a sort of 'tea boy' which is what I'd always *expected* to be!

For the first three months I was paid and established as a producer, and then they started up another station, the first of the regional stations in Birmingham, and I went there.

I went from there to the BBC and did *"That Was The Week That Was"*. I invented and started it back in the sixties. From that I went on and did some more BBC stuff. I became a movie producer for four or five years. Then the bottom fell out of that. I did *"Side By Side By Sondheim"* and in the *meantime,* I've been *writing* with Caryl Brahms, who died in 1982. That's a rough rundown on a life.

AF: Are you mostly directing these days?

NS: Sometimes I direct. I do a lot of *presenting* or *hosting* as it's called on the radio or the 'telly.' We do a lot of AIDS benefits, more and more as the time goes by. A lot of *"Noël and Cole"* evenings tend to crop up—Noël and Cole, Sondheim, always seem to bring the queens out, with either of those combinations.

We did one for Elizabeth Welch just before Christmas, who's eighty something. She was quite funny.

Noël said to her, "Oh, Liz," (she sang *"Twentieth Century Blues"* at his seventieth anniversary concert), he said, "Oh, darling Liz, it's *so awful* that we've *never* worked together!" She said, "No, *it isn't,* honey. If we'd worked together, we wouldn't be FRIENDS!"

[laughs]

If you look through his diaries, *every time* he starts a new project—*'The NEW leading lady is going to be PERFECT! She is the answer to all'*—you know—*'the LAST leading lady was TERRIBLE! The NEW one is just IMPECCABLE and WONDERFUL!'*

And then by the end of the thing, it's all in tatters, and, *'She can't remember!'*—and—*'She doesn't do it!'*—and—*'She can't get a laugh!'* and all those things. It was an absolute cycle like that.

Bea Lillie, or whoever it is, he starts out saying—'wonderful to be back with Bea, *again!* Oh, such a distinctive artist!'

241

Then, by the end, he's saying, *'she won't learn her line! she's not on, she's off!'*

It's an extraordinary pattern.

AF: I think of Sondheim in the same vein as far as the songs.

NS: Yes, he *hates* being compared. One of Coward's little foibles, I think, is to say to any songwriter who emerges with any sort of distinction, "Ah! You're the ME of today!"

Lionel Bart was always flattered when he said that. Lionel gave Caryl a rhyming dictionary inscribed,

"Do not let this aim to rhyming Bitch your talent or your timing."

I said to him, "What a nice phrase."

He said, "Oh, I only wrote that in it, because *that's* what Noël wrote in *MY* book!"

[they laugh]

I think Noël told Stephen Sondheim that Stephen was *'the Coward of the present.'* Stephen *didn't* think very highly of *that*. He thought that was more pejorative than praising.

AF: Let's get back to your being producer and creator of *"That Was The Week That Was"*.

NS: It was fun to do at the time. A couple of good years.

We had a very good Coward *parody* on *"That Was The Week"* with David Kernan. Lyrics were by Herbert Kretzmer, who wrote the lyrics for the English version of *"Les Miserables"*.

Have you come across that?

It won't take but two seconds to read it. It's very good. I forget what it was prompted by, but I think it was the beginning of all that 'loose living' in the 1960's.

[reading:]
Teenager, teenager, living so terribly fast,
Selling your soul to the nearest bidder,
Why don't you hesitate to consider Where it may lead at last?

Glittering child of tender years Who's only half alive,
You've lost your precious "honor'
In clouds of marijuana.
In Greek streets the urgent beat Of saxophones throb till five.
No wonder half you beggars Are preggers.
To tell the truth, when! was a youth,
Temptations were much fewer.
We drank May wine, but towed the line,
And kept ourselves quite pure.
For life devours our precious hours,
And we've terribly few to spare.
Teenager—
Better beware.
Teenager, teenager, your life's a merry hell.
Come fill the flowing cup and drink it.
You see yourself as just a trinket,
And sin a mere bagatelle.
Frivolous girl in frightful jeans Collecting scores of boys,
You add to your collection,
All manner of infection.
In Soho, they sink so low,
They sell erotic joys.
And if they're feeling seedy,
It's V.D. k's a terrible town, when the sun goes down,
And the Junky Jazzman sings.
And you can't dismiss the nemesis That's waiting in the wings.
Before you rot, cease your mad gavotte,
Or your end must be despair.
Teenager, better take care.
Teenager, better beware."
    [stops reading]
It's nice isn't it?

AF: Yes. In my effort to interview people there are some I've met, but some are no longer with us. I spoke with Stritchie [Elaine Stritch] just a little over a year ago, and she was a lot of fun.

NS: Yes! She *disgraced* herself on my radio program! I was trying to get the story of the first night in London of *"Sail Away"*—when Noël said to her.

"Now, you know, Stritch, you've got to **behave** yourself, because there are a lot of very *important* people—Vivian Leigh, Kenneth More, and all sorts of people are coming."

So, she dressed *extravagantly. She hadn't had a drink all evening,* and she *dressed extravagantly! And carefully!*

She had to go up in the lift to the top—the penthouse, or wherever it was being held at *The Savoy*—and she found herself in the lift with a very *pissed* Vivian Leigh and Kenneth More.

Stritch was being a *good little girl,* and *looking* like a good little girl.

She got out of the lift to be greeted by Noël Coward who said, "I told you to come *PROPERLY* dressed, but I *didn't* tell you to dress like a fucking **nun!**"

SHE **TOLD** THIS STORY ON THE AIR!

THEN she said, *"Oh, my god!* Oh, you can **cut** that *out, CAN'T YOU? You CAN edit that!?"*

I said, "No. It's *LIVE,* Stritch."

She said, "You mean *LIVE* television?"

I said, "No. *Live* RADIO."

She said, *"Oh, Christ!* I *needn't* have **bothered** to make-up my face."

[they laugh loudly] She is wonderful!

She did a *"Song by Song"* on Dorothy Fields, I think, immediately after she'd come out of the big diabetes thing. *Her dressing room was a mass of broken needles.* It was the first time she'd been shooting herself up, I think. She'd always had somebody to do it for her. She kept breaking the needles. She is wonderful!

AF: Yes, I had to do my interview with Stritch in Central Park, while she was having her lunch—

NS: I'm sure.

AF:—on a *half-hour's* notice! **But at least I got it!**

NS: There is a wonderful story of Peter Graves, who was, I think, Ivor Novello's lover. I'm *sure* this is apocryphal, and *not true,* but there is a wonderful story.

When his father was a baronet, Sir George Graves, who was also a wealthy bookmaker, and he is supposed to have come back from Ascot, or somewhere, past *Red Roofs,* the Novello house—in his Rolls, and chauffeured, and a bit *pissed,* and decided it was *outrageous* that *his son* should be with THIS MAN in THIS HOUSE!

So, he is supposed to have got out of the Rolls and started yelling, **"Give me back my son! Give me back my son!"**

When Coward heard the story, he is supposed to have said, "Ah, yes! Calling the sods!" [they laugh]

But, I *think,* that is totally *apocryphal!*

GRAHAM PAYN

b. April 25, 1918   d. November 5, 2005

Interviewed March 18, 1987

Graham Payn, actor and singer, who was Noël Coward's companion from 1945 until Coward's death in 1973. He appeared in numerous Coward shows, and today heads the Noël Coward Estate. He was interviewed in New York, where he was visiting to see the new revival of Coward's *"Blithe Spirit"* on Broadway, starring Richard Chamberlain, Blythe Danner, Geraldine Page, and Judith Ivey.

ALAN FARLEY: Tell us what your activities are today, as head of the Estate, aside from looking after productions and so on.

GRAHAM PAYN: I've got three appointments today, which is quite light for this visit to New York. I only came here for *"Blithe Spirit"* and then the other things mounted up. It's really for *"Blithe Spirit"* which I saw in Baltimore, and very good they were, too. Excellent. Very good, but it needed a bit of *lightening up,* in the playing, but they were all excellent, and a wonderful cast, and I think that what Director, Brian Murray's done—I haven't seen it yet, but all the reports I've had are that it is excellent. So, I'm looking forward to tonight, which was the original first night, which is why my timing is booked like this. I've got to get back for business.

AF: Day-to-day, what is involved in running the Estate?

GP: Oh, well, there's always *something,* thank goodness. The plays are being done *all over the world!* It really is *amazing.* Germany, France and Italy have discovered Noël Coward in the last two years. They *never* did his plays before.

AF: Are these done in translation?

GP: Yes, in translation.

AF: Who does the translation?

GP: Oh, don't ask me. I keep out of that. So, I wouldn't know anyway. But, there are things all over the place, and here, too, things in the air, which I suppose I mustn't speak about at the moment.

AF: But, it's up to *you* to make the decision, whether or not to allow productions to be done.

GP: Yes, mainly, and also the casting, because that's very important. Sometimes they think a big name would be good, and, it may be a big name and a wonderful actor, but it just doesn't suit the part, or the part doesn't suit him or her. So, we have to watch out for that.

AF: What are the most popular plays these days, as far as the *number* of productions is concerned?

GP: *"Private Lives", "Blithe Spirit", "Present Laughter* are done quite a lot, and surprisingly, *"Fallen Angels".* It's very high, especially in summer stock. They do that a lot, and *"Hay Fever",* too.

AF: I know that *"Hay Fever"* is being done, I think, this Summer at the Shaw Festival in Canada.

GP: Oh, is it? I didn't know that. Oh, thank you for telling me. Right.

AF: I look forward to seeing that. They did such a terrific job with *"Cavalcade.*

GP: I hear they did a marvelous job on that. And wasn't it clever of them to bring it down to commercial size, because it was a great big spectacle at Drury Lane. When they revived it at Chichester, they had *two hundred* extras! They were *amateurs*. Equity allowed the amateurs to come in and fit in, and that was the sort of production it was.

But the Shaw Festival has done a wonderful job and brought it down to commercial size so it can be toured.

AF: Yes, I hope to see it do that.

GP: Yes, because it's so good, it holds, it really does hold. It's excellent.

AF: The anti-war statement in that was so strong, and something I wasn't prepared for.

GP: Yes, well that *is* a pretty strong thing in his mind anyway. Or was, I should say.

AF: So. you were born in South Africa.

GP: That's right.

AF: How did you get from there to have a part in *"Words and Music"* by Noël Coward, when you were fourteen years old?

GP: Well, it's funny, but I'll make it short.

I was a boy singer, a boy soprano. I wanted to be a film actor. I wanted to be like Douglas Fairbanks—*"The Mark of Zorro"* the *"Black Pirate"* and that's it.

My mother said, "Well, come on, if you want to go on the stage, or cinema, we go to London."

So, we came over, and I did all right. Broadcasting, as a kid. Then there was a Noël Coward/Cochran review coming on called *"Words and Music"* I think it was called *"Set To Music"* in America, later.

Anyway, my mother said to me, "I don't think there's much chance for a boy soprano in the Cochran/Coward review, so in case they stop you, you sing and dance at the *same time.*

So I did!

I sang *"Nearer My God To Thee"* and did a *tap dance* to it!
Well, Noël was so impressed by this *extraordinary* exhibition, that he said, "We've *got* to have that kid in the show!"
And *that* was it. That's how I first met him!

AF: What did you do in the show?

GP: Oh, I sang bits and pieces, nothing very much. Oh, I did announce *"Mad Dogs and Englishmen"* my claim to fame.

AF: And who sang that in the show?

GP: Romney Brent.

AF: And Bea Lillie?

GP: She was in the *American* production. There were people I don't think were known all that well here. Steffi Duna was known here, wasn't she? She was in it. Doris Hare, Romney Brent, that's about all the names I can remember.

AF: After the war you were in *"Sigh No More"*.

GP: That's right, yes, because he came to see me in shows.
I didn't see him from 1932 until wartime.
I was invalided out of the army. I'd got the juvenile lead in a revue, called *"Up and Doing"* and he came to see it. He came backstage and he said how *good* I was.
Then a few years went by and I was pretty lucky and had lots of work to do. Kept busy. I was in *"The Lilac Domino"* and I got him tickets to the first night.
He came round in the second interval, and he said, "I've never seen anybody learn so many bad tricks in such a *short* time. You're *terrible* in the show."
He really ticked me off—at the interval in the first night! And then he *left!*

AF: What a time to do that!

GP: I thought, "Well, hell! That's a bloody cheek to come and tell me this when I've got the show to finish!"

I called him up the next day and said, "Well, actually, I *know* what you are talking about. I've been forced to *laugh* on every entrance with a girl on each arm and a glass of champagne in my hand, and *laugh* as I go off and sing very, very loudly. That's not the way I want to do it, but, I'm *told to* by the director. Can I come and sing to you as I really sing?"

So, I went with my singing teacher. I sang as I wanted to sing.

He said, "Oh, that's *quite* different! *Much* better. We'll try and find something for you to do."

AF: For that review, *"Sigh No More"*, he wrote *"Matelot"* for *you*.

GP: That's right. They had another song in its place, which was my solo spot in the second half, with the unfortunate title of *"It Couldn't Matter Less"*, which was apt!

I said, "I can't get this thing." That was the marvelous thing, he being a *director* who could *perform*. Which is why I said, "This is no good. I really can't do this. It isn't good enough. It isn't strong enough."

He said, "Of course it is. It's a *very* good song."

I said, "Well, would *you* get up and do it? *You* show me, because I can't do the *bloody* thing! (I mustn't say that, must I?) I can't do the *DARN* thing."

AF: Oh, that's okay.

GP: Anyway . . . That was so great. He could get up and sing the song himself. He did it once. Then the *second* time he said, "NO. You're quite right. It *isn't* strong enough. It won't hold. Go on, rehearse the bit to it to follow the song, and I'll write you another one."

And I thought, "Oh, yeah, I've heard that story before." I was none too pleased, I can tell you. But luck would have it, he pulled a muscle in his leg, and he had to stay home. Didn't come to rehearsal for three or four days.

He called me up on the telephone and he said, "I had this idea. I've *written* the song! Come down and hear it."

I heard the first eight bars of "*Matelot*" and I said, "That's it! That's wonderful!" And indeed, it *is!*

AF: I think it *remained* one of his favorite songs.

GP: Yes, it did. Very, very romantic song. Difficult to sing, but, also, the secret to that—if there is anybody listening who wants to sing it sometime—is to keep a *good tempo* and *then* put in the expression. The *song carries* you. Just do it *straight*

AF: I've talked to some other actors who've worked with him as a director, and I think they said that he made actors very *comfortable* by giving them precise *technical* instructions about what to do. None of this *feeling* and—

GP: No, no, none of this *inner feeling* stuff, just the *technical* job, get *that* right, and the *words. Think* what you're saying, and they'll come out right. He would get up and do it, and say, "I don't want you to *imitate* me, because that would be silly, but this is the *idea.* This is the *idea* of the way it should be. You do it *your* way on those lines, and that's fine. That's how it *works.*"

And it DOES work. But he was funny, too, because he could chide you a bit, which was all right. I had a number called "*Wait A Bit, Joe*" and he said after it had been running a couple of months, "Well, a little *charm* wouldn't hurt in that number."

"Oh," I thought, "that's funny. I thought it was all right." Anyway, I went on and I smiled a bit more, put in the *charm.*

He came through the pass door, and he said, "I *said,* a *little* charm—not *Mary Rose on* **ice.**"

[laughter] I was *overdoing* it again, you see. So, he got one right *and he* made you laugh. It was great.

AF: Did you sing *"Sigh No More"* as well—the title song?

GP: Yeah, and that's a sonuvabitch to sing, I can tell you. It starts so low and goes up so high. To open up cold, alone on the stage, as *Harlequin,* and had to *open* the show. Very difficult. Nerve wracking. *Especially* on the first night. after, one got used to it, it's a lovely song, a beautiful song.

AF: Bobby Short has done a marvelous recording of it.

GP: Yes, he has, very, very good, indeed, but it's not easy. It's wonderful, but I used to grumble at Noël through the years, with all of the shows we did, I said, "The RANGE is so big in your songs. It's all right for *you, you* have a composer's voice, and you can stretch it as far as you like. I have a limited voice, a beginning and an end."

He said, "Oh, you're always *grumbling.*"

Anyway, it went on, and a wonderful payoff came when Joan Sutherland, *Dame* Joan Sutherland recorded his songs, and after it was all finished she said to me, "They're *not* easy to sing at all, are they?"

So, I said, "If SHE finds it difficult—

You see what I mean?" [laughter]

AF: On some of his recordings, his voice is just fantastically high.

GP: Amazing range, he could sing it, the highest stuff *and* the lower notes, he could hit those, too. He had this extraordinary ear for music. He could hardly *read* music. He certainly couldn't *write* music. Somebody *else* had to write it down. He'd come back after seeing a show, if we went to the theatre together to see a musical, and I promise you, he'd *play* that score *right through*! His *ear,* his *ear* was absolutely *fantastic!* How he could do it!

AF: How did he work when he was writing a song?

GP: He just *played* it, *and* played it, and *played* it until he hoped he wouldn't forget it. Then he got somebody to take it down. A lady called Elsie April used to do it. Then, later, fortunately, the tape recorders came in, so he'd turn it on and that was it.

AF: What about the lyrics?

GP: Oh, well, that he'd do just at his desk and work those out. Wonderful rhymes there too.

AF: Oh, yes the inner rhymes are just—

GP: *Terrific* stuff.

AF: I think that's what first attracted me to his songs—his *lyrics*.

GP: And a difficult one, *"Nina"* is a difficult one.

AF: That was in *"Sigh No More"* also, wasn't it?

GP: That's right. Cyril Ritchard sang that, and Noël did it himself at the *Cafe de Paris* and dried up, or put one verse in the wrong place.
    All the way through the rest of the number he was thinking, how could he get back to the second verse to put it in the right place again?
    How he could concentrate like that was fantastic! How he could change the words around *while* he was singing! Several people have tripped on that one. I've heard three *go up* on it at charity concerts. It's a complicated lyric.

AF: I've noticed a lot of singers sing "O-LAY" at the end of it instead of "O-LAH" as it was written. Not that it makes any major difference, and that in the *"Bar In the Piccola Marina"* where Bea Lillie sings, "Picco-*LO* Marina."

GP: There are different pronunciations. Like in *"If Love Were All"*—in America they sing *"HIGH-Ho, If Love Were All"* and the English pronunciation is *"HEIGH-Ho, If Love Were All."*

AF: That's certainly one of his most wonderful songs. That is one that so many singers have done.

GP: So many singers, and they all sing it well, but again, they're inclined to take it a little *slowly*. The thing with those sort of sentimental songs of his is to keep them *going.* They really carry you. You don't have to *add* to it at all. He's done that in the lyrics and the music.

AF: That one has the lyric, "*The most I've had is just a talent to amuse*", which, of course, was used as the title for Sheridan Morley's biography of Noël.

GP: But it *caught on,* that phrase, *"a talent to amuse"* and it was used a lot *about* him, but *he* never thought of it.

AF: Cole Lesley's book is marvelously written for a first book.

GP: Yes, isn't it good? It really *is* good.

AF: Yes. When I started it, I wondered, "Well, now what is this going to be like? He's never written a book before." I've read some books by—oh, I remember one in particular by a famous musician, and he had written it sort of as *therapy,* after his wife died. I thought, "Well, now is this another one of those therapy books?"
But Cole Lesley's book is not like that by any stretch of the imagination, I mean, it is a first rate biography.

GP: Well, Cole Lesley was a remarkable man, and he really could write. He never had before. It was amazing.

AF: I guess he had helped Sir Noël from time to time in working on plays.

GP: Well, I think working with Noël so much he obviously picked up an awful lot of the technique. They worked together on *"Look After Lulu".* It was when they did the Feydeau farce. Coley worked a lot on that one. I think he did the original translation with Noël. I mean they didn't do a *literal* translation. You can't. You've got to do the English *version* of the French, or the French *version* of the English. You can't translate it *literally.*

AF: Are you writing *your* autobiography?

GP: No, I can hardly write a *letter,* let alone write a *book.* Good god, *no*! No, no, no! That's not my—no, there's nothing to write *about* It's all done in *"The Diaries* ["*The Noël Coward Diaries"* edited by Graham Payn and Sheridan Morley (1982)] really, but it's fascinating, to me, the work I've got to do.

Up there, he and Coley must be laughing their heads off and saying, "That lazy little sod's working at last! Getting down to business!"

[Ed: Payn relented, and in 1994 *"My Life with Noël Coward"* by Graham Payn and Barry Day, was published by Applause Books.]

AF: A continuing concern throughout *"The Diaries"* was his concern for *you* and your career, and always worrying about it.

GP: Yes, he was worried about that, but suddenly it dawned on me—I was awfully *lucky,* really. After several shows, I thought, "Well, you should be further on than this. There's something *lacking,* and it must be the *essential,* which is *star quality."*

This I did not have.

I *thought* I had. I *hoped* I had, but it didn't depress me. I just went on working, as long as anybody was silly enough to give me a job, I went and did it. So, *I worked! That* was the thing. I think, *he* thought that if I wasn't "so *nervous."*

But, I *was* nervous on the stage. I might have come through better.

He thought I *had* got a quality there. He said so.

He said, "Come on! You're too *nervous.* Don't *fuss* about it, go on, ENJOY yourself!"

AF: You also were in *"Pacific 1860"* with Mary Martin in her West End debut in 1946.

GP: Yes, that's right, Drury Lane.

AF: Yes, which, I guess, turned out to be the wrong place for that show.

GP: It was quite the *wrong* theatre for that. It was far too *big. Also, the poor audience!* It was the first show in there *after the war* and the heating wasn't working, and it was *freezing* cold. How Mary got through without getting pneumonia, I don't know. At least I was dressed in jackets and trousers and all that. *She* had these dresses off the shoulder. *Freezing,* it must have been. We could see the audience sitting with *rugs* over their knees, and sitting with their fur coats on!

Unfortunately, the show didn't work, which was a pity, because it's a wonderful score. It really is one of his best.

AF: What's your favorite song from that show?

GP: *"Bright Was The Day"* is a lovely one, and the one that a lady called Sylvia Cecil sang, called *"This Is A Changing World"*—beautiful song, but there are so many in it. Funnily enough, *"Uncle Harry"* comes out of that, which Noël made famous later. It couldn't mean anything in the show.

AF: I seem to recall reading that he had originally written *"Alice Is At It Again"* for that show, but Mary Martin didn't think it was *proper,* so he cut that.

GP: He cut that.

AF: Did it not yet have *"Uncle Harry"* at that time, or was that already part of the show?

GP: No, *"Uncle Harry"* was put in after he got the bad press.
He said, "We'd better *liven this up a bit!*
He had this number at the ready. We put it in to try *liven it up.* Mary *wouldn't* do *"Alice"* I don't know why. It's a very funny song. Mind you, he did *add* to it later, when he did it himself. The lyrics at the end are much stronger in a modern way, so that she *couldn't* have done that. I don't mean that she *couldn't* because she's not *capable,* I mean, it would have been *out of period,* so . . . The song was much stronger *later,* when *he* did it in cabaret.

If you read the lyrics, you'll find that they would be quite wrong for *"Pacific 1860"*.

AF: Yes, yes. *"Pacific 1860"* is set in *Samolo*.

GP: That's right. He *made up* this island.

AF: Also, his novel *"Pomp and Circumstance"* takes place there.

GP: Yes, and making up the *language*. There's a *dictionary* on that! I've got that. It's in the *bank*, if anybody wants to look at it.

AF: I guess it's based a bit on Jamaica.

GP: Yes, and the south sea islands. He loved all those places. He traveled a lot, as you know. Always, went away. He'd be around till the party, when the production opened, then two or three days later, he'd go.

AF: He really had a great love for Jamaica, didn't he?

GP: *Adored* it! *Loved* it! We all did. It's a beautiful island, and his house up at the top! First of all, he bought a house down at sea level, called 'Blue Harbour.' Then he found this place up on the top of the hill, which he called 'Firefly.' We used to go up there for drinks in the evening, and the *fireflies* would come out. It was marvelous! The view down the coastline is fantastic! So, he built the house up there, and that's where he is buried, because, we thought, when he died in Jamaica "Now where? What should we do? Should we take him back to England?"

    A great friend of ours from London telephoned and said, "Well, no. Why don't you leave him where he was so happy? He loved it there. It was his favorite spot." So, we put him where we used to sit and have our Martinis, before the house was built.

AF: Well, it's a fantastic site. I was lucky enough to see it last year.

GP: Oh, good.

AF: It's *beautiful,* the way the museum is situated there.

GP: I hear it's well looked after.

AF: Yes.

GP: They've told me that. Several friends have been to see it.

AF: Now, you maintain the residence in Switzerland.

GP: Yes, that's right.

AF: That's where, I guess, all the archives are located?

GP: Well, they're all in the bank. All the *original* manuscripts, and things like that. Naturally, I'm leaving those to theatre museums. There's *the* theatre museum, 'The Mander and Mitchenson Museum,' but I'm also considering leaving something here in *America.* He *loved* America so much, he really did. He *adored* it.

AF: It annoys me regularly when I see all these tributes to musical theatre in this country, and they always seem to leave out Noël Coward. It's always *American* composers, and *American* lyricists. It seems to me he was as much a part of American theatre as any other composer.

GP: Well, I don't know, because they were so marvelous over here, really, wonderful, Cole Porter's lyrics, and the music of Rodgers and Hammerstein—*marvelous.*

AF: "*Sail Away"* was created first in this country.

GP: And "*The Girl Who Came to Supper"* after that.

AF: Which had some *marvelous* songs in it.

GP: Yes. Now somebody brought that up a few months ago, that they wanted to try it out in England, but it's a very expensive production, so I said, "Well, you better try it out-of-town before you lose a lot of money on the production, in case it doesn't work." But, I think it should.

He wrote *another end* to it, which was never used here. It was a *happier* end. They ended up *together,* instead of their being separated. *I've got that script.* That last scene he wrote.

AF: There have continued to be publications all the time of unknown material. Not long ago, the autobiography was issued with forty pages of the uncompleted third volume.

GP: Oh, that's right. Well, the publisher, Methuen, has been very good in that, getting all the books back that have gone out of print, . the plays, and doing them all in paperback, and the short stories, lyrics, and even the songbook has been put in paperback.

AF: I just saw that yesterday, *"The Collected Verse",* which I had been looking for, for years under the old title *"Not Yet The Dodo".* I came across the new edition with many more verses in it, which I think is just delightful.

GP: It's very good isn't it? And they've done a good job on the presentation of it.

AF: What further productions are in store, do you know?

GP: Well, there's *"Fallen Angels"* coming on in London. That isn't quite set yet, but that should happen now in the next couple of months or so. I am very pleased that finally we are going to do *"Bitter Sweet"* because the Sadler's Wells Opera Company wants to do it. That won't be done again till next year, but I'm very pleased about that. That's a beautiful score.

AF: What other publications are coming out, do you know?

GP: No. There's nothing else to come out. I must say that Weidenfeld, the publishers, keep on saying to me, "Come on, isn't there *anything?"*

I say, "No, there really isn't. Nothing long enough worth publishing."

AF: When I talked to Sheridan Morley a while ago, I asked him about a book of letters, but he said he didn't really write that many letters. He used to telephone.

GP: The sad thing is, nobody in those days in his office thought of asking him to keep a copy of his letters. So, we have no copies. *He used to write quite a lot actually,* so Sheridan was wrong on that one. We don't have any *copies* of any of them. We've got lots of very interesting letters *back* to him, *answering* his letters, we've got all those.

AF: It's very frustrating.

GP: It is frustrating.

AF: The few letters that are published in Cole Lesley's book are fascinating.

GP: Oh, yes, and he was very funny in his letters, too. Even the short postcards he'd send. I suppose it is a natural thing. We don't keep copies of letters we write privately. Do you? At least, I don't think people do, do they?

AF: I know some people who do.

GP: He didn't, unfortunately, because it would be marvelous to read what he'd said, and how he'd phrase the things. But the funny thing is, people have got them, unless they've destroyed them. When Cole Lesley was doing his book on the life of Noël Coward, we advertised in *"The Times"* in *"The Telegraph"* and even *"The Stage"* for copies, if they'd just *lend* a letter to be contributed to the book, and *not one* reply. Not *one.* They just shut up like a clam. Everybody had letters, but "no, no, no" in case we took it away or something. We can't. Well, we CAN, because it is the writer's property, you see. Maybe they were afraid, and not one person replied or sent a letter.

AF: That's amazing.

GP: I think, somebody did write saying that Noël wrote them a "thank you." It said, "thank you very much for a lovely evening" and that's it. Not a letter. It was very, very strange.

AF: He was also in the habit of writing *verses* for people for special occasions.

GP: Oh, yes, like the one he wrote for the Cole Porter song, *"Let's Do It"*. He couldn't wait. He said it's one of the most wonderful rhyming constructions of Cole Porter. The original song was brilliant, wonderful to do. He couldn't wait to get off and do a little to bring it up to date with the people of today, at that time, I mean. And very funny, they are, too. Cole Porter *liked* them, too, which was nice.

AF: You were telling me the other day that you weren't able to see him perform in Las Vegas. You were working elsewhere at that time. He was certainly a great success in Las Vegas.

GP: Oh, it was an *enormous* success. I'm just so sorry I couldn't go, because he wasn't sure whether it was *going* to be a success or not. I mean, it's very special material he had, and whether the public who went for gambling would *like* it, or *understand* what he was doing—he wasn't sure, but it was an *enormous* success and they *loved* it.

    Frank Sinatra took a whole *party*, and flew a chartered plane over there for opening night! Acting most generously, he said during a broadcast to the public,

    "If you want to hear how a song *should be* sung, go and hear Noël Coward at the Desert Inn." Now, that's generous, isn't it?

AF: Extremely.

GP: You don't get that often.

AF: The recording, at least, is a fine document of that show.

GP: Isn't it good? Very, very good. It's well done. They took a lot of that from the actual live performance, you know. I remember him talking about that. Through several nights, they'd tape. That's where you get the reaction from, from the audience. I just wish I'd been there.

AF: Were you ever present at his recording sessions?

GP: No, not one, unfortunately.

AF: Was he present at your recording sessions?

GP: Yes, but he kept pretty quiet. He left that to the technicians.

AF: One show I didn't mention was *"Ace of Clubs"* which you did about 1950?

GP: Oh, yes, that was fun to do that one.
    Then he got *attacked* on that one. It was a bad period for him. The press was after him. *Nothing* he could do was right, and because the story was about a *sailor* and a *nightclub singer,* in a sort of fifth-rate little nightclub in Soho, the press that came out said he was *playing down to the public for writing about those sort of people.*
    REALLY, now! Come on!
    The story he wrote *is* a similar one, in a way—because it's got gangsters—to *"Guys and Dolls"* but *"Guys and Dolls"* is much stronger. Much, much stronger, but there are some marvelous songs in *"Ace of Clubs"*.

AF: Oh, there are! In fact, one I discovered when listening to the original cast recording was *"Three Juvenile Delinquents"*. It's a marvelous number, isn't it?

GP: Very good song. I wanted to get in on this one. *"But,"* he said, *"you can't,* because it doesn't fit the part. You *can't* get in on it. You're *not* a juvenile delinquent! Not a *juvenile,* anyway!"

AF: That was where *"Sail Away"* first appeared, isn't it?

GP: That's right. That was my sailor's song. He liked it so much, that he used it again.

AF: It was also his philosophy, wasn't it? *"When the storm clouds are rising, sail away."*

GP: Just go! It will clear up.

AF: I know he liked the navy and sailing. Do you share that love of the sea?

GP: Oh, yes. Wonderful manners they've got. I remember during the war, one would *go,* naturally, *out.* Physically, I wasn't fit, but I was lucky to be able to be working from my own point of view. *Every Sunday I did two troop concerts,* and went off for the Army and the Air Force, all very nice, very charming, but the *Navy* were the most wonderful hosts. I don't mean as an *audience.* I mean at the little *supper* party afterwards. Wonderful manners they've got.

AF: They are just about to do a series of Noël Coward short stories on Masterpiece Theatre.

GP: That's right. And very good they are, too—*"Me and the Girls", "Star Quality", "Mr. and Mrs. Edgehill"*—very, very good. Good *casts,* too. Very well done. I hope they will be popular here. They were in England. The short stories are very good.

AF: The *"Collected Short Stories"* were just recently published in one volume. I am amazed. I think that they would all make terrific productions.

GP: The trouble is a lot of them are of a *narrative* quality, without much of his dialogue, and it's very difficult for anybody to write his caliber of usage of words. That's rather tricky. So, it's better for the ones where the people *talk* a lot, and that they are his words.

AF: Maybe Tom Stoppard should be hired to do it.

GP: He could do it. He's very good, but he probably wouldn't want to. He's got his own things to do.

AF: Do you go to the theatre a lot today, yourself?

GP: Oh, yes, as much as I possibly can. I've just seen the Neil Simon play—

AF:—*"Broadway Bound"?*

GP: Yes, that's terrific. He's a great writer, I think. He's marvelous. All his plays.

AF: Who are your favorite playwrights today?

GP: Oh, difficult to tell, isn't it?

AF: Alan Ayckborn?

GP: Oh, yes, he's very good. Very, very funny, and he turns them out, doesn't he? Peter Shaffer, very good, and Pinter is excellent, I think.
  I'll tell you what's so funny about Noël and Pinter, because he didn't care for Pinter's writing when he first saw the plays. He thought they were *too slow.*
  Then he got 'round to *seeing* them, and he said, "He's a great writer." And he *is,* he's a marvelous writer, I think. I *could do without some of those pauses,* personally, but still, that's only my personal opinion.

AF: The production of *"Hay Fever"* at the National Theatre, in the sixties, was sort of the start of a major revival of Noël Coward, wasn't it?

GP: That was terrific, yes, Kenneth Tynan's idea. He used to be a critic, as you know. He was on the Board there, invited by Laurence Olivier.

    He said, "I think we should do *"Hay Fever"*!
    Noël, of course, was delighted.
    Edith Evans was remarkable.

AF: She had trouble with her lines, though, didn't she?

GP: Yes, she certainly *did*. She had *a lot* of trouble with the lines, oh dear. She *couldn't* get them in.

    But, Maggie Smith was in the play, playing a character called Myra, and she understudied Edith Evans. Noël rehearsed her and she was perfect. He said she was wonderful.

    He went to Edith one day, when she was at the hotel in Manchester, and she'd been *fluffing* the night before, and he said, "Why don't you take the matinee *off*, and just concentrate on *learning the words,* because Maggie Smith is marvelous, and *she* can go on *this afternoon!*"

    Edith was down there so fast! I can tell you there was *no way* that Maggie Smith was going to go on!

    [laughter]

    After that she concentrated more, and in spite of the fact that she was a bit **waffly** when she opened—it was a *genius* performance. She really was great. *That's star quality,* that she had. She could make herself look beautiful and really, in person, she was *not* beautiful. Marvelous *personality,* and she could make you believe *anything.*

AF: I've heard so many people talk about Noël Coward as being the *'greatest wit of the twentieth century.'* His wit sometimes can be expressed in a single word. I know there are probably hundreds of stories that will never be retold.

GP: He'd just come out so *quickly* with it. Just like *that!* He hadn't thought about them, it just seemed—it's a *gift.* One I wanted to put in, but couldn't put in the book, because it doesn't read very well, but I think it's quite funny.

... in Jamaica. He was in the swimming pool, and for some reason or other, I don't why, I started to *DANCE* around the edge of the pool, and he laughed his head off!

I said, *"Don't* laugh! *People* have paid *money* to see me dance!"

And he said, "Not very *many,* and not for very *long."*

And he went under the water and swam to the other end of the pool!

[laughter]

Well, I thought it was very funny, but he'd never say that if he thought it would hurt me. Of course, it didn't. It made me laugh!

AF: The process of editing *"The Diaries",* I guess it must have been a monumental task.

GP: No, it wasn't, as a matter of fact, because the only things we had to take out were plane departures and ship departures, and having lunch with 'nobody' that—You couldn't have a footnote on a person who he only met *once,* and wasn't of any interest to anybody else.

And. a very few libelous things, one or two, which I can't even repeat here on the air, *had* to come out. The lawyers advised us, they said, "You tell us if you think there's anything libelous, because it's got to come out." There were just a few. They were *very* funny, but unfortunately, they had to come out, but not many.

AF: Did he write *"The Diaries"* with a view that they might eventually be published? Do you think he had that in mind?

GP: I think that he did, yes. He started writing the third volume *"Past Conditional"* so he was going to use those as notes, really, because a lot of it is not his kind of writing. It's rather careless and just done, but we did it. That was it. Oh, yes, I think he was going to use those for the other book. That's why he just put them down to remind himself of *what* happened, *where,* and *whom he met, and so on. I think he says that somewhere, doesn't he?*—'what's going to be written about me after I've gone, I'd love to know? What sort of rubbish . . .'

AF: As you mentioned earlier, the critics just always seemed to have it in for him after a certain point.

GP: Yes, after the war, I don't know what happened. *Nothing* he could do was right. Except for *"Nude With Violin"* which ran for nearly *three years* in London, and even *that* got bad press. It started with John Gielgud, and then Michael Wilding, and then, of all people, Robert Helpmann, who played a very good part. What was the other one that Gladys Cooper did? Can't remember the name of the play now.

AF: *"Waiting In The Wings"*?

GP: No, but that's a good play.

AF: My fantasy was that Katherine Hepburn and Bette Davis should make a TV film of that.

GP: Oh, wouldn't it be terrific!

AF: They're so right for it.

GP: It would be marvelous.

AF: Because it's about a retirement home for actresses.

GP: That's right. And it's a very funny play. I think the idea that made people a little worried is that they didn't want to see tired, old, sad actresses, *miserable,* when they're not at all. When you see the play, the way he's written it, they're very funny. I think it's an excellent play, too.

AF: It's got that marvelous song, too.

GP: *"Come The Wild, Wild Weather"*—lovely song. Yes, I asked for that one, too, but it was a separate song. It wasn't in the original story, but there's a party that they give, and it was written in the script that I'd come and join them. He composed that song, and I thought it was marvelous, that song.

"Couldn't I use it in the show?" I asked.

"Oh, well, all right, I'll put it in," he said.

And it's a lovely song, it really is beautiful, but, again, you see the awful thing . . .

. . . the first night was a *sensational* first night, and the next morning *terrible* press. TERRIBLE press. That killed the business. It only ran for three or four months. But it's a very funny play. I'd love to see it now that they've calmed down a bit, and they're seeing things in perspective. To see how good it is. I'll tell you what, in Denmark, they're making a *film* of it, which I can't wait to see, how it holds up as a film, because then we could show that and give people the idea to do it here. As you say, it's a marvelous thing to do in America. [Editor: *There was a Broadway run of the play that opened in 1999 starring Lauren Bacall and Rosemary Harris, which ran for six months.*]

AF: As you mentioned earlier, the activity in all parts of the world is just amazing and very encouraging.

GP: What they do is terrific. Even in *Japan.* Japan has been working his plays for a long time. He was funny, because, when he was alive, they did *"Cavalcade"* and he laughed dreadfully about that!

He said, "Well, I wonder how they're going to represent the number eleven bus in Trafalgar Square?"

[laughter] Translate *that* one! Anyway, they do them a lot.

AF: In Switzerland, there must be a large record collection.

GP: Yes, I think I've got all his records, even the ones that were done—what are those things under the counter? They're put on the market, and when they're sold, that's when the company closes, and you can't catch them. No royalties from *those,* but they're well put together and they're good.

What *is* so wonderful is the music. I was talking to somebody the other day about the songs he sang at the Cafe de Paris, and that was splendid. When he came here to go to Las Vegas, that marvelous Pete Matz was going to play for him.

Pete looked at his orchestrations and said, "What!? You're *not* going to use *these* are you?" And Noël was quick to say, "No! I want YOU to re-orchestrate, please."

Which he did, and I must say, when you hear the record of Las Vegas, and the record of Noël at the Cafe de Paris, they're like two *different* programs! Pete did a marvelous job. They'd hold even up today, and that's many years ago, isn't it?

AF: Over thirty years ago.

GP: Must be about thirty years ago and they sound great. He *loved* doing it, and his *own* recording, too, of *"Sail Away",* very, very good.

AF: It's hard to find.

GP: It *is* hard to find. I think they can't have printed very many.

AF: They should reissue it. [Ed. It has since been reissued on CD.]

GP: I'm glad I've got that. His rhythm was impeccable. He had a marvelous beat there. When he first did the latest rendering of *"Mad Dogs and Englishmen"* which was usually done at a normal tempo, and he took it at this great *speed,* you know.

He said to his accompanist, "Just keep a *strict* tempo and go! I'll *catch up* with you, but don't try and wait for me, because you'll get it all wrong. Just you go ahead and *I'll catch up.*"

And I think it's a remarkable piece of work, that song, don't you?

AF: Oh, yes.

GP: The *speed* of it, you know.

AF: I guess he must have gotten tired of requests for that. I guess that was probably the *most* requested song.

GP: It *was!* That's *why* he did it at that speed. *He got fed up with it!* He said, "I'm *fed up* with doing this number!"

    The wonderful range he had, being able to write those *funny* songs, *witty* lyrics, and then the very sentimental ones with lovely melody. I don't think there's been anybody with his *range* of talent. *Talents,* I should say. When you think, you know, writing *plays,* writing *stories,* writing *music,* writing *lyrics, acting* himself. He was a very good comedian, indeed. Doing *cabaret,* which is a very special talent, one of the most difficult of all. Remarkable. *Directing* shows.

    And his *paintings* are jolly good, too, but that was what *he* called the '*amateur job*'. That was his *hobby.* He wouldn't exhibit *ever,* although he was *asked* several times.

    He said, "No, no, no, no, I do this for *fun.* I *don't want any criticism* to knock it and *spoil* it."

    He had a wonderful time. Mind you, when he was doing those paintings, things would be going on in his head about a lyric, or a story, or an idea, or something.

AF: He read a lot, didn't he? Voraciously.

GP: Ooh, yes, yes. He failed desperately there with *me.* He *tried* to make me read. I'm a very bad reader. I'm slow at reading.

AF: When I visited Jamaica, I saw most of the books there are not *his* books, but *other* authors' books. And when you read *"The Diaries",* just the *lists* of other works *referred* to is *pages* in the index. So, every time I finally come across something that I thought he might have read, I look to *"The Diaries"* to see what he said about it, or a film, or something like that, because, of course, he went to a lot of films, and saw, I guess, as many productions as he could.

GP: Oh, yes! Sometimes at a weekend, we would all get together—Coley, Gladys Calthrop, Joyce Carey, myself, and Noël, and we'd go off, and we'd take in about *three* pictures in one day! We'd go to the first showing, the middle showing, and the next one. Three different films. Had a marvelous time talking about them afterwards.

AF: How much of the time do you spend in Switzerland, now?

GP: All the time. That's my base. I travel a lot. It's so near everywhere. It's so central. It's marvelous. Near Paris, near Rome, it's not far from the coast. Thirty minutes flight down to the South of France, and it is an hour to London. That's great, you know. The house is beautifully situated up in the mountains, with a view across the lake to France. It really is lovely there.

GRAHAM PAYN

b. 1918   d. 2005

Interviewed October 15, 1987

This interview with Graham Payn was recorded in his home, Chalet Coward, in Les Avants, Switzerland.

ALAN FARLEY: You acted with Gertrude Lawrence in *"Tonight at 8:30"*.

GRAHAM PAYN: That's right. She really was wonderful to work with. The strange thing was, that I'd never *seen* her onstage before. I'd missed her. I'd never seen *anything* she'd done on the stage. I *knew* about her, naturally, you know, but I'd missed her, and then she'd gone to America.
   Then, the war came.
   After the war, I went over there, and Fanny Holzman, who'd looked after her affairs—see, we wanted to do a *fill-in* tour for Gertie—but they asked me to play Noël's parts in *"Tonight at 8:30"*.
   I said, "I'd be delighted."
   Noël said, "Uh, you *shouldn't* do that! They will *compare* you with *me,* and you'll get into trouble. There will be trouble for you. ***Don't*** do it!"
   "So," I thought, "well, maybe he's right."
   He went off to write a play, and I was in New York on my own.
   Fanny said, "Oh, *come on!* You *can't* resist this, can you?"
   I said, **"No!** I *can't.*"
   [laughter]
   "I really *can't!* It would be WONDERFUL to play opposite Gertrude Lawrence in those MARVELOUS parts!"

AF: How many of them did you do?

GP: We did *four.* I didn't do *one*—*"Fumed Oak"* I didn't do. That was *out of my range,* really. It was an *elderly man* character,

Cockney man, you know, just *beyond* my range, but the others I could manage—*I* thought, anyway.

Gertie was *wonderful!*

There was a bit of a problem over the *direction* at the beginning. Jack Wilson [Coward's American business partner and rival for Coward's affections] was *going* to do it—got a bit *sarcastic.* It *was* a bit silly. The producers, who happened to be there at this first read-through, were back at Noël's apartment, and by that time I'd *agreed* to do it, you know.

Noël said, *"Okay!* It's up to *you!* Do it."

They were there saying, "Hmm, there's a problem then, and Jack Wilson will have to go, because he's going to make trouble. He's just going to stir up trouble."

So, Noël decided to take over the direction *himself* and Jack was let out. Noël took over the direction, which was *great!*

I'm sure Gertie *longed* for him to be playing the part, but she NEVER let me feel that at all. She was most generous. When we'd been playing a couple of weeks in this one called *"Red Peppers"*—it's a music hall act, and I'm supposed to be the *leader* of the act.

She said, "Come on! You've got to *take over!* Because, if you *don't,* I'll *act* you *off* the stage! Now, *come on!* We're an act *together,* and *you're* the boss. *You've* got to *take charge* on this stage! DOMINATE me!"

Which was WONDERFUL, wasn't it? Because if it were anybody else, they'd just say, 'Well, forget it! If he can't do it, I'll get on with it and do it myself.'

But she didn't. She helped me ALL she could. She was absolutely *wonderful.*

Different towns we went to—Boston, Philadelphia, San Francisco, Los Angeles—she wouldn't have *one* meeting with the press *unless I was there* so she could introduce me and give *me* a helping hand! She was wonderful.

She *didn't* do the things with me that apparently she *used* to do with *Noël.* That was—*OVERDOING* things, and *NOT* making up lines, but putting in *NEW* business. Something like that used to drive him *MAD*

But he *adored* her, and in spite of all that, she *never* did that with me. Maybe she thought I wasn't capable of handling it if she'd done something different, you know?

We used to have a great time because we'd always get down in plenty of time for the curtain, and she used to *limber up,* vocally, and I would do the same thing—dancing a bit and kidding around—just loosening up. So, we'd usually have a good hour's work before make-up time, before going on. I really did enjoy working with her.

It wasn't *supposed* to come to New York, at all. It was just this *tour* finishing up in Los Angeles, and I'd *got so good!* I had got *good notices* in San Francisco! I was TOLD I got good!

Noël agreed that I *could* do it, because he said, "Well, come on and stay a hitch in New York, because it's great! It's working beautifully!"

SOLD OUT *and* **GOOD REVIEWS** and everything *fine!*

... but, of course, when we got to New York ...

... they **CLOBBERED** me over the head! They really did *attack* me! *One* notice is good. You see, if they rate it very, very *bad,* then you have to *laugh.* You *HAVE* to laugh! I didn't read *any* of them till *after* we'd finished.

So, I've got TWO first nights. *One* lot of three, and *another* lot of three coming up! So, *I* didn't read them.

But *Gertie* would cut out the bad ones, and say, "I'm FURIOUS with that one paper!" [quotes the paper:] **"*Payn* is his name, and that's what he IS!"**

I'm sorry. That does *not* fit me at all. That just makes me laugh. This critic was like a *child* writing there, and that's *nonsense.*

So, from then on, I *LIFTED,* and I was *fine!* We ran there, I'm afraid, for just seven weeks. It was odd how the critics *turned around,* because when Noël and Gertie did it *before,* the critics said that the plays were really 'very *light,* almost *rubbish,* but SAVED by these two wonderful *star* personalities.'

Now, when *I* came in doing this, they were saying that 'the plays are SO *good*," and that *I* wasn't *'strong* enough' to play in them!

So, there was a big *change mon décor.*

AF: Did she really *light up* the stage when she was on?

GP: Oh, *yes!* That's *star magic,* isn't it? It's something you've either *got* or you *haven't,* and she certainly *had* it! Walk onto the stage and THAT'S IT! It was ELECTRIC! Timing! Excellent!

She was so *pleasant* to work with. Wonderfully *generous,* you know? I mean, she was a much STRONGER personality than I, and she could have really trampled me down if she wanted to, but she didn't. Never. Never once. So, I adored her, naturally.

When we went to San Francisco I had a bad throat or something or other, and Noël was going to *have to* play my part.

This man came to him and said, "I'm coming to see the show."

And Noël said to him devilishly, "Oh, aren't you *LUCKY.* Because, *NOËL'S* on this afternoon!" So, that was it. Noël *loved* going on. Noël *couldn't wait!* I bet they had a *ball* that afternoon!

AF: They just did one matinee?

GP: Just the *one* matinee, that's all. I guess I should have let them play two or three together, shouldn't I really? But I hadn't thought of that at the time. I just wanted to get back on. But it was great.

AF: I was looking through *"The Theatrical Companion to Coward"* and saw in *"The Lyric Revue"*, and *"The Globe Revue"*, that you worked with Ian Carmichael in both of those shows.

GP: That's right, that's right, yes!

AF: He's gotten some fame—

GP: Yes, indeed.

AF:—as Lord Peter Wimsey, in a television series, among his other credits.

GP: He's a very, very *good* comedian. *Excellent.* We'd worked together before, actually, on television.

"The Lyric Revue" came along for the Festival of Britain that was going to take place. It was only going to be on for about six weeks at the Lyric Hammersmith—it was *suddenly* this ENORMOUS smash hit! We moved into The Globe Theatre! So, *"The Lyric Revue"* was playing in *The Globe Theatre*—very confusing, you see.

AF: Noël wrote *"Don't Make Fun of the Festival"* for that, didn't he?

GP: That's right! He wrote it for that, naturally, and he 'sent-it-up' ROTTEN, didn't he? [laughter] He couldn't wait!

Then he wrote for the next one, *"The Globe Revue"* which followed on after two years—*"There Are Bad Times Just Around the Corner"*—again, it is *prophetic.*

It's wonderful using his material because one was SAFE with it.

As he said, *"Don't put in any expression,* just DO it! *The lyrics will carry* YOU."

I've passed that on, now, to people. Some people are inclined to take his songs a little too *slowly.* It doesn't work. It just takes the BITE out of it, or the SENTIMENT, whichever way it's going.

The most famous trap of all is *"If Love Were All"* from *"Bitter Sweet".* THEY ALL TAKE IT TOO SLOWLY. The point is— don't take it at a *gallop,* but at a good, reasonable *steady tempo,* and then the words DO get to your heart, and *fx* you.

AF: The demand on you for giving your approval of productions of his plays continues very heavy these days, doesn't it?

GP: Oh, yes, it's *fantastic!* It really *is* wonderful demand for productions *all over the world!* It's busy now! All the things I have to ward off, sometimes, because otherwise we have *too many* shows running at the *same time,* so we *have* to sort of put them off as politely as possible, because people can't wait forever, either.

They get the stars lined up, and then you can't do it, and then they say, "Oh, that's too *bad.*"

I have to look out for him and protect *Noël. He* comes first.

So, we try and have one thing at a time, and not two or three running at the same time, because then, also, they'd run out very quickly, wouldn't they!

AF: You spoke to me before about the paintings that are going to be auctioned off at Christie's. These are paintings that *he* did.

GP: Oh, yes, they are all *his* paintings. He never exhibited, and he never sold. He *gave* some to *charity,* in the years back, for sale, naturally—that's a different thing altogether, but he wouldn't *sell.* He said painting was his *hobby.* He *enjoyed* doing it, and it was great *fun,* and that was *it.*

So, now we see them, and everybody seems to like them so much, and I thought it was a good idea to let the people have them, and put it up on the wall. There are so many, they can't *all* be tucked away. The proceeds go to benefit *theatre* charities, so that goes into a special trust, and that will happen when I go. Then they get it with the interest added on to it.

AF: That's a very generous thing to do.

GP: Noël, I thought, would have liked that, because he was always giving to the *theatre* charities anyway, but he wanted that, I'm sure. I think he would have approved to give them the money that comes from the paintings, which I intend to do.

AF: Thank you, once again, for being generous with your *time.*

GP: Oh, thank you, Alan. I'm just so glad you could come here and see the house, and be up in the mountains—get some nice fresh air.

HELENE PONS

b. circa 1898   d. 1990

Interviewed January 9, 1988

Helene Pons, designed costumes in New York for over two hundred Broadway shows from the 1920s right through the 1960s, and was the costume designer for Coward's *"Sail Away"*. This interview was recorded during a visit she made to San Francisco. Since this interview, Helene Pons' creative life has been archived at the HELENE PONS COLLECTION—Ohio State University Libraries which can be accessed at the following web address:

http://library.osu.edu/find/collections/theatre-research-institute/design-collections/helene-pons-collection/

There are several other websites devoted to her amazing work.

[Ed: I was very fortunate to know Helene Pons personally and was enriched by her friendship. As if she was rushing off to a costume fitting for Elaine Stritch or Noel Coward, Helene's speech had a very lively tempo, like a canary's song, even though one does not exactly grasp the melody. Her colorful accent freely blended sounds from Russia, Hungary, Italy, England, and the USA, sounding like a tender sister to Zsa Zsa Gabor, and a cousin of Sophia Loren; her rapidity of precise ideas, like Einstein. She seemed to possess unlimited energy, and was always stylish in her impeccable apparel. Her tongue was quick as her sewing machine's needle. She attributed her success designing costumes to her approach of designing *"from inside the character, out."* Helene directed her staff with a motherly, endearing bravura, and New York tough. Her bustling Broadway costume studio made her the clever, never-ending "bobbin of Broadway." Her resume is worth looking up.]

ALAN FARLEY: What songs do you remember from the show?

HELENE PONS: There are so many songs, but this one is the best one I remember, *"Why Do The Wrong People Travel, Travel, Travel, When the Right People Stay Back Home?"*—and this is the girl who was singing.

AF: Elaine Stritch.

HP: Yes. These are the *sketches* for the costumes that I made.

AF: Here's what Coward wrote in his *Diaries* about you:
[Reading from Noël's *"Diaries":*]

> "Helene Pons arrived from Rome with efficient and comprehensive dress charts for every dress, every character and every scene. Within five minutes of her arrival the library looked like a jumble sale.
>
> She really is a wonderful old girl, professional and thorough and, what is most important, she really understands the characters and her designs have humour."

HP: Yes. What I am trying to do is to write a book about all the things that I was working with on the stage. I have a story of how Elaine's costume happened. Would you read it? It's a short story, but it's a funny story.

AF: Shall I read it now?

HP: Yes.

AF: [Reading from Helene's unpublished book:]

> "Many productions from my past are still very vivid in my memory. The more I think of them, the better I see my crazy studio with all the cutting, stitching, draping, painting, dyeing, aging, *calling* the suppliers to remind them that I want all of the materials *yesterday. Pleading* with a stage manager to send the actors for fittings as a personal *favor*, and suddenly an IMPOSSIBLE request comes over the phone!

When I was designing *"Sail Away"*, I had one of these *moments.*

At first I was *stunned,* then suddenly out-of-the-blue the solution dropped in front of me! I climbed back on my high horse and galloped in the opposite direction.

The office called to tell me that Joe Layton, the choreographer, wanted an *AMERICAN FLAG hidden* in the blue chiffon dress!—the one that Elaine Stritch was to wear for the party on the ship. At the finale, as a *surprise,* she was to *pull the flag* OUT of her dress!

I thought the idea was *corny* and *not* practical, and *refused* to make it.

The scenic designer, was on the phone, "Helene they want the flag!"

"But *where* do you want me to hide it?" I kept on saying, "How could I *hide* an American flag in a blue chiffon dress? Even if I put pockets it would only be a small flag. It won't mean anything."

Oliver kept on repeating, "But Helene, they want the flag!"

I kept on saying, "It can *not* be done."

The conversation lasted for several minutes. Suddenly, a thought flashed through my head.

"Okay! *I will do it!"*

Oliver was *stunned,* "Helene, for *fifteen minutes* you are telling me you *won't* do it, and in a split second you say *'okay,* you *will.'* You are the *best* in those moments!"

At the final dress rehearsal in Boston I was sitting in the first row of the orchestra with Oliver. The curtain opened on a big stage. Elaine Stritch appeared alone dancing, whirling, singing.

Oliver leaned towards me and asked, *"Where's* the flag?"

I was all eyes, watching Elaine. I said, "It's *there."*

Oliver repeated a little louder, "Helene, where IS the flag?"

I said, *"It's there."*

Then I *jumped* from my seat to *run* to the back of the orchestra seats to see the effect.

Noël *caught me, "Where* is the *flag?"* He looked angry and worried.

I did not stop. I just said, *"There!"* and kept on running. Then I turned my head and saw Noël and his friends looking after me. "But they do not believe me," I said to myself. For a split second, a horrid thought flashed in my brain, *"Is* the flag there?"

At this moment Elaine Stritch slipped her hands behind her back, *opened* two snaps, *grabbed* two ends of the blue chiffon cape, and with a *quick* movement opened a *LARGE* American flag! which was hidden in the folds of the cape!

The unbelievers gasped! They were so surprised they could not smile—stunned, mouths open! *Then* they smiled!

I did not stay for the opening night. I was told that the *audience—my boss—*when *they* saw the flag they *screamed* and *applauded!"*

HP: It was very successful.

AF: Wonderful story!

HP: And that is what they wrote about—Mainbocher—you know who is he?

AF: Oh yes. [Ed: Mainbocher is a fashion label founded by the American couturier Main Rousseau Bocher, also known as Mainbocher. Established in 1929, the house of Mainbocher successfully operated in Paris and then in New York.]

HP: Well, Mainbocher wrote him a letter and Noël wanted me to read it, and sent it to me.

AF: Why don't you read it?

HP: All right. [Reading the letter:]

"Darling Noël,

You were an angel to send us seats for last night. A fabulous opening! Douglas and I had a wonderful time. We think you will have a terrific run. And what can I say, dear Noël, except that you are a genius and always have been.
All love, Mainbocher—Incidentally, it is one of the best-dressed shows I have ever seen!"

AF: Well, that's certainly a compliment, isn't it?

HP: You know, it *was* a wonderful effect, because it was so unusual. Suddenly I got scared. *'Was* it there?'

AF: After you assured everyone that it *was.*

HP: *Yes.* Because the *way* they were so sure that it *wasn't* there, that I am *lying.* [laughs]

AF: How did he choose *you* to do the costumes?

HP: I don't *know* how he chose. You see I was for *forty years* in the theatre!
    I want to show you the dress and how it was. You see? It [a huge American flag] was folded in the chiffon.

AF: It just looks *impossible* when you see the picture.

HP: I put it *inside,* because chiffon would show the color of the flag. Then I had to *line* it with white. And it was only *two snaps* held the whole thing! And she opened it like *that,* and it *was* terrific!
    She was wonderful when she sings that song I like best, "*Why Do the Wrong People Travel, Travel, Travel?"*

AF: "*When the Right People Stay Back Home?"*

HP: Yes, yes. It is a *very* good thing!

DONALD R. SEAWELL

b. August 1, 1912

Interviewed May 26, 1993

Donald Seawell is the founder and chairman for The Denver Center for the Performing Arts, and was also one of the original producers of Noël Coward's *"Sail Away"* on Broadway in 1961. In 1993, The Denver Center produced a revival—a rebirth—of *"Sail Away"* with the title *"Bon Voyage"*. The interview was conducted in his office at The Denver Center.

ALAN FARLEY: Of all of Coward's shows and musicals that I've become familiar with over the years, *"Sail Away"* is the one that I've been dying to see on stage, and so I'm glad to have a chance to see it here, even though it isn't exactly the same.

DONALD SEAWELL: Good. Well, I'm delighted you could be here and see it. It *isn't* the same. Actually, when Noël first came to me about producing *"Sail Away"* back in 1961, I believe he said he wanted to do a big, brassy Broadway type musical. We did it in New York with some success, and then London.

But, after the London production Noël said, "Don, don't you think that doing it big and brassy we've lost a bit of the *'Coward chic'?"*

And, in fact, we had.

Besides that, of course, it would be *impossible* today to put on *"Sail Away"* with the cast of *sixty-two,* so we've cut it down a great deal.

During the process of opening in New York, we were out of town. We did, in fact, make a great many changes. We were *forced* to, because a key member of the cast, as we had originally cast it, just didn't come through, and just before we opened on Broadway we eliminated that role entirely—which pretty much destroyed Coward's original plot.

"Bon Voyage" comes a little nearer the original plot, although we've combined a lot of the characters. We have

eliminated a few of the songs from the Broadway *"Sail Away"* and we've interpolated a lot more of his songs, as you saw, with the permission of the Estate. But when you change that much, you really *have* to change the title, because there are a lot of people around who may have seen *"Sail Away"* and they'll say, *"This isn't the 'Sail Away' I saw."* That's happened recently on Broadway with the Gershwin show *"Girl Crazy"*.

AF: Right. They called it *"Crazy For You"*.

DS: *"Crazy For You"*—they *had* to change it, because they had changed the plot so much, and threw in so much more of Gershwin's music. So, it's basically a night of wonderful, wonderful Gershwin music, and to some extent, we've done the same thing here.

AF: In fact, I spoke to Joe Layton a few years ago, and he told me about the process of—

DS: Joe was our choreographer originally. Did a beautiful job.

AF: How involved were you in the day-to-day preparations for the Broadway opening of *"Sail Away"*?

DS: When you are producing a Coward show, that Coward *himself* is directing, you get involved mostly to the extent that Noël wanted you to be involved. It would be heavy handed to suggest to Noël that *you should change this, that and the other!*

But Noël liked for me to *be there.* He liked to turn and ask questions—many of them rhetorical—[laughter]—and you really had to be diplomatic with Noël to change something. You had to try to make him believe it was *his* idea—as most things were, because Noël, let's face it—*the most COMPLETE man in the history of the theatre.* He was author, producer, director, choreographer, scenic designer, costume designer, actor, dancer, singer—he did everything. *No one else is all of those things.*

AF: That's certainly true.

DS: At least, not as well.

AF: What were his work habits, while he was working on that show?

DS: Noël's work habits were always *impeccable*. He threw himself completely into whatever he was doing. Although things usually came very quickly to Noël, he nevertheless worked very, very hard, and insisted on others doing the same thing.

Elaine Stritch was the star of *"Sail Away"* although, unfortunately, we never put her name above the title. There wasn't *room! Noël's name above the title was too big!*

At that time, Stritch had been drinking a great deal, but she did a beautiful job with self—discipline and overcoming it. She even took a job as a *bartender* to prove that she could overcome her alcoholic habits!

Noël took her out the night before and got her simply—well, *obfuscated*—polite term—and he called for rehearsal the next morning at nine o'clock, and she didn't show up on time. He simply gave her hell.

He was there. And she never again was late a single minute.

But it simply shows Noël's idea of discipline. Some would think it was a dirty trick to play on Elaine, but she understood it, and she laughed, and everything was wonderful—including Elaine.

AF: Well, actually, I had a chance to talk to her, too. I guess it was just about two years ago in New York.

DS: A real trooper.

AF: Oh, yes, yes. She told about some of the bad times she had when she was drinking. She was telling me about one time where some show—I don't think it was *"Sail Away"*—where she had to dash out, with just a coat over her underwear, to get a bottle of vodka to have *something* before the show—but, happily, those days are in the past now.

DS: *Stritch got her revenge on Noël* when the show was in Philadelphia, before the New York opening.

Noël and I took a train down. We got there on a matinee day, and the show was already underway. We went backstage just about the time when there was a crossover.

Stritch was standing there saying *'hello'* to all the passengers as they went by, and Noël said, [whispering], *"Let's join the passenger line."*

I said, "Not me, brother!"

But Noël did!

As he passed Elaine, she saw Coward *face-to-face* on the stage and she went *sky high!* Boy!—she *STORMED* off that stage, and when she got off, she said to me, *"Don't EVER let that AMATEUR on my stage again, or I'm walking off!"*

Noël was *very* contrite.

He rushed out and got her several dozen red roses, and he gave them to her, and they became friends all over again.

Noël wasn't usually that [laughing]—*something* just got into him.

AF: How did you first meet Noël?

DS: I first met Noël back in the early fifties. I was attorney for the Lunts, and they were doing a Coward play. Unfortunately, the producer—who had been a great old producer, but had become an alcoholic, and had budgeted the play so that at *capacity* it was *losing* a great deal of money.

So, the Lunts brought Noël to meet me, and *together* they said, "All right, you've got to take over the play. You've got to produce it. You've got to reorganize it."

And so, I found myself, in essence, producing a Noël Coward play starring Alfred Lunt and Lynn Fontanne, and where do you go from there? [laughter] You can hardly go up! The first thing I said to them, "Well, there's one way you can do it, but *you've* got to be the models. *Each* of you will have to *cut* your gross in *half* And I'll expect that you'll go to the company with that, and in consideration you'll get some of the profits, once we start getting the profit picture."

So, they all agreed. It was very simple. It worked out and everybody was happy.

AF: Just common sense.

DS: Yes, except for the original producer, whom we all liked, and had been a great friend of Noël's, but that was that. It had to happen.

AF: So, then, what did you do in theatre?

DS: So, we were great friends from then on, and I either produced or co-produced *everything* the Lunts did from *then on,* and worked closely with Noël on a lot of things that he did.

AF: I saw them once, just once, in San Francisco, in *"The Visit"* which was—

DS: Their last play.

AF: In 1960 or sixty-one, I think, something like that.

DS: I've forgotten the dates, lord, I should know, but they're handy in the next room. I've created The Lunt-Fontanne Room. It contains all of their memorabilia. All of their pictures from all of the productions they ever did, starting way back in Alfred's college days, and going right on through. So, we can look up anything that you want to about the Lunts, and a lot about Noël in that room. I think you'll be very interested in taking a look at it.

AF: I would appreciate that. That would be very nice. Was your association in theatre, then, *strictly* with the Lunts from then on, and with Coward?

DS: Oh, no, no. I had many other clients, indeed, in theatre, many other stars, and produced many other shows—*with* and *without* them. Lots more *without* them than with them, unfortunately.

AF: How did this—The Denver Center Theatre come about?

DS: Well, it was a sort of a crazy idea of mine to create this entire performing arts complex that you see here.

I was then publisher of the *"Denver Post"* and head of some foundations that needed direction, and I sort of looked around to see what was the biggest need of the community. I felt that we could do lots more with the foundations, and concentrating on *one* need rather than trying to be Santa Claus to everyone, and just getting a little bit done here and there.

I happened to be walking past this area. I stopped at a stoplight. I looked around. I thought, "Well, this would be a wonderful place to build a performing arts center." So, I sat down on the curb and pulled out an envelope, and mapped it out, and called an architect that I liked, and we were underway!

For good or for bad. You see, Denver is so *isolated* from everywhere else, so, we have to be pretty self-containing, and that is the reason that we have—that is, in many respects—the *largest* performing arts center in the entire *world,* in terms of the *number* of facilities, in terms of the variety of facilities, and in terms of the various things that we do, we are the *largest.*

In this one five-block area you see here, we have *nine* performing spaces; we have *fourteen* studios and rehearsal halls.

We have our own—unlike other performing arts centers—our own television, recording, theatre studios, and our own voice laboratories. I could go on, but we're talking about Noël, not about The Center.

AF: What is your fondest memory of Noël?

DS: My *fondest* memory of Noël? Well, there are so very many, stretching from his place in Jamaica to Les Avants, Switzerland, that if I started on wonderful memories I couldn't *stop*—but we were talking about *"Sail Away".*

Originally, I was in North Carolina, (where *mint juleps are* made, along with Kentucky, and other states in that area), but when we *opened "Sail Away"* in Boston, my suite was directly above Noël's.

The only way we could get crushed ice was to wrap it in a towel—and crushed ice was *essential* to mint juleps—and *BANG it on the hearth of the fireplace,* and Noël could *hear* it—*and he'd be up there in fifteen seconds for his mint juleps! He'd* never had them before, but he thought that was one of the *best* reasons for ever doing "*Sail Away*"—that he'd discovered mint juleps!

AF: I understand, too, that he had a great facility for making people feel at ease—unlike some stars, who are so infatuated with themselves—he was very generous.

DS: Yes, he was *extraordinarily* generous and very wonderful. I remember once he came to dinner at my house in New York. and he said to my son, *Brock,* "What are you playing in the school play?"

Brock said, "*Wendy* in *'Peter Pan."*

He turned to my daughter, *Brook,* and said, "And what are *you* playing in the school play?"

And Brook said, *"Prospero* in *'The Tempest".*

And he said, "Why don't you *switch* schools?"

[laughter]

I *wish* he were around to see what we are doing.

NEIL SIMON

b. July 4, 1927

Interviewed October 9, 1996

Neil Simon, the distinguished American playwright, had a Noël Coward connection early in his career. He visited San Francisco to talk about his memoir *"Rewrites"*. The interview took place at the KALW studios.

ALAN FARLEY: I was surprised to learn that after going to a play of yours, Coward actually had an important impact on your career.

NEIL SIMON: Well, especially because it was the *first* play, *"Come Blow Your Horn"* which we tried out in Bucks County, Pennsylvania, then moved on to Philadelphia, where we were a big hit, expecting that New York would be open arms for us, but we opened up to an advance of about three hundred dollars, which would have taken care of about forty seats for one night. So, we expected the worst.

The reviews came out that night and they were *mixed,* but the producer said, "Come on down and see the line tomorrow, and we'll tell how we're doing."

Well, I got down to the theatre—there was *no* line. There was just the man in the box office. There was a guy sweeping up, and they're having coffee, talking. NOTHING doing.

So, I walked into the theatre, and the two producers were there, saying, "We put the closing notice up for Saturday."

I said, "There goes my playwriting career!" because if you don't make it in that *first* one—which took me *three years* to write—it's *GOODBYE!*

But, we had a very smart company manager, and he said to everybody, "Listen, we were a big hit in Philadelphia, which means the audiences *loved* it. We've just got to get it *to* the audiences."

So, what they did was hand out tickets for FREE! And New Yorkers are very *skeptical*—they see a 'FREE' ticket—they throw it in the GARBAGE can.

They don't want to go.

But, we got *nurses* from hospitals, we got some *soldiers* from the USO. *A few people started to come! AND* they *liked* the play! Others came, but it was all for FREE. So, that closing notice was extended for a *few* days, and then it was OVER.

Until, finally, Irving 'Swifty' Lazar, a famous agent, came to the theatre one night with Noël Coward, because Noël would come over every season to see all the new plays. They had seen *everything,* and as Noël was about to leave, to go home the next day, he said, "Is there anything we missed?"

And 'Swifty' said, "Well, there's this *'Come Blow Your Horn'* play. I hear it's pretty good."

So, they *went,* and Noël Coward LOVED it, and during the first act—I later heard from 'Swifty'—Noël Coward said to him, "Keep your EYE on this kid, Irving, or just GRAB him, because I think he's going to be GOOD."

They went to a restaurant that night and the famous columnist, Leonard Lyons, (in New York at the time), came over to them and said, "Noël, what did you do tonight?"

He said, "I saw the *funniest* play in New York, *'Come Blow Your Horn"!*

And there were FORTY-FIVE people on line the NEXT day!

So, *THAT* was the power of Noël Coward!

AF: That's amazing. You also admired *him* as a playwright before that.

NS: Oh, enormously, enormously! And then, fortunately—I mean, he was so nice—he started *corresponding* with me! Wrote *ME!* Came to see *"The Gingerbread Lady".*

Called, and said, "Neil, you have tell—go speak to Maureen Stapleton. I know she's been in it for a year, but she's sort of walking through it, now. Gotta get back to opening night performance."

AF: I also read in his diaries brief references to *"Barefoot in the Park"* and *"The Odd Couple"*, how he just thought they were terrific plays.

NS: Right, right! He had written me about that! Incredible!

ALAN STRACHAN

b. in Dundee, Scotland—date unknown

Interviewed December 21, 1989

ALAN FARLEY: I'm in London with Alan Strachan, who has directed *"Noël and Gertie"* that just opened at the Comedy Theatre. Let's talk about *"Noël and Gertie"* and when you got involved. Were you involved from the beginning?

ALAN STRACHAN: Yes, I was. It goes back an awfully long time, *"Noël and Gertie"*. It has been through many, many different transmogrifications over the years. I first got involved about ten years ago, I think it was, when it was first done for a one-night-stand. It began as a charity show for an organization and is the COMBINED theatrical charities, which is basically to raise money for older actors. It was done for that one Sunday night at a, then, dark theatre, The Mayfair Theatre, on NO budget whatsoever, with four actors who had precisely three days rehearsal—two actors and two singers, and Sheridan Morley, who compiled the evening, doing his own narration. And that was the end of it, or so we thought. Then a few years later, the guy who had produced that Sunday night charity show, got it together AGAIN to take to the Hong Kong Festival, and then to play a brief season back in London, but it was still in its original format, then. It still had TWO actors, TWO singers, a narrator and a pianist. So, it was quite a BULKY show, not the slimmed down version that we have now.

    Then, believe it or not, it was done yet AGAIN about two years subsequent to that production at a theatre called The Kings Head in London, which is basically a pub theatre. It's a room at the back of a pub. Unlike any other theatre I know, it's run by a slightly lunatic, Irish-American gentleman, who still insists on charging old coinage prices. He hasn't gone 'decimal' so you still have to pay in pounds, shillings and pence, which makes life extremely confusing, and there is this little room at the back of this pub, which seats approximately a hundred people, and for which, for *"Noël and Gertie"* seated about a hundred and twenty a

293

night. He had people sitting on mantelpieces, on top of pianos and whatever. That was the end of it until recently, and then up it rears its head AGAIN!

AF: Well, as a matter of fact, I saw *"Easy Virtue"* at The King's Head in its final performance before it moved to the West End.

AS: And that was—what? Sixteen people squeezed onto that postage stamp size stage.

AF: Yes! Incredible!

AS: But they have done extraordinary things there. It's a very odd place to work. I find it a rather unsettling experience, but great fun.

AF: Did you work with Sheridan in revising the show?

AS: Yes, quite a lot. It has changed a great deal over the years. It was originally—and Sheridan would be the first to admit this—somewhat in the format of the *"Side by Side by Sondheim"* kind of show. What we call over here—I don't know if you have the phrase—we call them "book and stool" shows. Do you know what I mean by that?

AF: Yes, I know what you mean.

AS: Which tends to make it just a little bit "radio documentary"—certainly for my taste. So, in this reworking for just the two performers plus the pianist, quite a lot of re-stitching gone on for THIS version, the one that's now showing at The Comedy [Theatre]. A lot of material that's never been in before has gone in. Not so much the main extracts. Obviously, the *"Private Lives"* extracts, the *"Tonight at 8:30"* pieces have remained fairly constant over the years, but quite a lot of the 'linking' material has changed, and particularly the emphasis on both Coward's and Gertrude Lawrence's conception of themselves as stars—a bit of that has been slightly expanded for this version.

So, yes, over the years, Sheridan and I have ALWAYS tried, every time we've done it, we try to make it a little bit different, otherwise, it's a bit like climbing into a wet bathing suit, you know, you have to keep tinkering with it occasionally.

AF: Well, I must say, I found very interesting the resonances between some of his works and their lives, that I hadn't even thought about—the connections both in his lyrics and in the writing.

AS: Yes. There's a short story, which I'd totally forgotten, a thing called *"Star Quality"* which is very much about the kind of star that Gertrude Lawrence was. It is not a portrait of her entirely, but in that story, I think, Coward comes very close to analyzing his own conception of what 'stardom' actually meant. It's very clear that the kind of leading lady she was for him he adored her, certainly, but she also drove him absolutely mad at times, as well, and that comes out very strongly in that story. So, a piece of that has found its way, rather usefully, I think, into the latter part of the show. And, yes, some of the lyrics, too, must echo fragments, at least, of that partnership.

AF: I know, I thought, in fact, I have the recording that had been issued, I guess around a 1982 production.

AS: Oh, yes. That was from the production that was done at The Donmar Warehouse, which is another small, intimate theatre in London. I didn't direct that production. I think it's the ONE production I never have done. I don't think I was available at the time, and also, I had just done The Kings Head one the year before, and I thought, "Enough is enough. I must do *something* else."

AF: It had in it *"Come The Wild, Wild Weather"* and I thought, "Well, now, what's that have to do with it?" Because, of course, before I saw the show—Gertrude Lawrence was not ALIVE when he wrote that song.

AS: Certainly not, no. It was written for a play called *"Waiting In The Wings"* at least ten years after she died.

AF: Yes, but it's such a perfect song for it.

AS: I think it is, and I think there's also a song called *"I'll Remember Her"* which I don't know if it was in the previous version you saw, and that's a song that we use quite late in the show. It's about Coward singing about Gertrude Lawrence. I think a lot of the lyrics are very pertinent to what he felt about her. He describes her as *"somebody so alert, so impertinent, and yet, so sweet."* He talks about her "absurd exaggerating," which was something very true of Gertrude Lawrence.

And he also talks about his "sad and sweet, INCOMPLETE affair" which I think, also, has a certain resonance for the pair of them. But, the number had nothing to do with either of them, really, except he wrote it. He never sang it. She never sang it. It was originally sung EXTREMELY badly by Jose Ferrer in a musical called *"The Girl Who Came To Supper"*. (You don't need me to tell you all this.) But the lyric and the melody too seemed to belong very much, we thought, to that place in the show.

AF: That's why it really struck me. It's just a perfect choice.

AS: It's a lovely song. I don't know why that one's got lost. I suppose, because the SHOW got lost, and I think that score sadly undervalued. There are some very good numbers in that.

AF: I think Ferrer said—I talked to him when he was in San Francisco once about the show—and he said that he thought that that song was Coward's attempt to—*"I've Grown Accustomed To Her Face"*. That the whole show was sort of Coward's attempt to do another *"My Fair Lady"*.

AS: Yes, I guess, it was in its way, wasn't it? I never thought of it like that before. He has a point. I suppose, as a single number, as a melody, I actually find it more appealing than *"I've Grown*

Accustomed To Her Face", but I suppose, as a 'show' song, *"I've Grown Accustomed To Her Face"* is stronger.

AF: You're right. There's some great music in that, and I thought Florence Henderson in the recording was just superb.

AS: Yes. I never saw the show, of course, and it's never been done over here. I think there have been several plans to try and get it off the ground, but it's never had a full stage production. It had a very good radio production. I mean, a really splendid one with Keith Mitchell playing the Prince, with great charm, which I think, was probably one of the faults with the Broadway production, by the sound of it, but Florence Henderson sounded great, I must say.

AF: Well, now, one of the particular challenges, of course, when you're recreating some people who really lived, and there are still many people around who saw them, how do you deal with that?

AS: I think the first thing you have to deal with is that you have to say very firmly to the performers that nobody is expecting, nobody would want, and it would probably be rather embarrassing if there was any attempt to do it. It is NOT—and I don't think it ever should be designed to be—an IMPERSONATION of those two people. That particularly applies to Coward. Memories of her are a bit dimmer. She never had a movie career, really. I mean, she MADE films, but she was never a MAJOR film star, like he was. Of course, her career was much shorter. Oddly enough, I think there are comparatively few people around, even in this country, who saw her because of the fact that her LATER career was primarily based in America.

So, over HERE, I don't think HER legend, her aura is still quite so pungent. With HIM, of course, you're dealing with what has to be described as an 'English *monstre sacre*'. It really is. And everybody assumes that they KNOW the quintessential Noël Coward. It's quite extraordinary. I find it AMAZING that all these years after his death, you can still turn on the television and see television commercials which still use his voice, his persona, and, indeed, there's a CURRENT commercial being shown over here—I don't even know what the product's it's for—the commercial itself is so bad, you don't notice. But it, actually, uses somebody MADE-UP to look like him (not very successfully, I have to say) and doing, again, (not very successfully), an attempt, at least, to do a total impersonation.

So, the PERSONA still has extraordinary pungency, BUT I don't think on stage there would be any point whatsoever in doing that. Otherwise, it would be turning the evening into a kind of . . . um . . . parade of animated waxworks, and I don't think you can do that. I think all you can do is to EVOKE some sense of the very many different facets of BOTH the persona with affection, I hope; with a certain amount, too, of detachment—especially in the case of Gertie, who was a very complex personality. So, one has to try and get over NOT just how incandescent she was in performance, but also how VARIABLE she was in performance. So, it's a fact of her performing self that you can't ignore. But I do think any attempt to say, 'This is the DEFINITIVE Noël Coward'—'This is the DEFINITIVE Gertrude Lawrence'—in this day and age, would be IMPOSSIBLE. You can't do that.

AF: I think that *"Mrs. Worthington"* that song, for instance, I think it's just the greatest performance I thought that I've ever seen of the gradual—

AS: Yes!

AF: It's right there in the lyrics.

AS: Yes. We worked quite hard on that, unfortunately. It was largely because of *"Mrs. Worthington"* that we had some 'hiccups' on the road. Simon Cadell, who plays Noël in this version has done it before. He was in the version I did at The King's Head, and I think it was in THAT version of it, that *"Mrs. Worthington"* for the first time, was put into the show. The song wasn't in the very, very original version, and it always seemed to us that that early part of the show when you have get quite a lot of information about their early years and that LOST world, really, of child actors—that always seemed in the early versions just a little bit thin, and it needed a bit of boosting. *"Mrs. Worthington"* of course, is the ideal song. For the first time we put it in the Kings Head version, and obviously—there was no point—again this comes back to what I was saying about not impersonating. Coward's own recording of it is splendid, although, interesting enough, it misses out a final chorus, the RUDEST of all the choruses.

I don't quite know why he didn't put that on record. It must have something to do with the censorship of the time, although it's not really RUDE. Anyway, we have the FULL lyric. I and Simon worked out, I think, an interesting way of doing it, which was start with immense politesse—silky charm. Someone who is very used to fending off importunate stage mothers.

But, I think you have to imagine the person to whom he is singing the song. I mean, it's actually very important that you get an image of Mrs. Worthington, and THIS Mrs. Worthington is someone who ISN'T brushed off terribly lightly at all. This Mrs. Worthington is somebody who is extremely persistent.

So, the song builds, and, I think, by the end it's quite risky, because he's using vocal muscles that perhaps shouldn't be overtaxed. It builds into a positive crescendo of long pent up bile.

> *Don't put your daughter on the stage, Mrs. Worthington,*
> *Don't put your daughter on the stage,*
> *One look at her bandy legs should prove*
> *She hasn't got a chance,*
> *In addition to which*
> *The son of a bitch*
> *Can neither sing nor dance,*
> *She's a VILE girl and uglier than mortal sin*
> *One look at her has put me in*
> *A tearing bloody rage,*
> *That sufficed,*
> *Mrs. Worthington*
> *Christ!*
> *Mrs. Worthington*
> *Don't put your daughter on the stage!*

So, Mrs. Worthington becomes the target for ALL the stage mothers that plagued him over the years. And he [Cadell] does it extremely well. I mean, it's like a bomb going off. Very funny, but very real, I think, as well. Unfortunately, doing it like that in rehearsal is absolutely fine, but then, when we got to Guildford (which is where we were doing the pre-London try-out of the show, partly because everybody was a bit low with flu bugs—Simon Cadell did get the flu, and his voice, therefore, was rather vulnerable, and *"Mrs. Worthington"* which, having DONE it that way—) he found it impossible to tone DOWN. He simply COULDN'T reduce his voltage. He HAD to play the number that way or he couldn't do it at all, but it so shredded his voice that he then lost it totally, and actually missed something like eight performances in Guildford, which is all we needed. Not an easy thing to have to cope with when you're just trying to bring a show to the boil. It was all a bit of a problem, all that, but YES I think he does *"Mrs. Worthington"* splendidly.

AF: From the first time I saw it, as each refrain was yet another—some time passed and she came back.

AS: Try it again! Yes, yes.

AF: Because, actually, I think that somewhat naively he wrote the song initially to fend off—but it only encouraged—

AS: Exactly! I think he said himself, "The road of the social reformer is PAVED with disillusionment." I mean, *Mrs. Worthington*'s guiding spirit, I mean the INTENTION behind it sadly failed. I mean, the letters came flooding in all the more, USUALLY with, *'I'm not like Mrs. Worthington at all!'* And, of course, they were WORSE!

AF: I guess it must have been really hard to choose the songs, because there are so many songs.

AS: Well, some of them choose themselves. Obviously, since the main body of work that Coward and Lawrence did together was *"Private Lives"* and *"Tonight at 8:30"* the songs from those shows (well, there's only ONE song, really, from *"Private Lives"*—*"Some Day I'll Find You")* that automatically had to find its way in. And, I think, we've got, virtually, ALL the songs from *"Tonight at 8:30"*—yes, I think we have! The other ones were a bit more of a problem, and some have come and gone over the years.

There used to be a song called *"Where Are The Songs We Sung?"* which we used towards the end, but that's gone. That went in this version, largely because of the increased prominence that we gave to the songs that we've already mentioned—*"Come The Wild, Wild Weather"* and *"I'll Remember Her"*. It seemed both to me and to Sheridan [Morley] that those songs were strong enough and full of impact on their own, that we didn't need yet another elegiac lyric number relatively near the close of the evening, and *"Where Are The Songs We Sung?"* we just have a—we originally had quite a long version of that in. So, that's GONE, and, I think, with profit. It always began to put the clouds over the evening, which meant that the final numbers didn't quite work as they should.

I don't think that there's anything that I'm DESPERATE to get in that we've never had in. As I say, over the years, songs have come and gone. I think NOW the selection is probably the BEST of all the versions that we've had. There's enough of the 'point' numbers, the elegiac strain, the lyric strain, I think, is very well taken care of, and a nice mixture, too, of the known and the unknown.

Another number that's never been in before is a song that, frankly, we HAD to put it—well, we didn't have to put THAT particular song in, but we had to put A song in because we had to cover a COSTUME change. Patricia Hodge, I think, beautifully sings a little known number from *"Tonight at 8:30"* from a play called *"Shadow Play"*. Everybody knows *"You Were There"* which is the big number from *"Shadow Play"*.

There is another song which recurs as a refrain throughout the play, sung by different characters, called *"THEN"* which is a very BLEAK, rather almost 'Sondheim-*esque*' song. It's odd the music for that. Quite often we'd startle people who came into rehearsals. We would play it and say, "Who do you think that's by?" More often than not they would say Sondheim rather than Coward. It has something to do with its descending, slightly minor scale. It's a very strange number, and that one isn't known at all. People have forgotten that. It's rather nice, occasionally, to REMIND people of gems that have got forgotten, as well as, of course, give them the ones that they all want.

AF: And then, of course, there's the one song from *"Lady In The Dark"*. Is that the only, as I think about it, the only song that's NOT by Coward in the show?

AS: It IS! Yes. We were very keen this time—again this is new. I mean, one of the problems with the show, has always been [that] their relationship ENDED. One, it didn't end, of course. It went right up to the end of her life. But their PROFESSIONAL collaboration ended when she started to base her career in America, although, each thought that they would work with the other again—of course, she died so young. But this time 'round we thought it would be a good idea to put something in that BOTH—reflected her American career, but ALSO reflected her strongly. She still relied on Coward's advice, influence, even when she wasn't working with him, and it was very much Coward who finally steered her into that show. She was doing her usual dithering about, much to Moss Hart's rage and impotent fury, and it was very much because of Coward that, finally, she was steered into harbor.

We originally wanted to put in *"The Saga of Jenny"* which is also from *"Lady In The Dark"* largely because the lyric of that—"a lady who couldn't make up her mind"—seemed quite appropriate, both to Gertrude Lawrence and to the circumstances of her doing the show, but you really can't do *"The Saga of Jenny"* without—two things, really, it doesn't quite work with JUST a piano, which is all we've got here. Deliberately, it was never a show designed to have even a small orchestra. It's always been designed for just the sympathetic accompaniment of a piano. But *"Jenny"* really needs an orchestration. It ALSO needs the refrain from the chorus. It doesn't quite build unless you have that. Also, it is probably true to say, it would have been very unfair to ask

Patricia Hodge to sing THAT, at that stage in the evening, when she'd already had quite a tiring second half. You can't do *"The Saga of Jenny"* without pulling out all the stops.

Also, most people know that song, whereas, *"My Ship"* certainly in this country, has rather got left by the wayside. It's one of the ones that got away, and it's also, I think, an absolutely beautiful song. Also, it illustrates a side of Gertrude Lawrence that we see quite a lot in Act One when she's singing some of the more wistful numbers that Coward wrote for her early on in her career, things like *"Parisian Pierrot"* but there isn't too much of that in the later material. I think it's rather good that an audience see, quite late in the show, (because *"My Ship"* comes at quite a late point in the show,) they see AGAIN something they've seen in Act One, that extraordinary ability that she had, (which Patricia Hodge also has, I think,) which is to invest an apparently very SIMPLE lyric, (because *"Parisian Pierrot"* is a very simple lyric, and so is *"My Ship"*) but to invest them with such genuine BELIEF that the pathos really becomes quite moving. That they are not just rather emptily romantic numbers, but they have a certain foundation to them, and I think Miss Hodge manages that in both those songs. Anyway, the other reason is that *"My Ship"* is a personal favorite, so that's why I booted for that one.

AF: I was interested to see the dancing, the choreography for *"Parisian Pierrot"* and for *"Dance Little Lady"*. How was that done, is that purely invented, or was there any way of actually finding out what was done?

AS: We tried to find out a bit more than we, sadly, in the end could do about *"Parisian Pierrot"*. There's a lot of photographs about the original production of *"London Calling"* the revue from which *"Parisian Pierrot"* came. We dug up some of the reviews of the original production. It was staged—it was quite a BIG number. Gertrude Lawrence BEGAN it, singing it to a Pierrot doll that she carried, and then gradually the number built, so that the chorus was sung by the chorus of the show singing it to Gertrude Lawrence. It began very simply, but built into what was a big company number. Well, we don't have these resources, of course. I mean, in those days, London revues really were very LAVISH affairs, indeed! They brought in people like Leonid Massine would choreograph numbers.

AF: And Fred Astaire!

AS: Fred Astaire doing quite a lot for Coward at some stages. So, we didn't' have those resources, nor did we want them. So, the staging of that number was very—I staged that number, that wasn't actually done by the choreographer, who's done splendid work elsewhere. We didn't want to make those numbers too busy. The important thing, Coward always used to say this himself, was to concentrate on his LYRICS. He used to get very angry with director/choreographers who did too much business, who ILLUSTRATED too much. I think he's absolutely right.

AF: I recall a story that Joe Layton told me about that, regarding *"The Girl Who Came To Supper"*.

AS: Yes, and indeed, there's a rather rude entry or two in *"The Diaries"* about Joe Layton. I mean, he was very fond of him and admired his work hugely, but, I think, got irritated by that habit, which is perhaps more endemic with Broadway director/choreographers than it is over here—this slight mistrust of words alone—there's a tendency to embroider, perhaps, to over-illustrate.

So, we really didn't want to do that with numbers like *"Parisian Pierrot"*. So, that was very much based on a few photographs that we found from the original production—an attempt to EVOKE the world of intimate revue at that time, rather than to REPRODUCE it literally. As I say, we didn't have the resources to do that, anyway. Really, the main brief to David Toguri, who has done the choreography and done it extremely well, was to keep it simple—not to dress up—not to dizzy up too much.

Some of it is difficult, because the numbers in the *"Red Peppers"* sequence, *"Has Anybody Seen Our Ship?"* and *"Men About Town"*, have to tread that very difficult line. It's meant to be a rundown music hall act. Broken down vaudevillians really, so they have to be rather BAD, but they have to be bad without the audience thinking that the PERFORMERS are being bad. It's a very tricky middle line to tread, and I think he's done that extremely well.

AF: You've had a lot of experience with Coward's works. Back to *"Cowardy Custard"*.

AS: Yes, over the years and *"Cowardy Custard"* is a long time ago, now, of course, my goodness, it's nearly twenty years ago!

AF: That was the seventieth birthday year was it?

AS: I can't remember. I don't know. I don't think it could have been, because we did it in 1972, so, no, it wasn't for his seventieth birthday. The original reason for doing *"Cowardy Custard"* at that time, was that there was a thing known as the 'City of London Festival.' That was its first year, 1972, and the theatre that *"Cowardy Custard"* was done in was the Mermaid Theatre, which was bang in the heart of the City of London, and indeed in those days, not anymore, alas, was very much linked with the City. So, it was the city institutions that provided the springboard for doing *"Cowardy Custard"*. They wanted to celebrate a great Londoner, I think. That was really why the idea of doing a revue based on Coward's material came up.

 It was ORIGINALLY going to be a much more complex show. It was going to be a "revue of revues. It was going to be a kind of history of twentieth century English revue, but that was not a good idea. It would have been far too bulky, far too unwieldy, also, I suspect, it wouldn't have been very good. I was saddled with all the research for it, and basically, it was a very depressing experience, as you found out that, really, an awful lot of the material had sadly dated, and that really the stuff that had lasted, was more or less, ALL by Coward! Which is why, in the end, the show distilled itself around that one talent. But that's such a long time ago.

 It's just been revived. They've been touring it, but I haven't seen that production. And then, I've done a lot of Coward plays.

305

Again, at strategic intervals, I don't want to do nothing but—and when I was running a theatre down in South London at The Greenwich Theatre, we made a kind of policy, really, of every second year we would do a Coward play as part of the repertoire. They became a kind of tradition and a very successful one. Three of those, *"Private Lives", "Present Laughter"*, and a much rarer play, *"Design for Living"* all did very successful Greenwich runs, and then subsequently transferred into the West End. So, yes, over the years, it's been quite a strong link, I suppose.

AF: Did you have any interchange with Coward at the time you devised *"Cowardy Custard"*?

AS: A little. He was very—once the decision to do the show based entirely on his material had been made, he sent quite a long letter to Bernard Miles, who of course, was a professional collaborator of Coward's on *"In Which We Serve"*. They had been in the movie together and knew each other, were old friends. Coward had quite often gone to the Mermaid to see plays over the years. But he wrote to Bernard, (and I was working at the moment full time then,) he wrote Bernard saying, "Fine. Carte blanche. You can do whatever you like. I would like to see the script, obviously, but basically, I don't want to interfere."

So, when the script was ready it was sent to him. As far as I remember, he had a few minor niggles—something to do with the PLACING of numbers, more than CHOICE of numbers. He in no way interfered with what the selection was, but I think, rightly he pointed out that in the first half there was perhaps too much concentration on the lyric numbers, and not enough on the comic material. So, a little bit of redistribution went on. We also had to cut it quite heavily, and he was quite right. He pointed out when he'd read the finished script that he thought it was a might long. He was dead right, because when we first previewed it, it ran for three hours, which was much too long. So, we had to make quite a few snips, rather hastily, because in those days one didn't get the luxury of long preview periods.

Then he came to see it.

He came to the first night, which was a fairly memorable occasion. He was, by then, rather old and clearly not a well man. I think there was a feeling in the audience that night, (a night I remember fairly well,) that this might just possibly be the last time he was seen in public at an evening of his own material. It turned out it WASN'T, because there was a revival very shortly afterwards of *"Private Lives"* with Maggie Smith and Robert Stephens, which he managed to attend.

Then he came back, and indeed this was the last show of his own work he saw. So, he came back to *"Cowardy Custard"* about six months into the run and to see it again. Not to check up on us so much, as I think, he genuinely like the show, and of course, I think the surprise to HIM, (he was the first to admit,) was that he'd forgotten a great deal of the material. There were things in that, as I say, back in 1972, songs that had got totally forgotten, and indeed, songs that I think that had never seen the light of day. There was a song called *"Touring Days"* which indeed is in *"Noël and Gertie"*. I was just going to ask you about that—he didn't publish it.

It was never published. We FOUND that at the bottom of a trunk in the flat of his, then, London representative, who hoarded over the years, scrapbooks, all the things he hadn't bothered to take either to Switzerland or to Jamaica with him. At the bottom of this trunk was this rather ragged piece of sheet music. I think he'd written it when he was something like nineteen. I think he had totally forgotten it himself. The memory of that song had totally left him. I mean, he didn't deny that he'd written it, but he'd actually forgotten writing it. That's a very affectionate little number about the joys or miseries of life on the road, obviously written out of personal experience. Some of the other songs, some of the earlier stuff—things like *"Mary Make Believe"* he hadn't heard for fifty years. So, I think the show both pleased him and rather worried him that he'd written such a vast output, a lot of which he'd totally forgotten.

AF: I guess it was the line quoted from—After he had seen *"Oh, Coward!"*—"I came out humming the tunes!"

AS: Oh, yes! [laughs] By then, he'd seen *"Cowardy Custard"* of course. *"Oh, Coward!"* followed *"Cowardy Custard"* here is always a slight source of pique, I think, to those of us involved in *"Cowardy Custard"* because it was bought. The show was bought for America, but then, of course, *"Oh, Coward!"* came along and rather, as we say over here, "queered our pitch." There was no way that TWO shows, all based on his music, could run in New York at the same time. So, sadly the show never made it to New York, which we were all rather disappointed about.

AF: Yes, I wish it HAD—WOULD make it to the States some time.

AS: Well, maybe there's still time, we shall see. It's done occasionally in stock, summer stock companies do it over there, and it's done a lot in regional repertory companies over here, but it hasn't had a major London revival, and I think, obviously, while *"Noël and Gertie"* is on, it couldn't possibly. Some of the material, to a certain extent, is duplicated.

AF: How did you get interested in theatre?

AS: Well, my parents used to take me a lot. I never planned to be a director. It all was a complete accident. I was all set to be—I don't know if you have the phrase over there—we call them "dons." Do you know what I mean by that? University teacher. I went to two universities. I don't know what I'm doing in the theatre. I've got TWO degrees, for goodness sake! I first of all went to the University very near my home, which was in Scotland. That was a very OLD university in Saint Andrews, the home of golf, but also the home of the second oldest university in Great Britain. After that, I went to Oxford to do a post graduate degree, and I was all set to stay on. I was going to be a university teacher. It was largely because of America, oddly enough, that I became a director. I did a tour of the campus circuit with a production that was formed by a company from Oxford students and a company from Cambridge students. We were directed by a professional director ALWAYS. The year I did it, it was directed by Jonathan Miller!

When I returned after doing the tour, which was over our Christmas vacation period, I had a few months to fill in before I started this position at my old college at Oxford. To fill in, and also to earn some money, I needed a job, and Jonathan Miller very kindly offered me a job as his Assistant Director on ONE production only at the Mermaid. It was a production of *"The Tempest"* way back in 1970. I went for five weeks on five pounds a week, and I stayed for five years. I never did go back to college. I had to write a very polite letter, which I don't think pleased them, saying "Awfully sorry, but I won't be coming. I think I've found something else I'd rather do." I don't regret it at all, but, as I say, it was never planned.

The interest began at a very young age. I was born in a Scottish town called Dundee, which had a very good repertory theatre, and my parents used to go to every production, virtually, and from quite an early age used to take ME. So, that's where the interest in the theatre began. The desire to work in it really wasn't kindled until I started to DO it. I did a bit of student theatre, a bit of undergraduate theatre, and some acting. I used to do a lot of revue. I was a very bad actor. I don't know why Jonathon really wanted to employ me at all, because I was very BAD in the production of his play. It was the worst part in Shakespeare. It was Fabian in *"Twelfth Night"* which is the least rewarding role in the entire Shakespearean output, in my opinion. I think he wrote it to make some actor very miserable.

[laughter]

I did a lot of revue. I could do that. I found that much easier than plays. You know, changing characters every five minutes. I didn't get bored doing that. And I used to WRITE revues, as well, and a bit of directing. Basically, that was just for fun. There was no intention whatsoever of doing it as a career, and here I am twenty years on. Here I am still doing it. Still thinking, "When am I going to get a proper job?"

AF: What are you planning next? Do you have some—?

AS: I'm going very soon, in fact, to America. I'm going to the Long Wharf Theatre in New Haven [Connecticut] to do yet another musical revue based on another English icon figure, a comedienne called Joyce Grenfell, who was a very popular figure over here. [She] died about ten years ago. She was the "English Ruth Draper" I suppose, is a thumbnail description of her. Oddly enough, they were distantly related, too. She was a diseuse, monologist, wrote some rather good songs, most of which had music by a composer, in a kind of "minor Coward" vein. A guy called Richard Addinsell, who wrote some songs for *"Sigh No More"*, a Coward revue, in which Joyce Grenfell starred. I don't know HOW it will go down in America at all! I wouldn't have thought Americans had ever HEARD of Joyce Grenfell, but it is performed by a BRILLIANT British comedienne, called Maureen Lipmann, who is also a dazzling actress.

The show was a big success over here. Guys at the Long Wharf saw it, and seemed to think it would work for their audience. So, that goes on in January over there. Then I come back to do a play for my old friend, Alan Ayckbourn, who runs a theatre in Scarborough, where I work fairly regularly. I did an American play this year up there, and I'm going to do, (not quite sure yet,) a new play, I think, for him in April. I always like to keep it varied. I never like to stay doing the same thing for too long.

AF: What do you think the chances are of *"Noël and Gertie"* going to the States?

AS: I honestly don't know. I think it would probably work rather well with a sophisticated audience. I think in certain cities, from my knowledge of American audiences, I think it would probably play quite well in New York, probably play quite well in San Francisco. The problem, of course, is that it does demand two extraordinary performers. I think we have them over here, but then one runs that old problem of trying to get them Equity tickets. So, whether they would ever allow Patricia and Simon in, I just don't know. I'm not sure that it would be a very good idea, necessarily, to cast it with American actors. I'm not being rude about American actors, because I do think that they can occasionally play Coward extremely well, but THIS show, which is so steeped, because THEIR roots were so steeped in a very English touring and variety theatre in the early days, I honestly don't think it would quite work without quintessentially British performers.

    Certainly, I'd love it if there was chance of bringing the two of them over. I think two years ago there was a possibility of Patricia doing it in New York, but they found it very difficult to cast the Noël [part]. So, we shall see. Let's hope it happens. It would be great fun, anyway. It's been great fun to do here, and it would be fascinating to see whether it could work with an American audience.

AF: Well, I hope so! I really appreciate your taking the time to talk with us today.

AS: Pleasure!

AF: I enjoyed the show immensely.

AS: Good.

AF: Was moved to laughter and tears both.

AS: Well, that was the plan!

ELAINE STRITCH

b. February 2, 1925

Interviewed June 7, 1993

Elaine Stritch is an actress and singer who created indelible roles on Broadway in Rodgers & Hart's *"Pal Joey"* (1952), Noël Coward's *"Sail Away"* (1961), and Stephen Sondheim's *"Company"* (1970). She received much acclaim for her Tony Award winning one-woman show *"Elaine Stritch at Liberty"* (2002).

Noël Coward became an outspoken admirer of Elaine's talent in 1958, when he saw her playing in a hopeless musical, *"Goldilocks"* and soon after in 1961 he gave Elaine her Broadway breakthrough part as the lead in his new musical *"Sail Away"*.

The next year she won the hearts of London audiences in the West End premiere of *"Sail Away"* and then returned to Broadway in a starring role in Sondheim's *"Company"*. In addition to her outstanding work in musicals, she has gathered many accolades and awards for her straight dramatic roles, including a Tony nomination for her work in Edward Albee's *"A Delicate Balance"* in 1996. This interview took place on a park bench in New York's Central Park.

ALAN FARLEY: I've been reading in *"The Diaries"* and in Coley's book about Noël—how he first met you, and how he saw you in *"Goldilocks"*. Hated it, but loved you.

ELAINE STRITCH: He came backstage that night and he said, (which is poetic justice reigning supreme), *"This musical has no book, no lyric, no whatever—and the only talented thing in it is Elaine Stritch, and she's in tears in her dressing room. Something must be very, very wrong."*

What a funny man he was. I get Noël 'Cowarditis' if I start talkin' about this man, I just, you know, he's kinda like the male Judy Garland for me. Once you start telling stories about Noël, you can't stop.

AF: Many people who tell me stories automatically get into imitating his style of delivery.

ES: He had such a presence. When he was there, he was *so* there. I'll tell you at the end of this interview something he said to me later in his life. Let's go in step by step.

Another thing I think that made him come was Leonard Bernstein. He saw me do a benefit at Carnegie Hall, I think it was, and I sang two songs from *"Wonderful Town"*. I did the duet, *[singing] Why, oh why, oh, why-O'* and I sang the wonderful song that Rosalind [Russell] did in the original. *[singing] One Hundred Easy Ways to Lose a Man!*

He called Noël and said he had seen a performer that he thought Noël would like. And that's what made Noël come.

It's a small world, the theatre, and when you—I've never seen it to fail! When you think either in life or the theatre, I'm just beginning to realize it happens in life, you know, that cliché—*"It's always darkest before the dawn"* is really true. It reminds me of one Noël used to use, *"It'll never get well if you pick it."* Isn't that in one of his lyrics?

AF: Oh, in *"Red Peppers"*.

ES: Right. Anyway, that was it. I was going to do *"SailAway"* and *"Goldilocks"* ran about six months, but not very happily. Then I did *"Sail Away"* with Noël, and *it took two years of my life,* what with the American rehearsal, playing, and the London rehearsal . . . visiting him in Switzerland.

You know, it's interesting in life, Alan, we never really—it kind of goes back to *"youth is a wonderful thing, too bad it has to be wasted on the young"*—it's the same principle. You just look back on your life and say, *"Jesus, did I really appreciate where the hell I was?"* Did I *appreciate* the fact that I was *sitting in a hot pink dining room, or a living room in the mountains, at Les Avants, in Switzerland, listening to Noël Coward play the piano?!*

AF: I got a chance to visit Graham there, and just seeing that, and seeing the 'john' *papered with the sheet music!* Joe Layton gave me a tape that Evelyn Russell [Ed: Broadway/Film actress, b. Aug 4, 1926, d. Feb 4, 1976] had made of Noël playing the piano in Les Avants. About a half an hour just sitting here playing away, when she visited him one time. She had an early little portable tape recorder.

ES: I noticed an interesting thing about Noël, when he would do that after dinner at night. *He never played his own music.* He played Rodgers and Hart, he played Rodgers and Hammerstein, he played Schwartz and Dietz, he played Otto Harbach, he played anything, but not his own stuff. Interesting. I think that was one place he behaved like a civilian—in his own home.

AF: *"Sail Away"* was remarkable, in that, during the trials it was almost completely changed, and you were given, essentially, the lead role.

ES: Low self-esteem reigned supreme! The night that I was told that I had to be in Noël's suite at twelve midnight, that he wanted to talk to me, I thought I was going to get the sack. So, there is no logic in the theatre. I was stopping the show every night with *"Why Do the Wrong People Travel?"* . . . and I thought I was going to get fired.

AF: For stopping the show?

ES: Yes! And then I found out that I was going to get the whole basket, you know! So, it was thrilling! It was a challenge, and *I learned her* [Jean Fenn's] *part and her songs in two days,* Sunday and Monday, and opened Monday night. God forbid we should lose a night, you know.

And then, Tuesday night I was out of commission. *No voice.* Not because of the strenuous singing. It was the whole emotional experience. It took my breath away, my voice away, everything. And of course, he got sore at me, told me that if *I didn't have the five beers I'd had at the Variety Club I could have gone on.* It was the only time I ever got mad at him because he was a perfectionist. I must say he never demanded anything of anybody else that he didn't do himself. I looked at him and said, "You're lucky it was five beers and not a quart of bourbon!" I was absolutely emotionally drained.

But Wednesday I got on again, and then we went on to New York and I got brilliant notices in New York. It was thrilling. And the idea of working with him was so wonderful. And Joe Layton, who was a very big *'power behind the power'* of that hit show.

Then he wanted me to do it in London. I didn't know whether I wanted to do it. *Imagine!* ME wondering *'whether I wanted to go to London to play the lead in a Noël Coward musical . . .'*. It astounds me. As I say, again, in retrospect . . .

So, off I went!

Noël did not get his proper credit in New York in the reviews. Some good things, but it was much better than they said it was.

AF: That is the one show of his I'd love to see revived. It's got such great songs, such great lyrics.

ES: So, between New York and London I went to Switzerland, which was a thrill. Went gambling at Evian. It was a tiny little period in my life where I was literally among the elite. And coming from a Midwestern town, Birmingham, Michigan, I was not aware of it, and I think that's why Noël liked me.

AF: I gather that he also had the ability to put you at ease in a situation like that.

ES: Sure, because he's the 'other side of the tracks,' you know.

AF: Right, from Teddington.

ES: Absolutely! I love the story about Noël Coward. *his mother thought they had to pay!*—remember that famous story? When they said he got the part, and she said, *"How much?"* and they said, *"Twelve pounds fifty,"* and she said, *"We can't **afford** it."* Wonderful story.

Anyway, we opened in London. Again, the same thing happened. I was the 'big discovery' and I got all the notices. You know what they don't understand is, *what would I have done without Noël Coward? That's what made it work.*

AF: I heard a great story, (I can't repeat on the radio), about Harold Fielding [Producer of *"Sail Away"*] and Mary Ellis' friend, Alan Wheatly, said that Noël said about Harold, *"If you pour hot water on him—instant shit."*

ES: I must say, Harold was a pain in the ass, he really was.
    Anyway, a couple of lovely stories about Noël . . .
    Noël had a very fatherly attitude towards me. I think he really cared about me. You know, most people like that in the theatre care about you because they want you on the stage every night making money.
    I think it went beyond that with Noël. I think he really loved me.
    I remember once having an interview with Mike Wallace about Noël Coward—Mike Wallace is *such* an asshole—
    He looks at me, and he says, "Was Noël Coward a homosexual?"
    And I evaded it completely.
    I said, "Oh, Mike, for heaven's sakes! What a question! But let me tell you this—when I was out for an evening with Noël Coward, I felt like I was with more of a man than about ninety—eight percent of the men that I've been out with. Put that in your mic and smoke it."
    Noël really *cared* about me. He *cared* about my health. Noël was worried about my drinking. *I drank a lot.* I remember once I went on the wagon, temporarily, for my health, and he wrote me a letter, and I told him. I wrote him a letter in Switzerland and said, "I've stopped drinking."
    He wrote me back a letter and the gist of it was, *'. . . you know, it's wonderful! WONDERFUL! You're so talented, and you have so much to give! . . .'* and *'. . . that drinking would get in your way . . .'* and DAH-dee-dah, but, you know, it takes one to know

one. And then at the end of the letter, he said, *'Oh, and Stritchie, think how pleased your friends will be!'*

I always thought that I *had* to drink to be popular, you know. It was all fun for me.

AF: I think he tried stopping drinking at one time and also tried stopping smoking.

ES: Oh! Tell me about it!

AF: I remember reading in his diaries how self-satisfied he was about it, but he never wrote about the fact when he *started back* drinking and smoking again.

ES: No, never. So, I remember, while we're on the subject of booze, we had a party one night on a boat that went around the Thames. It was the night the Queen of England came to the theatre. (Which makes me think of *another* story.) On our way up to the box to meet the Queen, Noël was so nervous that I wouldn't do it right. Noël looked at me and said, "You know, Stritchie, you have to *curtsey.*"

I said, "Noël, I went to Sacred Heart Convent for twelve years. That's ALL I did!"

Anyway, he gave this party. All the kids, me included, were up on the top deck turning Noël Coward songs into rock and roll, or whatever we were doing, I don't know, whatever the swing thing was at that time, and we were drinking *champagne,* and then I got this dopey idea of throwing the champagne glasses overboard when we finished the toast. We were all trying to pretend we were Vivien Leigh or somebody.

One funny line he said—I got absolutely crocked at this party—and he said to me that I was *the only actress he ever saw fall UP a gangplank!*

Then the other thing—

He came to my dressing room the next day. I didn't usually drink that much, but I *did drink that much* that day, because it was such a relief. And the Queen had seen it and gone. It was all pressure, you know.

He came to my dressing room early the next day. It was a matinee day. All producers throw parties the night before a matinee. (I'm certain they are sadistic!) He'd asked me to come in early. He wanted to talk to me. He talked to me for about an hour and a half, and it was so sweet. He really was concerned.

I said, "Noël, we all make mistakes. So, I got drunk. I'm better now, and everything's okay, and I'm here and in one piece and ready to do the matinee."

"All right all right," he said. He warned me, "You *must* get married, and it would be good for you to be married," and he went on and on and on. He got a little teary.

Then he kissed me good-bye, and he walked up those long steps that go up to the stage door at the Savoy Theatre. The Savoy Theatre is underground. That's where everybody wanted to play during the war so they wouldn't get bombed. They were in a bomb shelter to start with.

Anyway, he gets to the top of the stairs, and after all this wonderful meeting, and so emotional, and 'kissy, kissy, koo-kee' and everything was terrific.

As a matter of fact, I was standing there thinking, "This could not be the last line of this scene. There's got to be something coming, because I don't think he'd go out on that note." See?

He gets to the top of the stairs, and he turns around and he says, "Oh, and incidentally, *Stritchie,* throwing champagne glasses into the Thames went out in twenty-nine!"

Well, my dear, [laughing] the one thing I never wanted to be in life, was *boring,* and I'm telling, you he *really let me have it.* It pushed my buttons, and of course what I did was *burst out laughing!*

After we closed in London, I remained a great friend of Noël's and he of mine.

We saw each other occasionally, not often.

I remember that I told you that I would tell you something that happened very shortly before he died.

He used to say to me that one of the things that really worried him most about life was that he would not be remembered. Which is kind of funny, isn't it? It shows you that he suffered from the same low self-esteem that a lot of artists do.

And I remembered saying to him—and I was very young, and I didn't know much about Noël Coward, and I went to work for him—I said to him, "Listen, Noël, anybody who wrote *"Brief Encounter"* is going to be remembered."

I don't know why I picked that film, but I did. Isn't it funny? Because you know why, I think? I just thought of it now. I think it's because it's a serious, sensitive subject that he dealt with so masterly, and with such feeling, and such understanding, and simpatico, and *tenderness* that that really is what made the man. That's what was there, in spite of his humor and because of his humor and everything.

I thought that he was so dear that he would say that. Certainly, today is living proof that Noël is remembered. How long has Noël been dead?

AF: Eighteen years.

ES: Oh, my god. He said to me, about two months before he died—the doctor had told him that *if* he exercised and *if* he stopped drinking and *if* he stopped smoking he could live another ten years. He was terribly afraid of dying when he was young, but as he got older. I guess we *all* get prepared for the big adventure. *he really didn't want to go on.*

I asked him *"why?"* one night. I said, "Why wouldn't you be? You've got all your faculties. Everything. You're sharp as a tack."

Honestly, Alan, he said something to me that was so moving, and the reason I think it's so moving, and I'm going to say this at the risk of sounding very egotistical, but I do have the same problem, maybe that's why I recognized it in Coward—maybe not to such an extent, but I know what he's talking about—

He said, "I am so bloody tired of *entertaining.*"

It was a startling remark.

He elaborated a little bit on it. **He said, "Every time I leave the flat, or the house, or the hotel suite, or wherever I am, I *'assume the position.'* I get out of that door and everybody expects—*TA DA! Curtain up!*"**

I'm telling you that that can be the drag of all time, and once you've established it, it's very hard to get out of it. There are just a handful of people in the world that will go and spend time with you *socially,* and just sit there, and not demand a one-woman, or one-man show. That's the time for someone to give up the ghost, I think, and go to that, you know, that—what am I trying to say?—I was going to say 'go to *writer's paradise'* but in Noël's case you'd have to say *actor's, writer's, composer's, lyricist's, director's'*—wherever that paradise is, I'm sure he's in it. He was such a—he had such high principles. I think he was a very *good* man, actually.

AF: It was said that that *persona* was his own greatest creation. I guess, in a way, he was trapped by it.

ES: *Mmm-hmmm!* Absolutely!

AF: What was the toughest song to learn in *"Sail Away"?* Were they all tough, or were they all about the same?

ES: No, none of them were tough. I enjoyed Noël's material so much. It was good material. *Good material takes half the energy,* you know. God!
   Let me tell you about a few shows I was in where the material wasn't any good. It's like taking nine lashes on some—you know. It was just awful. So, it's a holiday to have good material! I mean, it's hard work, but you know what I mean. You're confident when you go out there. You've got something to say. But, if you go out there with nothing to say—I won't do it anymore. I've been trapped a couple of times in bad material. It's not worth it. It's too embarrassing.

AF: *"Later Than Spring"* is one of my favorites. I don't think it has gotten as much play as it should have.

ES: I sang that the other night at a fifty year tribute to Vincent Sardi, and they loved it, the audience, they loved it. It's such a lovely thought, and as I get older, it gets more and more pleasing and tender to listen to.

AF: I think one of the songs that you sang in a BBC program I heard recently was *"Marvelous Party"* and you said that Noël had forbidden you to sing it.

ES: —*until he died,* because he was the best at it, and he *knew* I'd be *good* at it. Oh, I loved that! That's wonderful! That was a hard lyric. Some of his stuff was hard to learn because it was so active. All those names! But, no, I found no trouble with his stuff at all. It was FUN to do his material, and certainly fun to do his dialogue.

AF: Have you ever played in any of his other plays?

ES: I did *"Private Lives"* at the Theatre d'Lys in New York. I loved *Amanda*. I just loved it.
    Another thing I think is in Noël's favor is that—[hushed confidentiality]—I have *left* my fifties. That's as honest as I'm going to get. I could play Amanda today.

AF: Joan Collins is doing it.

ES: Oh, please! This program is about Noël Coward, isn't it? Okay. No, no Joan Collins, in the opinion of *this reviewer,* is not right for *"Private Lives"* but I give her credit. I shouldn't even say that because I haven't seen it. She might be divine. However, I would like to even do *"Design For Living"*. What I am trying to say is, there are certain actors—I mean certain playwrights who write plays that can be done by actresses of any age. It doesn't make any difference. Tennessee Williams is one. You know, '. . . *the play is the thing* . . .' and if you look appealing and in good shape, there is no reason why you can't play it. There is no reason why you can't do *"Brief Encounter"* at any age.
    Also, the interesting thing is that the theatre doesn't honor that anymore. *Age is such a big deal!* It's the first question everybody asks.

AF: It's always in every newspaper story. It has to give the age of people.

ES: Unbelievable!

AF: I don't understand. There *may be* times when it's relevant, but ninety percent of the time it isn't.

ES: Absolutely. It makes you angry because it has nothing to do with—look at all the great actresses of the past that played *Juliet* at sixty! I mean, that's an exaggeration, let's face it, but you know what I'm getting at.

Oh, I'll tell you what I was going to tell you, having given up the 'sauce' as they call it, is another instance in which Noël was yet again, right!—that if you love alcohol as much as I did, true, it interferes, because it is *an escape.* It doesn't make you have the feelings that are being sent to you day by day *for real.* And that's my strong suit—*reality*—in my work. Since I am not drinking, I feel so much better about my work. My only regret is that he is not hanging around to appreciate it.

I remember hearing that Noël Coward was in the audience when I did *"Who's Afraid Of Virginia Woolf?"* I found that I was out of vodka, and I *always* had a drink before I went on the stage, *just one,* I mean, I didn't overshoot the runway, but I had to come down a little bit, because my nerves were so jumpy.

I remember having to go out in my bra and pants, and *raincoat* to the liquor store to get a bottle of vodka so I could have that *one* drink to give me the courage to do it in front of Noël.

Then, you know, you get fooled, because Noël Coward said *it was the best he'd ever seen.* So, you say, 'well, it must work.' You know what I mean? So it takes you a lot of years later, and a lot of maturity, and a lot of 'quiet times,' I guess, for want of a better expression, to come to the conclusion that—I came to the conclusion that I wanted to find out if I could do it *without* that—stuff, *and I find that I can!* And that I'm *much* better, and that raises your self-esteem. I'm a little sorry Noël didn't experience that, you know?

I think we're in a generation of sobriety. An up and coming generation of sobriety, and yet you hear that kids are taking alcohol like it's going out of style.

AF: And younger and younger kids.

ES: And younger and younger. But there are an awful lot of people my age that don't drink today, I'll tell you that.

AF: Well, I've found that though it's never been a real problem for me, that the older I get, my tolerance varies. Sometimes I can have one drink and it affects me, and other times not . . . so, I have to watch myself.

ES: Getting old is a lot of fun, isn't it?

AF: Did you see that picture of Noël when he was two years old? He looked like a girl. Long hair. I don't know if it was a dress, or was it? I do a slide show, slides and tapes of Noël's songs. Who'd have guessed that this little two year old would grow up to look like this. And then I found a photo in Coley's book of Noël and Gerald du Maurier in drag at a garden party. So, I go from that one, to that one.

ES: Oh, that's great!

AF: I kick myself, because I was living in Los Angeles in 1955, when he appeared in Las Vegas, but I wasn't interested then. I just wish I had gone at that time, but I'm just glad I've got a chance to meet these people. I've met and interviewed Joyce Carey.

ES: Isn't she lovely!

AF: Such a sweet lady, and such a wicked sense of humor, too. So, I go back to London every year now, just to see people and do interviews. Have you seen or read *"Waiting In The Wings"?*

ES: Yes, I've read it.

AF: That's one I would love to see done.

ES: Yeah, I like that play, it's a wonderful play.

AF: I think you could play an older woman like that.

ES: Oh, sure! Absolutely! Certainly I could now! Don't be so silly! I told you I left my fifties, Alan!

AF: At one time my ideal casting was Bette Davis and Katherine Hepburn for a TV movie. I thought it would have been great, but it never happened. I just heard a BBC production, a radio production with Mary Ellis, Evelyn Laye, and Dinah Sheridan.

ES: Oh, nice.

AF: It was! I like it, I really like it. There was a rumor a couple of years ago it was going to be done in this country. [Ed: It was finally produced on Broadway in 1999 with Lauren Bacall and Rosemary Harris.]

ES: It was never done? Ask me some more questions.

AF: I'd like to talk about the lyrics.

ES: Okay.

AF: Did you ever see Noël at work on his songs?

ES: No, never. Oh, no, no, no. You mean composing? No, no. Oh, god no.

AF: I guess he was sort of unhappy at first, that you hadn't gotten his words 'word perfect' the first rehearsal.

ES: Oh, Noël and I differed in that respect. He liked someone to know all their lines, all their lyrics, and all their music from the first day of rehearsal. I don't agree with him. I like to find my way as I go along, and learn as I experience the rehearsal. But, *I did it his way, because he knew more than I did,* so—and those are the *only* kind of people I can work with—*somebody who knows more than I do.*

The trouble begins when you work with someone who knows *less* than you do. Then you can't take it, and then you argue, and then you end up—

Noël told me that. He said, "Never work with anybody who knows *less* than you do, because they will end up your enemy, because they're mad at you, because you do *know more!*"

He was certainly right about that.

I remember sending a script to Noël. I could have kicked myself I didn't take his advice. I sent him a script to ask him if I should do something. He read the script.

He called my service and left word. The lady at the service said to me, "Mister Noël Coward called and he said the script will be with the doorman. He thinks *he* might rather enjoy it."

And then 'Miss Dummy' here, went ahead and *did* the play, and it was AWFUL! So, I *shoulda* listened! I *shoulda* listened.

AF: How would you compare Stephen Sondheim with Noël Coward?

ES: I know that Steve is very fond of Noël's work. I think the *seriousness* of Noël's work is so covered with such subtlety, that it *seems to be easier* material to do. I don't think it is.

I just think that Steve's work is so *thought provoking* that you have to work at lightening it up.

Noël gives you a little bit more of a *lift.* And Noël's music is easier to sing than Steve's. For instance, there never was, in the opinion of this reviewer, a good comedy song that didn't have a good melody, *ever.* And Stephen Sondheim's melodies are GOOD but they're *difficult,* and they're *offbeat.* They're interesting, which makes them very unique, and of course, they're HARD to learn. *hard to learn.*

One of the funniest lines that Sondheim ever wrote in *"Company"* was in that chorus thing that the four girls did about *"Bobby, Bobby"*, when we are talking about him. We're listening in on an affair he's having . . . I had a line, talking about this girl who's *". . . not right for you Bobby. Don't waste your time on it . . ."* and *Joanna's* line was

[singing] *"She's tall enough to be his mother."*

I thought it was just *weird!*
That's 1970, you know. But Coward's melodies are so simple and sing-able. *"Why Do The Wrong People Travel?"* when you hear that, you'd almost—it sounds like an MGM musical, [singing] *"Why do the wrong people travel, travel, travel? When the right people stay back home?"*—It's so sing-able.

And then you get Sondheim, [singing] *"Here's to the ladies who lunch. Everybody laugh!"* It's TOUGH! Minor, major . . . *do do do do* . . . all over the place. But they're *similar artists* because they're so *thought provoking.*

It's an interesting observation that comedy songs, if they have a good melody, they usually work. I remember one Arthur Schwartz did with the wonderful lady lyricist, Dorothy Fields. [singing] *"He'd say 'pardon my glove' politely when he shook my hand."*

Remember that? from *"A Tree Grows In Brooklyn"*.
[singing] *"He'd only use four letter words I didn't understand, he had refinement."*

It was a wonderful song and it was so melodic, you know, reminiscent of the old musical comedies. It was so wonderful that Steve Sondheim had a chance to write that satire on the old shows with those songs.

[singing] *"I'm just a Broadway Baby . . ."*
That stuff was so much fun to do, because it's not difficult. *It's loaded.* You know, so loaded with fun, and satire, and all that jazz.

AF: *"I'm Still Here"* is one of my favorites.

ES: Oh, yes! My god, I'm going to *wait.* I want to be in my seventies before I touch that song. I've always disliked the idea of doing it. It's a great song. I'm not ready for that. As a matter of fact, not because of her age, because the girl who did that the best is Yvonne De Carlo, even though she couldn't sing very well. She was *right* for it. She was saying, *'goddamit I'm here!'*

AF: I saw Dolores Gray do it in London.

ES: She's good. Oh, a wonderful voice. What a voice!

AF: But I was hoping you would do it at the end of *"Follies in Concert".*

ES: No, I'd much rather do *"Broadway Baby".* Much rather. Carol Burnett should never have done it. She's too young.

AF: Yeah, but you have such great character in your voice.

ES: Exactly. And Carol is silly. She's in her prime, for god's sake. She didn't '. . . *stuff dailies in her shoes* . . .' neither did I! I think there has to be a certain credibility, or why do it?

HARRY ALAN TOWERS

b. October 19, 1921   d. July 31, 2009

Interviewed February 16, 1996

Harry Allan Towers has worked as a producer in radio, television, and films for over fifty years. In 1947, he persuaded Noël Coward to record thirteen half-hour radio programs about his songs, for international syndication. The interview was conducted over the telephone.

ALAN FARLEY: How did you first meet Noël Coward?

HARRY ALLAN TOWERS: I met Noël during the war when I was in the Royal Air Force. At that time I was in charge of an outfit called The Overseas Recorded Broadcast Service, which is the equivalent of the Armed Forces Radio Service. So, it was used to put programs on disks, which we sent all over the world to British troops.
    How I met Noël Coward . . . He did a kind of program, a biographical program. We became friendly. Then after the war I started my own business, Towers of London, making and selling radio programs all over the world, which ultimately ended up with Orson Wells, and Laurence Olivier—all the big stars involved.
    The very *first* big star to work for me was Noël. The other one was Gracie Fields. At that time he had reopened the famous Theatre Royal, Drury Lane, with a show called *"Pacific 1860"*. It was, unfortunately, *not* a big success. It was called, in the trade, *"Soporific 1860"* but it had some nice tunes in it.
    I went to him with an idea that we would do thirteen half-hour radio programs. Well, Noël was a man who attracted enormous *loyalty* from everybody who worked with him and knew him, including myself.
    He said, "Okay, I'll do thirteen half-hour radio shows with only *one* condition. We'll use members of the cast, and the orchestra leader of the rather unsuccessful show *"Pacific*

1860"—(which was being kept alive by infusions of cash at Drury Lane),—"as long as they all get work out of it." So, that's how we did it. We had in the show, Joyce Grenfell, Graham Payn, of course, and the music for the show was done by Mantovani, which was long before he was associated with big orchestras. We had an orchestra of about fifteen people. We made the show. It was recorded in pieces. Noël did the commentary separately, which was largely biographical.

He was interested entirely in his works, and in each show he, of course, sang one of his point numbers—needless to say, *"Mad Dogs and Englishmen", "Stately Homes of England"*—he had thirteen point numbers, and we had thirteen shows. Oh, no—on the thirteenth show, his own personal contribution was the 'toast' speech from *"Cavalcade"*. He always used to put it together with *"Mad Dogs and Englishmen"* as a party piece. The shows did quite nicely, though I don't think they were ever broadcast in England. I can't really remember. I know we sold them foreign. We didn't sell them in the United States. Noël also did the commentary in both French *and* Spanish, and we sold them in France and Spain. They sold, I think, in Canada, if I remember rightly, certainly in Australia and New Zealand, and all over the Commonwealth, the English-speaking world.

That was really the start of my radio business.

[**AF** notes: Through the diligence of record producer, David Lennick, copies of those programs have been found in Canada. Excerpts were issued on one CD, and copies of the entire series now reside in the Coward Archive in Brimingham.]

HT: Also, at that particular time, I was associated with Lord Rothermere on the London Daily Mail, on promotional schemes. I came up with the idea of launching what became the British Film Awards. Of course, they're altogether different now. To begin with, they were a *newspaper* stunt, and I organized them.

Through that, I got to know Lady Rothermere, who was, of course, the much publicized nymphomaniac wife of Lord Rothermere, and she ultimately went off with—

AF:—Ian Fleming?

HT:—who wrote the *James Bond* stories.
She invited me to lunch with her, because she had decided to help Noël Coward and bring back the 'theatrical garden party,' which had been a great pre-war event, and which they couldn't have launched on the same basis, because the old venue of the 'theatrical garden party' in pre-war years had been in the circle of Regents Park, in the center of London. But, the only place she could get for a place for a garden party was out in Hurlingham, which is, of course, a famous polo ground.

So, I agreed to organize it, and had the full resources of Lord Rothermere behind me, and thus, I became involved with Noël Coward, *again.*

At that time, I was rather bright, twenty-six years old, with a big business, and all the rest of it, and I'd put on a lot of shows all over the place.

I'll never forget the first day of the 'theatrical garden party,' which was a most elaborate affair. We put together all the tents, and marquees we could get hold of in England just after the war. We had a 'Circle to the Stars'—*everything.* Rex Harrison—every star you could think of there.

I'm getting in the rented car with my production manager on the morning of the 'theatrical garden party,' when I said, "You know, it's really wonderful. Here I'm *only* twenty-six years old, I've *done* all these things—I've done *this, that,* I've put up shows at the Albert Hall!—*everywhere*—the only thing I *haven't* staged, yet, is a *WATER SPECTACLE.*"

So, my production manager rolled down the car window, put his hand out, and said,

"Harry, your dreams have come true."

AF: [chuckling] Oh, no!

HT: It pissed with rain! It *pissed* with rain—*IT POURED!*
Right at the end, in the marquee, the tent, when everybody had gone home, Noël Coward was *reclining* on a cushioned bed, with his brow being *mopped by* the Duchess of Kent! and his feet

being *massaged by* Richard Attenborough! and the man from Price Waterhouse came in with the figures. *I'd actually succeeded in losing ten thousand pounds!*

AF: Oh, no!

HT: [chuckling] Noël looked at me with those sad eyes and said, "My dear Harry, I don't fault your *enthusiasm,* but remember that forevermore the three bloodiest words in the English language in my vocabulary will be *'theatrical garden party."*

I went in to see Lord Rothermere on the Monday morning, and he sighed and said, "It wasn't a great success."

I said, "Rain stopped the play."

He said, "How much did it cost you?"

I said, "We lost ten thousand pounds."

He said, "How much will it cost to keep the orphans housed and cared for?"

I said, "Oh, fifty thousand pounds."

So, he sent for his checkbook, and wrote me out a check for sixty thousand pounds!

AF: Wow!

HT: I went *straight* round to see Noël at his apartment at Gerald Road and *gave* him the check. He said, "You have amended yourself. God bless Lord Rothermere!"

AF: Oh, my!

HT: He was *very* sweet. I can only give you *two* other stories of Noël Coward.

He went to Australia during the war. Noël's problem was he always wanted to be useful, and ended up singing *"Mad Dogs and Englishmen"* at intimate parties. So, he went to Australia and gave shows for weekly broadcast on the ABC, which was supposed to boost British morale. I am not sure it did much good at all, except that he was going into the famous (closed now) hotel in Sydney, called, The Pub.

Saturday night, and *it was a really rowdy crowd of 'diggers' in the pub.* Noël gets into the elevator.

A large, fat gentleman from the outback, smelling of beer, gets into the elevator.

They are the *only* two people in the elevator.

Noël is rather nervously adjusting his little bow tie.

As the elevator ascends, the Australian says, "You're Mister fawkin' *Noël Coward,* aren't you?" He says, "I don't give even a fawkin' DAMN! I heard you every fawkin' day on the radio *trying to build up the fawkin' Australian* MORALE! *You've been here FIVE FAWKIN' WEEKS in Australia! Say something AUSTRALIAN!"*

Then, the doors open.

Noël steps out, adjusts his lapels and his bow tie. and says, **"Kangaroo."**

[laughter]

And the final story—*everybody knows. That* one I've *never* heard told. The *other* one, which I *have* heard told, is:

Noël goes to the coronation of the present Queen, and, again, it *pisses* rain—Needless to say, and he's sitting there next to—not to Joyce Grenfell, to Joyce Carey, you know the English actress in many of his movies—and the procession goes by.

Of course, it was *pouring rain!*

The Queen was with the King in a coach, and a crown on her head, and all the rest of it, and there was Winston Churchill, et cetera, *all* the 'greats of the day,' as they say, the apt expression of the British Empire.

There was *one* person *ignoring* the rain. That was Queen Salote of Tonga, who was in an open carriage—*stood up in the rain*—wearing a kind of sarong sort of dress, which queens of Tonga used to wear in those days. She was a *very large, stout, form, an ample lady.* There were only so many carriages to go around. The potentates of the British Empire were kind of 'paired off.'

Sitting next to Queen Salote of Tonga was an *insignificant, little man,* in full morning dress with a top hat. He was actually the Sultan of Zanzibar.

Meantime, the overpowering presence of Queen Salote went on *waving* to the crowd in the *rain,* as they are going down Oxford Street.

Noël is seated next to Joyce Carey, who is studying her programme, and she says, *"Oh! This is Queen Salote of Tonga!"* and she says, *"I wonder who that little man is in the carriage with her?"*

Noël says, "Probably her LUNCH!"

WENDY TOYE

b. May 1, 1917   d. February 27, 2010

Interviewed October 3, 1990

Wendy Toye is a theatre director and choreographer who worked with Coward on *"Sigh No More"* in 1945, and much later was involved in the production of shows featuring Coward material. She was interviewed in her London home.

ALAN FARLEY: You started as a dancer, is that right?

WENDY TOYE: Yes, I did. When I was a child, I was a dancer. I also studied singing and acting. I was the original *Marigold* in *"Toad of Toad Hall"*. My first professional appearance, I think, which was before *"Marigold"* was when I was twelve was at The Old Vic in *"Midsummer Night's Dream"* in 1929. I was one of the four fairies.

I'm not sure, but I've got a feeling that Master was at the Charleston Ball. There was a tremendous gathering here at the Charleston Ball, organized and produced by that great impresario Charles Cochran, who Noël wrote *"Words and Music"* for, and many other things. It was a great big event which was to find the champion amateur Charleston champion—'man and woman,' and 'professional man and woman,' and then the 'best chorus'—because, in those days, I think it was 1929, everybody was doing the Charleston, so most of the shows had the Charleston in it.

I was entered for the women's section. Of course, I was the only child that was entered. It was 1925 when I was nine years old, I think. That's right, I was eight and a half, or something like that. The judges were Ziegfeld, Fred Astaire, and the Dolly Sisters, and all sorts of people like that. I've got a feeling that Noël was there, or amongst the judges, and *I won the women's!*

AF: Did you see *"Words and Music"* in 1932?

WT: Yes.

AF: Do you remember Graham Payn in *"Words and Music"*?

WT: You know, I *don't* remember Graham in *"Words and Music"*. I didn't know he was in it. I remember him in lots of other things, but I didn't know he was in *"Words and Music"*.

AF: As a juvenile, just a very small part.

WT: Was he! How interesting! Then, of course, he probably met up with Coward much later again.

AF: Yes, after the war. Was *"Sigh No More"* the first show of Coward's that you were involved in?

WT: I think it must have been. Although, I seemed to know him very well when I started on that. So, what could I have done before with him? I'm not sure, but I've known him most of my life, because I started very young in the profession, and I'm sure we had met before. I think he had wanted me to do the dances in other shows of his.

But, *"Sigh No More"* you might have heard this story—but he actually said to me—and I don't think there's any way he could have repeated it. I'm sure this was first off.

> The opening was three wonderful looking harlequins springing onto the stage in a very 'dancy' fashion. One was Tommy Linden, and another was Graham Payn, and the third was a young man called Grant Tyler, who hadn't had very much experience on the stage, and had never danced, and had obviously never worn *tights* before.
> The boys in the dressing room had obviously not been very helpful to him, because he hadn't got a jock strap on underneath his tights, and he did this great leap onto the stage, and then stood still for a moment.
> Noël turned to me, and said, "Wendy, go 'round and tell Grant to take that Rockingham tea service out of his tights."
>
> [laughter]

Wonderful . . .

I didn't do all the work in that show, because I working in *"Strike It Again"* with Sid Fields at Prince of Wales at the time—but I was overall in charge of the actual dancing and staging of numbers. It had three or four different choreographers, but I did the ballet of *"Blithe Spirit"* and somebody else did *"Nina"*—it was Cyril Ritchard doing it—and all of Noël's songs. You know them probably better than anybody in the world—*the less you do, the better the songs are.*

Somehow or other, Cyril, in this particular production of *"Nina"* was wearing a GREAT BIG HAT, a GREAT BIG CUMMERBUND, a *white* suit, and he was *wriggling* about a lot, and . . . *Noël wasn't very happy about it. And* there were some other dancers up in the corner of the stage *also* which was a *bit* distracting! So, he said to me one day, "Wendy, will you go up and do *something* about this?"

So, I *did.* And apparently, when Coley [was readying] *"The Diaries"* [for publication], there is a page in one of *"The Diaries"* [where Noël] says,

"Thank GOD Wendy went up and in twenty minutes improved 'Nina' tremendously."

It wasn't actually printed, but it was so nice for me that it was *in "The Diaries".* What was very interesting was (after I re-choreographed *"Nina"*) Cyril did much LESS in it.

Then one day Cyril was ill. There was nothing else to be done about it, excepting for *Noël to go on.* So, *he* went on. *Master* went on. Did absolutely NOTHING. *Didn't wriggle.* [laughs] And he was just terrific. It is how his work *should be* done.

AF: The television special with Mary Martin, in which *"Nina"* is one of the numbers he does—it's all in the eyebrows, in the face, in the hands.

WT: *Absolutely.* When I did *"Cowardy Custard"* with Alan Strachan and Gerald Frow, I was kind of very nervous when I went to see him [Coward] in Switzerland, and I stayed with him for a bit, and I said, "Now, you will come for our first week's rehearsal or so, won't you, and help us?"

He said, "No, I'm not going to. I've got lots of faith in all of you, and I will be there for the first night and get a lovely surprise."

Which was a great compliment in a way, but of course, on the first night we were all absolutely *petrified.* John Moffatt, who sang *"Nina"*—and sang it *brilliantly*—actually *dried* at about the second verse. Of course, with Master being in front of you, you can imagine what *that* must have been like for him!

He just stopped and said, "I'm very sorry, I have to go back to the beginning."

And he did! It worked perfectly all right.

AF: You know that happened to Noël the very first time *he* sang it, as well.

WT: I didn't remember that.

AF: He and Norman Hackforth were touring, I guess, in India, and he wrote it one day, and they decided after a few hours rehearsal to do it *that very day,* and Noël dried up, and they had to restart. First thing was, Norman prompted him, *but with the wrong lyrics,* so they had to start all over. He took it well, but Norman said afterwards that Noël was absolutely furious with *himself.* He said, *never again* would he *"do anything before two weeks rehearsal!"*

WT: Yes, I know how he feels.

AF: So, he must have had some sympathy for John Moffat.

WT: Oh, I'm sure. Oh, yes. But you know, it is extraordinary about his work, because I've just received a notice from America where they have been doing *"Cowardy Custard"* and the whole point really is they did an extraordinary thing, and showed that it can be done in so many *different* ways. That's why I think it doesn't *date.* The songs don't date, do they?

AF: I don't think so. I've been surprised and very pleased over the years with my series on *"The Songs of Noël Coward"* that it continues to be the most popular program I've ever done. It's young people, as well, who are fascinated by his lyrics.

WT: He's one of the greats who was not appreciated enough in his lifetime. He was, of course, by the people in the profession and by the public, but I don't think the critics gave him credit for the depth of his work.

AF: He directed *"Sigh No More"* didn't he?

WT: Yes, he did.

AF: Let's talk about the songs. *"Wait A Bit, Joe"* was in that, wasn't it?

WT: *"Wait A Bit, Joe"*—I remember, yes. That was a lovely kind of 'bluesy' number, but I don't know any history about it.

AF: *"Merry Wives of Windsor"*?

WT: That was great fun! This again, was a sketch with music. Have you found the music of that?

AF: Yes.

WT: Yes, but I think it had some dialogue in it. The ballet of *"Blithe Spirit"* had no singing. That was just the ballet of it, which he was very keen on doing it. I was a bit scared, because I think I always feel that if there's been a very, very good play, it's always risky turning it into a musical. I felt this a little bit with the ballet. I felt that the *words* were so important, and it was such a marvelous script, that to make a ballet of it—*would* it work? *wouldn't* it work? But Noël thought it did. He was happy with it.

AF: I've grown quite fond of *"High Spirits"* after listening to it many times.

WT: Yes, but that was *"Blithe Spirit"* wasn't it? It still isn't as good as the play, though, is it, when the play is well done?

AF: No, although I think there are some good songs and some good lyrics.

WT: I really did feel worried about doing *"Blithe Spirit"* but I enjoyed doing it, and I was glad he was pleased, and the audience all liked it, so that was good.

AF: How did you do it? What was the process? Did you have a completed score, and was it up to you to interpret it?

WT: No. I think that Master and I, and composer, Richard Addinsell, *talked about it, and talked about it,* as you do, with a ballet—and if you're lucky enough to have a composer, or if you have somebody arranging other classical music for a ballet—you say, *'this section is this, and has to be that rhythm, and this section is this. Then we need a little interlude, because somebody has to make an entrance. Then this is a pas de deux, so you want that.'* I think, we just talked it through like that. Of course, Noël being so good with his own tunes, I think he did a lot of sketching it out with me on the piano, I seem to remember, to start with.

AF: And, of course, you had dancers representing all of the different characters.

WT: That's right, we had *Madame Arcati,* and we had *Edith,* the maid, and we had a lot of *Ruths,* and a lot of *Elviras.*

AF: How did you realize *Madame Arcati?* Anything particular about what she did?

WT: She was just very eccentric. It was Daphne Anderson, who was a lovely actress and very good dancer. It was easier to do *Madame Arcati,* really. The *Elviras* and the *Ruths*—the *Elviras* were done in a very dotty, kind of 'flimsy' way, and the *Ruths* were very 'down-to-earth.' This was Noël's idea, of having groups of them. I think they had one leader, but then we had them as though you'd see them in dimensions, though it was 'the person'—

AF: In one performance there were several?

WT: Yes, yes, yes.

AF: I saw a production of the ballet *"Romeo and Juliet"* which had multiple Romeos and Juliets. [Editor: The ballet was choreographed by Oscar Araiz in 1978.]

WT: Oh, no! I didn't know that. Really?

AF: That was the first I'd seen that, but here is Noël Coward doing it back in 1945.

WT: Yes, it was '45. It was a long while ago.

AF: *"The Burchels of Battersea Rise"*?

WT: I think it was a quartet. It must have been very strong, because we've got things like *"That Is The End of the News"* and I think *"There Are Bad Times Just Around the Corner"*—was that in the show, too? I think it might have been, and if *"The Burchels"* was placed last, it must have been very strong. On the other hand, it hasn't lasted, has it?

AF: No, it's not been recorded as far as I know.

WT: No, no. I did *"Noël and Gertie"* in Monte Carlo. We did it at The Princess Grace Theatre, and it was very nice, because *all* the royal family came. At the last minute the narrator fell out, so I did the narration, as well, and joined in with some of the numbers, which was quite fun.

AF: Well, let's talk a bit about *"Cowardy Custard"* and the process of putting that on.

WT: *"Cowardy Custard'?* Well, it was very interesting, really, because Gerald Frow and Alan Strachan had done a great deal of research on the story, and the life, and what they wanted to include.

I said to them, "Well, honestly, I think what we ought to do now is for me to think of how we can use the songs, and how we can use them best. I'll get on with doing that, and then we'll get together again, and then we'll see whether you want to rewrite anything that's going to go on in between them, or whether I must change some of the songs."

So, we really did it *separately* for a few days, and *then* we got together and worked on it very *closely* . . .

It all came about, you know, from his birthday party.

Noël's *seventieth* birthday party . . .

It was decided that *we*—all of us in the profession—wanted to give him a 'birthday performance.' Martin Tickner and I organized most of it. There were one or two other directors directing separate *sections* of it, but I really did the overall thing. Martin and I got hold of everybody, and we had—oh! *everybody* you can imagine was there at The Phoenix.

AF: I certainly have heard about that event!

WT: We worked out the running order of the *show,* and then the *second half* was like a *party with everybody on stage—ALL* the stars on the stage, and *then everybody came out and sang his songs—ALL* the big stars came out. It took a lot of rehearsing!

There was a big day when somebody said, "We ought to televise this!'

I don't know whether I was the *only* one, but I felt so strongly that if it was *televised,* it would become a 'different thing.' It would become—'who had to be top of the bill'—'who was going to do this'—'who felt they weren't in the right position in the show'—and all *those* sort of things, which nobody would want to have to bother about. The artists wouldn't want to have to bother about it on his *birthday.*

So, it was decided NO! *We would just do it for HIM.* In a way, it's terribly sad, because it was the most *exceptional* show, as you can imagine . . .

It started off in The Phoenix Theatre, and we all waited until we knew he was outside, and then we shone a light on the box, and we started *"Happy Birthday to you...."* before he came in.

Then he came in to the show and Princess Margaret was there! It was really a very nice, *friendly* birthday party evening, *'specially for him.*

AF: It started at midnight, did it?

WT: I guess it did! Yes, I think it was a 'midnight matinee', and it *went on.* It was *very* long! Most of these things we tried to keep short and don't succeed. But this one, we didn't *really even try to keep short,* because we wanted everything to be done, and we wanted *him to see everybody. We wanted everybody to see him.*

So, it was really a very exceptional evening, *and he* came down! He made a speech from the box, and he *also* came down and saw us all after. *We had a party on the stage.*

It was after that that Bernard Miles said to Alan, Gerald and me, "Would this not make a good show?"

I said, "Of course! Yes!"

We all thought it would like anything! So, he got in touch with Noël. Noël approved and agreed. That was at a moment in time when Noël had decided he didn't want very much Coward to be done. He wanted there to be a bit of a rest from it. And so, we were very lucky. We went on when there hadn't been a great deal of Coward going on. It ran at The Mermaid, as you probably know, for a long while. The Mermaid really wasn't allowed to keep things on for longer than so many weeks. I'm not sure how many it was.

AF: Well, I think it was originally planned for eight weeks.

WT: Something like that. And, of course, we could have gone straight into the West End. Everybody wanted it, but of course, it was making a lot of money for The Mermaid, which was very necessary at that moment. So, although we were disappointed that it didn't go into the West End, we were delighted that it was doing so well for the Mermaid, which we were all very fond of—Lord

Miles and his wonderful wife, Josephine. We were just so glad that it was doing well. But, of course, then it missed the boat to go into the West End. Everybody keeps saying it's time for a revival of it, but I'm not sure.

AF: To get back to the process, you were the one who worked on the songs.

WT: Yes.

AF: How did you *decide*. It must have been almost torture to—

WT: No, no it wasn't at all. No, it wasn't, because™ of course, this was very much in consultation with particularly Alan, who is also a director—a marvelous one—and it fell into place completely, because, for instance, [I had this] one thought, "Oh, it would be lovely to do that whole section from *"The Girl Who Came To Supper"*—

AF: The 'London sequence'?

WT: The 'London sequence' seemed, to me, right, "We must do the London sequence, and that needs costuming." Now, if it needs costuming, and everybody's got to change, there's only one position for that, which is the opening of the second half. So, that became the opening of the second half.

I thought, "What one needs is to do a lot of songs that people *know well,* but little, tiny bits of them, and let's do that for the *opening!"*

So, there was the opening. So, we had the opening and the opening of the second half.

Then I thought, "well, we've got to have a *montage* of songs for the *end* of the show." So, that was the next thing.

So, one then decided what were the little bits of songs for the first bit, and one wanted some slow bits, and quick bits, one or two that people had never heard of before and didn't remember. Everybody said to me, after that opening, which lasted about eight minutes, they said, "It was quite incredible! There were eight or nine songs in that we had no idea he had ever written." Which is really what we were trying to achieve.

We knew that *"Why Must The Show Go On?"* would be wonderful for the finale of Act One. We all agreed with that. As the story was the story of his life, sometimes it went back and we did a flashback, but mostly it was in advance as it should have done, so there were moments for certain things to happen where there couldn't be anything else. It fell into place very, very easily. What was difficult, Alan, was *cutting* it, because it lasted twice as long when we first did it. We had wonderful little things in it like Una Stubbs did a little song called *"Miss Mouse"* which I don't think anybody would remember. I think it was in a play of his. It was quite delightful. She just—*sprang on* and did it, and *sprang off!*

We had to cut a lot of things, and that was most heartbreaking for the artist and for all of us. It wasn't a bit difficult getting the shape of the show. He's just so versatile, you see.

I've been asked very many times to do the same sort of thing with Ivor Novello. You can't do it, because all his music is beautiful, it's lovely, but there's no variety. He has written exactly one lively song, which is the one he wrote for Cecily Courtenage. It's a song about vivacity. That's the only really quick song he's written.

AF: Interesting, because after my Noël Coward series was on for a while, a friend, whom I met because he was fan and sent me some records, said, "Well, I've got a big collection of Ivor Novello, if you'd like to do a series about him.' He gave me some of the records, and I listened to them, and at the time I thought, "No, I don't think so." Now, since that time, I've certainly gotten to appreciate his wonderful melodies, but you're right, there is just no variety. A lot of it is a bit much.

WT: It's very alike. You can do two shows. Actually, there is another one called *"Glow Worm"* I think, which is a lively song. I worked for quite a long while on a Novello show, and we took one or two songs from other shows to put in to get a little bit more variety, but no, you can't do the same thing with Novello.

AF: Were you involved in the Cole Porter revue that The Mermaid did?

WT: No. Not in the one called *"Cole"*, but I was in the one called *"Oh, Mr. Porter!"* which I loved doing! Absolutely loved it.

AF: Next to Noël Coward, I think Cole Porter is probably my favorite.

WT: *"Oh, Mr. Porter!"* was written by Benny Green. It was the most marvelous idea. They've done one complete show of Cole, which was called *"Cole"*, which was lovely, and that one I think Alan Strachan directed. Some months afterwards they wanted another one. So, Benny and I did *"Oh, Mr. Porter!"* and we didn't use one song that had been in the first show. But, of course, they *wanted to use the unusual songs,* which they did. They used songs that hadn't been played so much. So, we were left with the really popular ones.

AF: I'm always looking for the unusual ones, too. So, Coward was not involved at all in the creation of *"Cowardy Custard"*?

WT: Absolutely not at all. He didn't even want me to come over again and tell him what I was going to use. Which I thought was surprising. I thought it was nice of him. I thought he would want to say, 'Well, I would love this in the second half.'

We did "*Matelot*" and we did it in a very different way, which I thought worked awfully well. The way we did it, we did the whole thing so simply, there was *no furniture—no props at all! We* had some newspapers, but I don't suppose you ever saw it when we did it. It was all black and silver, and just *bits of the rostrum pulled out* and became seats, or became a desk, or became *whatever* you wanted them to.

When John Moffat and Patricia Routledge sang *"We're A Dear Old Couple And We Hate One Another"* people have said to me since—*"I loved that scene on the boat, when the two people were sitting in deck chairs under the awning on the boat, singing"*—this song.

There was no awning! There was no boat! There was nothing! She had a very flat hat on and a shawl, and he had, I think, one of those white Panama hats, and they were both reading a paper, or she was knitting. There was no awning. No boat. Nothing.

But the idea we were trying to give was they were on a cruise, sitting on a boat. And it worked! *It is extraordinary how people use their imagination.*

AF: That reminds me that, of course, you do some of the songs from *"Sail Away"*, the one show of his that I would like to see revived.

WT: So would I. I'd love to see it done again.

AF: It has so many wonderful songs; both romantic songs like *"Later Than Spring"* and *"Something Very Strange"*—and those brilliantly witty songs. *"Useless Phrases"* and *"The Customer's Always Right"*.

WT: Yes, yes, we used those two. We made a little section of it, without calling it *"Sail Away"* we just called it *"English People Traveling"* or *"American People Traveling"*—that marvelous bit of the two Americans looking over the church. It's very funny.

AF: He came up with the title, I understand.

WT: Oh, isn't it awful, yes he did. We wanted to call it *"Master Piece"*. It would have been super, 'cause it's sharp and it's neat and it's quick.

Then somebody one day said, "Oh, what about '*Cowardy Custard*'? He loved it! I always thought it was a bad title, because I don't think Americans know what '*cowardy custard*' means.

AF: No, perhaps explain it for Americans.

WT: Well, *'cowardy custard'* is a terrible thing that children shouted at each other over here, *if they didn't like each other,* they would shout, *"cowardy, cowardy custard!"* because somebody was a coward, and somebody was not behaving very well. It seems to me an old fashioned name, and it's not used now, and it's nothing to do with Coward. *If anybody was courageous it was Coward!* I thought *"Cowardy Custardy"* was a horrid title. I *hate* saying it.

Do you see that? *"Cowardy, cowardy custard"*—that lovely picture on my wall, which is an old print, that Coley [Cole Lesley] gave to me after Master died. On the back it's signed *"From Joan Sutherland and Richard"* [Bonynge] her husband. It was a present to Master on the first night of *"Cowardy Custard"*.

AF: You also directed the show, the gala that was held after the Westminster Abbey ceremony at Drury Lane, didn't you?

WT: No. I only did *one* item. There were lots of us doing it. Again, Martin Tickner, I think, was in general command of it. I did one section. We got the original cast of *"Cowardy Custard"* back.

Oh, I've never known such a nervous lot of people! 'Cause they hadn't done it for years, you know. This is the worst thing. If you haven't done anything for a long while, and you don't have much rehearsal, it's almost worse than doing something new. I don't know what it is, but when you're doing Coward, there's such an *edge* to it, and there's such *a way of doing it,* and such a way of not doing it, that one is always nervous to get it right.

Of course, he was such a perfectionist, himself, that you feel you can't dare let him down. Graham Payn, who comes and *sees everything* that's done of his, now, is very generous, very helpful, and if *anybody knows how it should be, it's him.* They all came on the first night, Noël and Graham and Coley, and they didn't see it before that. They didn't even see a rehearsal of it.

AF: What did he say?

WT: Oh, he was delighted!

AF: I guess it was *"Oh, Coward!"* about which they quoted Noël saying, **"I came out humming the tunes."**

WT: That's very nice. [laughs]

AF: That started around the same time in the States.

WT: Yes, it was just *after,* I think. Roderick Cook did it. Then they brought it to England.

AF: Have you directed other of Coward's plays?

WT: [incredulously] Do you know, I *haven't!* It doesn't seem possible, but I haven't.

AF: I saw the revival of *"Bitter Sweet"* at The New Sadler's Wells Opera a couple of years ago.

WT: I saw Peggy Wood in the original London production [Editor: 1929-1931].

AF: You couldn't have!

WT: Oh, I could and I did. Yes, I did. I saw it three times. Loved it!

AF: I guess it was a big success at that time, wasn't it?

WT: Oh, enormous, yes. We talked about *"Bitter Sweet"* when I was staying with him, both Graham and he.
    I said, "I always longed to do it at Sadler's Wells."
    He said, "Well, you must one day."
    I said, "Do you think it ought to be changed *a bit? Do* you think it ought to be rewritten *a bit?"*—(Because the script isn't all that strong.)—he said, "Oh, yes, I do! I definitely do think it should be re-looked at."
    Now, whether they did, when they did it, I don't know.

AF: I don't think so.

WT: It just didn't seem to work, did it? It didn't transfer.

AF: I was surprised to learn that Norman Hackforth had a walk-on part in that first production of *"Bitter Sweet"*.

WT: *Did he!*

AF: Later on he played *Vincent,* the pianist.

WT: Yes, that's nice. Well, another one I didn't know was *"Would You Like To Stick A Pin iIn My Balloon?"* I didn't know, that song.

AF: Was that from the show *"Ace of Clubs"*?—the show *within* the show?

WT: I bet you're right. I'm sure you're right.

AF: Of course, he says in the book of lyrics that it wasn't going to be complete. He wasn't going to publish the lyrics for everything, because he thought some things not worth publishing, but of course for someone like me, I want to see everything that exists.

WT: Yes. How many songs are there in the book of lyrics?

AF: think, about three hundred. [Ed: Thanks to Barry Day in *"The Complete Lyrics of Noël Coward"* 1998, we now know he wrote over five hundred songs.]

I'd like to ask you to talk about working with him. You worked with him, obviously, before this. You worked with him on *"Sigh No More"*.

WT: I've never known him to lose his temper. I've been with him at other times, when he's been working on other things, and had a lot of tiresome things going on, and I can't ever remember him—not *ever* losing his temper—but he could be *gritty.* He used to be able to be very *gritty,* and he used to be able to say the most *startling* things to people, all of which I'm sure you know. None of which I can ever remember—which is much, MUCH worse than somebody who'll fly off the handle at you. But, a marvelous man to work *with* and *for,* because *he knew what he wanted.*

AF: I read in Coley's book about when he and Basil Dean were working together. He said he found it a little bit unusual that Noël would work with Basil Dean because of Dean's, reputation for being cruel to small people. Because of Noël's *own* attitude, he found it remarkable that Noël would be willing to coexist with this.

WT: Yes. The only thing that there is often a query about, was his absolute demand that everybody on the first day of rehearsal *know all their words.* I don't think he expected them to know all the words of the *songs.* I think he expected people to learn that as they learned the music. But he definitely expected them to know words on the first day of rehearsal. A lot of actors feel that if they learn the words, they're going to learn an interpretation, which can't be quite the same when you're working with another person. If they give you a line with a different inflection, and a different meaning, you've got to answer it in a different way.

I don't think Noël ever meant you to learn it as an *interpretation,* only so that you *knew the words.* He knew so well how to *get* the comedy, and *how* he wanted the thing said, and I think that he just really meant to learn the words so you didn't have to have the book in your hand.

A lot of people feel very uncomfortable. A book's like a *cozy,* you know, you don't have to use your hands if you're holding a script, and it is quite hard to start on the first day of rehearsal without a script in your hand. It's a lot to ask. It's the sort of thing that Noël himself, Master himself, could have done.

AF: Did you see him perform at the Cafe de Paris?

WT: Oh, *yes,* ever so often, with lots of his different guest artists introducing him, including Marlene. It was wonderful!

I can sit and listen to the records of him doing all the songs, and I sit in a kind of *despair,* because I think, "Nobody can do them better. Why do them again? Why do them at all? Because, *he* does them so wonderfully well."

And, it's very interesting. I've got a record that he gave me, *"Mad Dogs and Englishmen".*

AF: It was the thirties, because it was in *"Words and Music"* in 1932.

WT: Well, he gave me this record, signed, with his name on it. It hasn't got anything else on the label. It's just got a white label and I think it's got *"Wendy, love from Noël Coward"* which you can't read anyway, because you can't read his signature, can you?

I've also got the latest one that he did at Las Vegas, and the *difference* in it! He used to do it quite *slowly,* and then he got *quicker and quicker.* Every year he got *quicker and quicker.* Now, he *rattled it off,* didn't he, when he last did it in cabaret, or at the Las Vegas places?

AF: Yes, in fact, he said that Cole Porter was in the audience for one performance, came back to him afterwards, and said—it's the first time he's *"ever heard a song sung in one breath."*

WT: [laughs] *And heard every word!*

AF: Exactly!

BARBARA WARING

b. August 1, 1911   d. April 1990

Interviewed October 18, 1987

    Barbara Waring is an actress and singer who appeared in supporting roles on stage, and in a number of films in the thirties and forties in the U.K. The interview was recorded in her residence in Reigate [an historic market town in Surrey, England, at the foot of the North Downs.]

ALAN FARLEY: I understand that you worked in *"Cavalcade"*. Tell us about that.

BARBARA WARING: Very long time ago. When I was at RADA [Royal Academy of Dramatic Arts] you see, believe it or not, I won the Sir Bob West Award for my year for playing Hamlet.

AF: Hamlet?

BW: Yes, I played *Hamlet,* believe it or not!
    Noël was doing auditions at Drury Lane, and I *escaped from* RADA and went to Drury Lane, and said I wanted to *understudy* Binnie Barnes singing *"Twentieth Century Blues"* in *"Calvacade"*.
    So, I went downstairs into this sort of basement part of Drury Lane. He was doing auditions *upstairs.* I went *downstairs—and practiced.* I was singing *"Twentieth Century Blues"*—practicing it. *I could sing it like a dream!*
    Then, *Noël* came down, and as soon as he came in—
I *couldn't sing a word.* I was actually terrified!
    So, he said, "Well, now don't worry, just go on practicing for another half hour, 'cause I've got to be upstairs doing more auditions. So, go on practicing, and I'll come back in half an hour." And he went out. *As soon as he'd gone out,* I could sing like a dream!
    HE WAS LISTENING OUTSIDE!

He came in and said, "Okay! You've got it!"

AF: Well, how *considerate* of him!

BW: Wasn't it marvelous! He was like that. He was a *lovely* person. So, I got it! I was in *"Cavalcade"* and I was doing sort of, you know, what do you call it? Not models. What are they called, you know?

AF: A spear-carrier?

BW: That's right. That *sort* of thing and doing things *like* that. Not the *chorus,* but you know, in the—whatever-it's-called—*singing.* And then Binnie Barnes got married and was off for two weeks, so I was on! It was absolutely fantastic! I couldn't believe it!

The next day in the *"Daily Express"* it said, "Little Barbara Waring's voice never deteriorates into a croon."

And every time Noël saw me, he always pointed at me, and said, "Little Barbara Waring's voice never deteriorates into a croon." [laughs]

AF: I can hear him saying it!

BW: He was absolutely *marvelous!* I loved him!

AF: Well, what was it like going *on* for the first time?

BW: For the first time, well you know, I was only *eighteen* or something, maybe *nineteen.* In *those* days, you were very 'young for your age,' if you know what I mean. I *knew I* was the greatest singer in the world. It didn't worry *me!* [laughs] I wasn't frightened. I *did* it! It was *great!*

AF: It *must* have been great to be associated with such a spectacular success as *"Cavalcade".*

BW: Yes, it was.

AF: Did you work in other of Noël Coward's shows?

BW: Oh, *yes,* I did. I was in *"Design for Living".* I was in *"Words and Music".*

AF: I guess Noël was in that *himself.* Were you on stage *with* him?

BW: Yes. I do remember *that.* What was the other thing I was in with him? Something Edith Evans was in. What was that?

AF: *"Hay Fever".*

BW: *Must* have been! It was terribly funny because I will always remember.

> **I was only playing, you know, a *small* part, and Edith Evans came on and stood in the *middle* of that stage, which *I was standing in,* and she *pushed* me aside! You know, *SHE stood in the middle!***
> She never would let me—I had to come on! I was playing *something,* and she *PUSHED* me aside!
> I said to Noël, "I can't *stand* it! She never stops *pushing* me aside! She *won't* let me come to the *center!"*
> He said, "Darling, she's one of those people that *does* that sort of *thing.* Don't worry. Nobody cares. *Everybody will notice you* because *you're lovely* and *she's not."*

> [laughs]

> He was *heaven!*

AF: I understand that you went to parties with Noël Coward.

BW: I went to parties with Noël, yes. I didn't necessarily go *with* him, but he was *at* the parties, and we were good friends. I used to go with him to some places, because he didn't want to be seen with another *guy,* or just *himself* and another guy. So I used to go as his *girlfriend.* So sweet!

AF: So, he was anxious about that?

BW: Well, only purely for the publicity. See, in *those* days it *wasn't* done, if you know what I mean? Different than today.

AF: Did you know Gladys Calthrop, the designer of many Coward productions?

BW: Oh, yes of course. I knew her very well. She was a good friend. She was, naturally, much older than me. I was very young in those days. If she *couldn't* go—or if she *didn't want* to go to some show, or if she'd *seen it before,* or something, you know—to some party or something, she'd say to me, "Will you go?"
    I'd say, "I can't wait!" and it was really lovely. So, I would go with Noël instead of her going.

AF: When you went to the theatre with Noël Coward, what kind of an audience member was he? Did he form instant judgments?

BW: Yes, but not publicly, if you know what I mean?
    He used to go backstage afterwards and say somebody was *"absolutely wonderful!"*

    [chuckles]

AF: With a twinkle?

BW: Yes!

    [She laughs]